LUMBERJILLS

BRITAIN'S FORGOTTEN ARMY

JOANNA FOAT

The
History
Press

Cover illustrations: *Front:* Women of the Forestry Commission section of the Women's Land Army carry logs on their shoulders in Suffolk, 1 December 1941. (Photo by M. McNeill/Fox Photos/ Hulton Archive/Getty Images) *Back:* Women's Timber Corps using a mobile sawbench 1945 (Images © Crown Copyright. Courtesy of Forestry Commission)

First published 2019

The History Press
The Mill, Brimscombe Port
Stroud, Gloucestershire, GL5 2QG
www.thehistorypress.co.uk

British Library Cataloguing in Publication Data.
A catalogue record for this book is available from the British Library.

ISBN 978 0 7509 9090 5

Typesetting and origination by The History Press
Printed and bound in Great Britain by TJ International Ltd

Contents

Foreword

I grew up hearing wonderful stories of adventure, hard work, glamour and – above all – friendship from my mother, who had very proudly served in the Women's Land Army, Women's Timber Corps and North German Timber Control during and after the Second World War. Having heard her tales, it came as some surprise to me that there had been no formal recognition of their work, and there was little readily available information on the Lumberjills and the crucial contribution these remarkable women made to the war effort.

My mother was delighted that Joanna had asked her to contribute to this book. Not only did it give her the chance to reminisce about one of the most extraordinary times of her life, but it was also an opportunity to talk about these women whose work had largely been forgotten. Now it seemed hers, and many others' stories, would be told, in their own words.

The Land Army and Timber Corps waited a long time for the recognition they so deserved. It was only in 2008 that they were given some credit, when the British Government issued a commemorative badge. A decade on, I am delighted that Joanna has given a voice to the Lumberjills. As many of them reach the end of their lives, she has captured their personal experiences in their own words ensuring that their stories endure for future generations.

I first met Joanna in 2018 when she invited me to attend a talk she was giving about the Lumberjills at the WI's Centre for Learning. Just a few months after my mother's death at the age of 94, I found the stories she told of these women's shared history moving, humbling and fascinating. She has uncovered so much about what these young women coped with, from the sheer physical effort they made undertaking extremely dangerous work, to the terrible living conditions, lost loves and the loneliness of being posted miles from home at such a young age. Alongside this darker side of their experiences, Joanna has also captured the adventures, the fun, the glamour and friendships that were made.

My mother's own experience in Devon was of horrible landladies, flea-infested billets, bombs, the hazards of felling trees, and working alongside prisoners of war. But most of all, she loved to talk about the fun times had with the women she worked and lived with and grew to love. 'We were a great gang, always going around together and trying to look glamorous,' I remember her saying of those women, whose friendships were to last the rest of her life. My brother Michael and I were brought up within that extended family, with Betty, Fran, Evelyn and Olive becoming our aunts and their children, our cousins.

Contributing so much to this country and its war effort produced so many strong, capable women. Having worked and thrived as Lumberjills during the war, many went on to have successful careers, raise children, travel the world and have other great adventures – none of which, it could be argued, would have happened without that early freedom, training, discipline and comradery that came with the difficult circumstances of being young women in a war.

Joanna's book brings to life the stories of those women and represents a love letter to all those who served working in the forests in wartime.

Mary Collins
Daughter of Hazel Collins (née Hacker)

Acknowledgements

A special thank you to all the Lumberjills and their families for sharing their stories and giving permission to reproduce their photos: Edna Barton, Audrey Broad, Mary Broadhead, Rose Burton, Hazel Collins, Peggy Conway, Katie Dowson, Joyce Earl, Olive Edgley, Frieda Ellerby, Gladys Fife, Margaret Finch, Patricia Frayn, Joyce Gaster, Brenda Harrison, Nancy Harrison, Edna Holland, Kathleen Hutchby, Mrs Lawrie, Enid Lenton, Eileen Mark, Ann Moffat, Betty Morley's son John Morley, Doreen Musson, Dorothy Naylor, Ethel Oliver, Violet Parker, Molly Paterson, Winnie Renshaw, Dorothy Scott, Irene Snow, Dorothy Swift, Evelyn Taylor, Joan Turner, Diana Underwood, Lilian Veitch and the only lumberjack Alfie Weir.

Thank you to my family and dear friend Sophie Artemis for their unrelenting support and belief. Thank you also to those people along the way who have offered encouragement and advice, especially Ann Kramer.

A special thanks also goes to the Imperial War Museum, The National Archives, Forestry Commission, European Ethnological Research Centre, Ex Libris Press, *Best of British Magazine*.

★★★

I would like to thank the following Lumberjills and their families and the one and only lumberjack for kindly providing interviews, letters, personal photographs and Women's Timber Corps memorabilia for this book:

Edna Barton (née Packwood) – Born 1920.
Women's Land Army 1941–42, Women's Timber Corps 1942–45.
Training at Culford, Bury St Edmonds, Suffolk, felling at Coombe Abbey on the outskirts of Coventry. (With kind permission of Peter Barton.)

Audrey Broad (née Wilcock) – Born 3 October 1925.
Women's Timber Corps 22 March 1943–14 February 1948.
Worked in Arundel, Poynings and Southwater, Sussex, as a measurer, calculating wages based on piecework. (With kind permission of Jenny Ansell.)

Mary Broadhead (née Swannick).
Women's Land Army, Women's Timber Corps 1940–46, when married.
Training at Culford, Bury St Edmonds, Suffolk, felling near Elveden, Brandon and Lakenheath and sawmilling in Chartham, near Canterbury, Kent. (With kind permission of Robert Broadhead.)

Hazel Collins (née Hacker) – Born 7 July 1923.
Women's Land Army 1940–42, Women's Timber Corps 1942–46, North German Timber Control May 1946–50.
Felling timber for Thornbury Mill, Holsworthy, Devon. Sawmill in Kingston, Devon. Office work for the Control Commission in Hanover, Germany. (With kind permission of Mary Collins.)

Katie Dowson – Born 1926.
Women's Timber Corps 1944–48.
Felling, brashing, planting and fencing at High and Low Muffles, Pickering, and calculating wages at Dalby Forest, North York Moors, North Yorkshire.

Olive Edgley (née Spoor) – Born 9 June 1924.
Women's Timber Corps 1940–45.
Acquisitions from Western-super-Mare, Somerset, to Cleveland, North Yorkshire, Savernake Forest in Wiltshire to Malmesbury, Stroud, Winchcombe and Westonbirt in Gloucestershire and Monmouthshire reporting to the Ministry of Supply HQ in Bristol. (With kind permission of Rosamund Edwards.)

Frieda Ellerby (née Hardy).
Women's Timber Corps 1940–45, when she got married.
Worked in forests in North Yorkshire loading pits props into trailers for the Bevin Boys in Durham, loading lorries heading for Thornton Dale Station.

Gladys Fife (née Holtby).
Women's Timber Corps 1943–48.
Based at Cropton, North Yorkshire, worked in felling, brashing, planting

and fencing at High Muffles, Pickering, and other forests in the North York Moors.

Margaret Finch – Born 1924.
Women's Timber Corps.
Training in Wetherby, Yorkshire, sawmilling, felling, loading and driving timber haulage lorries in Kings Langley and Epping Green Corner, Hertfordshire.

Edna Holland (née Lloyd) – Born 28 March 1925.
Women's Timber Corps October 1942.
Trained in Wetherby and worked in felling, haulage using horses and driving caterpillar tractors at Dalby, Boltby, South Wood and other forests in the North York Moors, North Yorkshire. (With kind permission of Fiona Jane Holland.)

Lillian Julian (née Veitch).
Women's Timber Corps 1942–44, Women's Land Army 1944–46, and left when married.
Brashing on an estate between Coldstream and Berwick upon Tweed, Northumberland.

Enid Lenton (née Anderson) – Born 11 July 1915.
Women's Timber Corps 1940.
Feller and supervisor at Alyth and Blairgowrie, Perthshire, in charge of forty girls. (With kind permission of Anne Ogden.)

Eileen Mark (née Worsley) – Born 1923.
Women's Timber Corps 1942–46, when she was married.
Trained at Culford, near Bury St Edmunds, Suffolk, and worked in Walderton and Compton, West Sussex, clearing brush, making fires, planting, stacking and loading and driving tractors. (With kind permission of Kevan Mark.)

Ethel Oliver (née Bailey) – Born 28 June 1923.
Women's Land Army 1941, Women's Timber Corps 1942–46.
Training in the Lake District and became a measurer in Chopwell Wood, Tyne and Wear, and Barnard Castle, in Teesdale, County Durham. (With kind permission of Randle Oliver.)

Violet Parker (née Talling) – Born 24 June 1924.
Women's Timber Corps 1942 until the end of the war.
Based at Lostwithiel, she worked stacking timber onto lorries at a sawmill in Lanhydrock, Cornwall.

Molly Paterson (née Douglas) – Born 1922.
Women's Timber Corps 1940–44.
Clerical work for the timber section of the Ministry of Supply in Ardbrecknish Forest, Argyll, Scotland. Later calculated wages, cubic feet of timber, preparing dockets for the stationmaster and loading. (With kind permission from Alison Tomlinson.)

Joyce Elizabeth Rampton (née Gaster).
Women's Timber Corps 1940–15 May 1946.
Trained as a measurer at the Forest of Dean, worked at Haltwhistle in Cumbria, Northumberland and Alice Holt Forest in Hampshire and was one of six women to represent the Women's Timber at the Victory Parade on 8 June 1946. (With kind permission from Shirley and Maurice Rampton.)

Dorothy Scott (née Turner) – Born 1923.
Women's Timber Corps 1942–45.
Training in Wetherby, Yorkshire, and worked felling in Stapleford Wood near Newark, then to Leicestershire and near Tideswell and Snake Pass, Derbyshire.

Muriel Patricia Shopland (née Pat Frayn) – Born 26 November 1923.
Women's Timber Corps.
Worked in Bradridge Woods, Launceston, Cornwall, Keepers Lodge Wood and Tower Hill Sawmills. (With kind permission from Angie Barr.)

Irene Snow (née Hannam) – Born 9 June 1923.
Women's Land Army 1941, Women's Timber Corps 1942–45.
Felling trees in Dulverton, Porlock Hill and South Molton in Devon.

Joan Turner – Born 1923.
Women's Timber Corps 1942–January 1946.
Training at Culford, Bury St Edmunds, Suffolk, felling, planting and fencing Slades Wood, Monmouthshire, Stoke Rochford, Grantham, Lincolnshire, Derby, Derbyshire and Tamworth, Staffordshire.

Diana Underwood (née Fortescue) – Born December 1922.
Women's Timber Corps 1940–autumn 1943, when she married.
Trained at the Forest of Dean in Parkend as a measurer and then went on to work in the New Forest working inside sawmills. (With kind permission from Mary Hobbins.)

Thanks also goes to Rose Burton; Brenda Harrison (née Simmons); Nancy Harrison (née Lowe) (with kind permission of John Harrison); Grace Hollands (née Hatch); Ann Moffatt; Sylvia Mole; Doreen Musson; Daisy Pragnell (née Lodge); Winnie Renshaw; Dorothy Swift; Evelyn Taylor; Maisie Triggel (née Arnold); Lillian Veitch; and Alfie Weir.

Introduction

I first heard about the Women's Timber Corps when I was working for the Forestry Commission as a public relations consultant. I was working for the best boss I'd ever had, David Williamson. He gave me freedom to choose the stories I worked on. He was so encouraging and supportive and asked me to speak to the staff and find the best stories I could.

It was, in fact, one of my conversations with him which led me to discover the Women's Timber Corps. He spoke about his all-female management team in the Chilterns based at Wendover Woods, Buckinghamshire, and how proud he was of them. (Little did he or I know at the time that this was in fact where the very first women had worked in forestry in the UK in the First World War.) This piqued my interest, as it seemed a far cry from the bearded, ale-drinking men one more commonly associated with forestry. So, with little to go on, I pitched the idea of 'Women in Forestry' to a BBC Radio 4 *Woman's Hour* reporter, whom I had been working with on another story.

She said she'd done a piece on female lorry drivers before and so she thought it could be of interest. But she needed something more to go on, something topical or newsworthy, to make it work. So, I began to research into women in forestry and found little to begin with, until I spoke to a wonderful woman in the Human Resources department at the Forestry Commission. She said, 'You know it is nothing new women working in forestry, the first women to work in forestry was in the war.'

This was what interested both the *Woman's Hour* reporter and me. So, I spoke to male and female foresters I knew and what was intriguing was that no one had ever heard of them before. I researched the Women's Timber Corps and found one page on a website about the Scottish members of the Women's Timber Corps.[1] But there was very little information online back in 2010.

I tried to contact people with connections to the website, but they were now living in Canada, having married Canadian foresters they met during the war. I couldn't work out whether the Women's Timber Corps was part of the Land Army or a separate division and I felt thwarted in my quest to discover anything about these women. Eventually, the *Woman's Hour* contact went cold.

After this I discovered that the first statue dedicated to the Women's Timber Corps went up in the Queen Elizabeth Forest Park, near Aberfoyle, Scotland, in 2007, some sixty-five years after the Women's Timber Corps was formed.[2] Following an appeal by Forestry Commission Scotland 100 of the original women got in touch and many attended the unveiling. I became fascinated by the story of these women and wondered what had happened to the women who worked in England. Where were they now and what was their story?

So I kept researching and making new contacts with people who may have known these women, until one day I was politely asked not to do any more work on the Women's Timber Corps, as there were other stories that might be more fruitful. But I didn't stop. Everything I did now was in my own time. My first port of call was The National Archives in Kew.[3] Here I found one folder with a note saying all the records on the Women's Timber Corps except one sample folder had been destroyed.

It felt like the story would stay forgotten unless something was done; after all, who would believe that the women could fell trees as well as the men? I knew Churchill's attitude to women and that women had to give up their wartime work, often to go back to domestic service, so the men could return to their jobs after the war.[4] My gut feeling then, as it is now, was that this was a cover-up: the government wanted the Women's Timber Corps to be forgotten, or worse, the women's contribution was regarded as insignificant.

My continued research found that even in Women's Land Army history books, the Women's Timber Corps at most receive one chapter, at worst a passing reference or a few lines. But I felt inspired by what little I had heard about these women. I had an affinity with them: I had always been proud of my own physical fitness and strength, I loved being in the forests, felt passionate about my job at the Forestry Commission and I was fascinated by the varied nature of forestry work and exploring the relationship between forests, people and the economy. If I had been a young woman during wartime I would have signed up with the Women's Timber Corps.

Then, eventually, I made contact with Stuart Olssen, who had campaigned for years to get the Women's Land Army and Women's Timber Corps acknowledged for their work. He explained that, like the Women's Land Army, the Women's Timber Corps received no recognition after the war, no gratuities, medal or pension, and they were excluded from Remembrance Day events. All his years of hard work eventually paid off when, in 2000, the women were allowed to march past the Cenotaph for the very first time in over fifty years since the war had ended. He was also instrumental in the prime minister, Gordon Brown, awarding medals to veterans of the Women's Land Army and Women's Timber Corps in 2008.[5]

Stuart Olssen invited me to the Remembrance Day Parade in 2011 at the Cenotaph, dedicated only to the Women's Land Army and Women's Timber Corps. This was the first time I met the Lumberjills, Eileen Mark and Audrey Broad, and they had wonderful stories to tell. I was even more enthused by the story of the Women's Timber Corps, so I enlisted support from colleagues across the Forestry Commission to help me uncover photos and any more information we could find. Richard Darn, PR consultant, had already begun the search for the forgotten Women's Timber Corps in the north of England.

So I visited the Forest Research Library and was invited to search the archives in Kielder Castle. To my surprise, the archives were no more than a jumbled storage space in the attic filled with old rusting forestry tools, dusty boxes and files covered in bat guano. It took me and my best friend Sophie two days to go through every box and shift each piece of machinery to discover, at last, some photos of the Women's Timber Corps, a rare book *Meet the Members: A Record of the Timber Corps of the Women's Land Army* published in the 1940s, a brass badge bearing the two crossed axes and a most prized armband from the Women's Forestry Service in the First World War.[6]

The stories, facts and photos I gleaned told the story of the powerful strength and potential of women and nature working together behind the scenes to support men on the front line at war. My enthusiasm for the story caught on in the organisation and, by good fortune, for the first time in almost 100 years the Forestry Commission had a female chair, Pam Warhurst. So, under her lead the organisation launched a nationwide search to rediscover the forgotten Women's Timber Corps of the Second World War and she commissioned a sculpture to be dedicated to the Lumberjills.

Over 100 women came forward, many in their late 80s and 90s, but we discovered from family members that many had sadly passed away. I then began a nationwide tour to meet the women from Cornwall to Suffolk, and from Yorkshire to Argyll in Scotland. I met many amazing, spirited women during the course of my research, who never imagined that their wartime contribution was of interest to anyone after all these years. Many were still either upset or angry that they had not been recognised for their contribution during the war for so many years.

I travelled four hours by train to meet Edna Holland, one of the first Lumberjills I met, but when I arrived at 10 a.m. and called to let her know, she didn't answer. I waited all day in a cafe, tried calling her every hour throughout the day, but there was still no reply. Just when I had decided to leave at 5 p.m., I thought I'd try one more time and to my surprise she answered. She said she was feeling unwell and didn't want to see me. I could hear she was upset, nearly in tears. She said, 'Don't waste your time, no one cares about us old people now. We are the forgotten army.' I replied that this wasn't true because I cared. Reluctantly she agreed to meet me. She was quite unfriendly when I arrived and shared little of her memories, at which point I was wondering why I had bothered. So, as a last resort, I showed her the brass crossed axes badge I had found at Kielder Castle, and she suddenly changed. She had lost her badge in the forest back in the 1940s and it brought back a fondness and memories close to her heart. She showed me the end of a pit prop she had kept as a souvenir from the 1940s and all of her memorabilia from that period. By the time I left, she was laughing, smiling and wanted to tell me all of her stories.

So, this is the true story about the thousands of women who worked as Lumberjills in the Second World War. The overwhelming feeling you get when you speak to the original Women's Timber Corps is that they were given little respect for what they did in the war, quite unlike the heroic images of the fighter pilots you see on postcards at the Imperial War Museum saying, 'Never was so much owed by so many to so few.' That was quite simply untrue. There were millions of others who played their part in the war, among them the heroines of the Women's Timber Corps.

It is important to say that the Second World War was not the first time women worked in forestry. The first pioneering women to ever work with an axe and saw were in the Women's Forestry Service in the First World War, which was also a branch of the Women's Land Army. This is an amazing story in itself, but one that even less is known about. After just twenty years of the interwar period between 1919 and 1939 it seemed it had all been forgotten, but for a few key women in the Women's Liberation Federation. By the time I started researching, it was too late for me to meet any women from the First World War. Although, bizarrely, I discovered the great-grandmother of my first boyfriend from school days was one of those Lumberjills. Unfortunately, his family had been left no photos or memories of her life and work. So, for completeness, I have included a chapter about the Women's Forestry Service in the First World War at the end of the book.

1

Women Didn't Wear
the Trousers

Life in the 1940s

In the 1940s people didn't believe women could work in forestry, they didn't believe they could fell trees, they didn't believe they were strong. As Laura Bates says in her book *Everyday Sexism*: 'Disbelief is the first great silencer.'[1]

The Lumberjills were laughed at, they were ridiculed, and their competence was questioned. Life was very different to today in so many ways that we might find it difficult to imagine. Firstly, women did not wear the trousers! I don't mean they only wore a pair of jeans at the weekend. I mean they never wore trousers. It was as acceptable for a woman to wear trousers in the 1940s as it would be for a young man to walk down the high street in a skirt today.

Women wearing trousers were also regarded as being more 'sexually available'. They were thought to be 'provocative' and 'promiscuous'. And why? Because they were able to open their legs more widely in a pair of trousers perhaps? But then, skirts provide easier access. It didn't make much sense then and it certainly doesn't today.

In the 1940s women were regarded as the 'fairer sex'. Women were expected to be genteel, well-behaved, polite, quiet, coy and feminine. They were told by their parents to be 'good girls', which implied they mustn't talk too much, voice their opinion or sound precocious. The young women were actually called 'girls' in the 1940s and referred to themselves as 'girls', and it never occurred to them that this might be patronising. We are far more aware of this discrimination now with campaigns such as Always' #Likeagirl.[2] But worse still, 1940s society generally accepted that women were inferior to men; women were the weaker sex, less intelligent and more incompetent than men. There was an assumption that the standard human model was male, and the female version was a variant and as a result worth less.

I really do mean worth less. In the 1940s there was no such thing as equal pay. Women were paid less than men, even if they did the same job better. The government, under Churchill's leadership, did not believe women deserved equal wages. Earning money was connected to status and so women were only permitted a modest amount of financial autonomy when they went out to work during wartime. The fear was that working women might become working wives and ruin marital harmony, not only because it presented a threat to a man's identity as the 'bread winner', but also to the concept of the full-time housewife.

To help maintain the status quo and keep women in their place, women were not allowed responsibility for household finances or even their own finances. It was not until 1975 and the Sex Discrimination Act that a British woman could open a bank account in her own name, without her husband's permission.[3] Single women still couldn't apply for a loan or credit card in their own name without a signature from their father, even if they earned more than him.[4]

The best career path for women was to gain experience in domestic service to prepare them for looking after their own homes when they were married. So when you begin to read the Lumberjills' stories, don't forget the default destination for all women was to become a housewife. When I met Lumberjill Audrey Broad, she spoke of the pain she felt to be told by her parents that she could not continue in education like her brothers, because she was needed at home to look after her baby brother, Fred. Over and over again I heard stories of the young women being pulled out of education because their families could not justify the expense when they would be getting married, having babies and staying at home. There was no need to invest in a career for women.

I began writing a fictional account of Lumberjills in wartime, but when I shared this novel with the Lumberjills I had interviewed I felt that they did not want their story told as a piece of fiction, glorified and exaggerated for entertainment. Because for the Lumberjills their stories were true and yet no one had believed, acknowledged or remembered what they did in the war for their whole lives. By fictionalising their war work it downplayed the challenges they faced, the stigma they experienced and the incredible advances they made in eroding a view of women as substandard. In the 1940s they smashed down what society thought women were physically and mentally capable of, they forced men to rethink what women could achieve, and they proved women could do things differently to men and still succeed.

So, to give these women a voice, I have written the book using their words as much as possible to let their voices shine. This is their true story. I have used first-hand accounts of the lives of these women, which I had the incredible good fortune to meet, in order for you to immerse yourself in a personal and intimate retelling of their journeys. They have made me laugh and cry with their stories, they have inspired me and been my role models since I met them. They are wonderful. When I have found life tough, I always knew that writing about the Lumberjills would make me feel strong again and they have been there for me in spirit, pushing me on.

I happened to be the person who stumbled across their story and it fired up a storm in my belly. The teenage young woman in me said loudly, 'I would have been a Lumberjill.' I have no doubt that, had I been born at that time, I would have signed up for the Women's Timber Corps. I was very good at maths, I was really strong, very practical and I love being out in nature. My father, who passed away more than a decade ago, even gave me an axe for Christmas one year, long before I had ever heard of the Lumberjills. Bless him! It was one of the most gratefully received and surprising presents I have ever had.

There is another important factor which needs to be brought to your attention. The Lumberjills worked in the forests of Britain. It is an environment which released the young women from their limitations that were preconditioned by society, and gave them a clarity and confidence that they could do anything they wanted. It has long been recognised that being outdoors in nature is a human need, which brings us joy and a natural happiness.

Meet the Lumberjills

Let me introduce you to a few of the Lumberjills to help you to get to know them a little better. You will hear more from the following women throughout the book.

Audrey Broad is the first woman you will hear from and was the first Lumberjill I met. She worked in Southwater, near Horsham in West Sussex, during the war and stayed there for the rest of her life. She was upset that she was not allowed to continue with her education so she could become a teacher like her best friend. When I met her at age 86, she was lovingly placing canes next to rows of gerbera in her large garden to ensure the stems remained perfectly straight. Reluctantly and modestly, she shared how she had often won first, second and third prize in the annual flower show, vegetable growing, jam-making and cake competitions she entered. She was adorable, generous and very astute.

I met **Mary Broadhead** at her home in Barnsley, South Yorkshire. She had a very pronounced Yorkshire accent and I soon discovered that she had lost a thumb in the sawmills in Kent while working as a Lumberjill. She worked in a sawmill in Kent by day and volunteered to be a Red Cross ambulance driver by night, to help provide emergency medical services bringing casualties from boats and trains to hospital. She was a tough woman.

I first met mischievous **Margaret Finch** when we were doing filming for *The Great British Menu*. The film production company wanted one of the chefs to create a menu inspired by the story of the Lumberjills, so we met in a local hotel in Upton upon Severn, Worcestershire. She was well dressed in a trouser suit and wore a glamourous cream head scarf. She was an adventurous woman and had some amazing stories about driving articulated lorries loaded with timber. She made me laugh so much I cried that day.

Violet Parker was one of the most soulful women I met. She knew I had arrived even before I knocked on the door, and had a wonderful peace and happiness about her. She was unusual in that she openly said she flirted around and had a wonderful time in the war with all forces based in Lostwithiel, Cornwall, and didn't marry until she was 33 years old. She didn't want me to leave until I had watched a film with her, *The Magdelene Sisters*. It was about young girls who had fallen pregnant, had babies taken away and were put to work in a convent laundry. It was deeply upsetting how the young girls were treated. She was involved in filming some of the convents recently, because she worked in one after the war which was just like that. It was terrible.

Dorothy Swift was 'an outdoor girl at heart' and trained to become a Lumberjill in West Yorkshire.[5] There she became a timber measurer and then moved all over the country, working in forests from Greater Manchester to County Durham and Herefordshire. She campaigned successfully to get underwear listed as part of the official Women's Timber Corps uniform.

On a trip down to Cornwall I met **Enid Lenton**, one of the Scottish Women's Timber Corps, and having read about these strong, determined and professional forestry workers I was not disappointed. It was very fitting that I met Enid not long after the London 2012 Summer Olympics, as she had just missed out on the chance to compete at the Olympics before the war as a swimmer and was a role model for young women in the 1940s to encourage them to do exercise and sport. The pictures of the muscular

Lumberjills reminded me so much of the female Olympic athletes that exciting summer.

I went to see the gorgeous **Irene Snow** in her house in South Molton in Devon. Straight away she said, 'No one ever asks me about what I did in the war. I didn't think anyone was interested after all these years.' I knew she'd be surprised by my enthusiasm and how much I knew, and we shared stories as if we had been there together. She was a size 18 in the war and always ordered her clothes too small, and it made me laugh when she said, 'Every time I lifted my leg [to climb on the lorry] I ripped my dungarees a bit more.'

In April 1939, **Barbara Beddow** married a boy she had known from school days.[6] But in September of the same year he was killed: 'He was in the Irish Guards, in barracks in Dover where they were shelled from across the Channel.' So, later that year she went to the Forest of Dean to be trained in forestry. Later promoted to forewoman, she was put in charge of a special project in the New Forest to extract a highly valuable shrub which was used by the military for making high explosives.

The war brought an abrupt end to **Margaret Grant**'s dreams of becoming a professional singer.[7] She was a pacifist, attended meetings of the 'peace pledge' union and was determined not to join any service. However, on second thoughts she decided to volunteer to work in forestry, in case they sent her to munitions factories. Although she found it hard to begin with, her life was transformed, and she discovered an idyllic and peaceful existence working alongside the banks of Loch Awe in Argyll.

All of these women were adorable individuals with different stories and takes on their time at war. But they all had a common shared experience of fighting from the forests to help win the war. All along in my journey with these women, I could hear their voices saying, 'We were never appreciated for what we did,' and, 'We have been forgotten.'

2

Domestic Servants, Shop Assistants and Hairdressers

In September 1939:

> Just after war was declared we were in church and the siren went off to test it. So it felt that no place was safe. It was a very frightening thought for a fourteen-year-old. The start of the war had a great effect on my life. It upset the house where we lived. It was strongly built with big beams and so we did not need an air-raid shelter. Our parents moved our iron beds belonging to Myra, Arthur and me to the downstairs room and that's where we had to sleep. One night in the early hours of the morning I heard a screeching plane coming down. So I remember rolling out of bed on to the floor and getting underneath it. That plane ended up in Swanbourne Lake in Arundel. It was a German plane and the pilot died. That was an awakener and made you think about the war.

For the young women like Audrey Broad, age 14, the beginning of the war was very frightening. It is hard to imagine what it would be like today to hear the prime minister declare we are at war. But at 11.15 a.m. on 3 September 1939, families sat around the wireless to hear Neville Chamberlain broadcast the following statement to the nation:

> This morning the British Ambassador in Berlin handed the German Government a final Note stating that, unless we heard from them by 11 o'clock that they were prepared at once to withdraw their troops from Poland, a state of war would exist between us. I have to tell you now that no such undertaking has been received, and that consequently this country is at war with Germany.

The outbreak of war meant families had to make difficult decisions. There were new financial constraints and the practical problems of travelling to and from school or work. Many young men were being conscripted, leaving behind young women and children; it naturally fell to the young women like Audrey Broad to look after younger children in the family.

At Christmas time in 1939, I was just over 14 years old and it was just a matter of looking for a job. I passed a scholarship to go to college. But, when war was declared my parents advised that it was better not to spend any money on going to college. Mary, my best friend, went on to high school and became a teacher. I was quite upset, and it still hurts that I wasn't able to go to college and become a teacher and that it could not be changed. Although, I would not want to speak badly of my parents as they did what they thought was right at the time. They were very sorry about it. Mum had a new baby, my little baby brother called Fred, and I was needed to help look after him.

We came from a middle-class family with five children. Bernard was the eldest, then Arthur, me, Myra and Fred. Bern went to the boy's service in the navy at 15 years old and Arthur joined the navy later during national service, after some time as a carpenter. Bern benefitted from going to the navy, where he had a lot of encouragement and education in the navy to do well. He did do very well and stayed in the navy for twenty-two years.

Audrey was so determined to prove herself like her brothers. 'In 1942 I was already training with the girls' brigade and became a sergeant. I must have been very authoritative as a sergeant in the girls' brigade. I can't believe it really as I was so withdrawn when I lived at home.'

Education

Across the country, many young women like Audrey Broad were discouraged from continuing with education beyond the age of 14. Molly Paterson would have liked to have gone on to Oban High School and Hostel. However, the system in the Highlands of Scotland in those days was for those living in the outlying areas to stay in the hostel all week, because it was not practicable to travel on a daily basis:

But even though I was probably bright enough to get through the entrance exam Mum said that I would have to go out to work. So I went to Dundee to stay with my aunt and get a job. I started work as a needle-work apprentice in a large department store where I had to sweep floors, make tea and learn the stitches.

It was common practice in the day that only young women from wealthier families, like Olive Edgley, should remain in education:

My twin sister, Vera, and I were born in Newcastle, moved to Wooley Bay when we were 2 years old and when we were 7, father bought a house on the side of Lake Ullswater where we spent holidays. Then when war broke out we stayed in the Lake District and went to school at Queen Elizabeth Grammar in Penrith.

In the 1940s, Britain was divided by class and women from poorer families had no choice but to leave school and start work at 14 years old. When Irene Snow grew up she lived between Bradford and Bingley, West Yorkshire, in a village called Wilsden: 'After I left school I worked in the woollen mills. I was one of seven children. We didn't have a lot of money but always had enough food as we were tenants living on a farm.' Edna Holland also worked in the woollen mills and was a spinner.

In the south, working-class women were employed in factories, making products such as medicine, poison or baby bottles in a glass factory or cigarettes, snuff and cigars in a tobacco factory.

Domestic Service

The beginning of the war signalled very uncertain times and big changes were on the way. Most young women were still under parental control in their teenage years and it was commonplace in the 1940s for women to be sent to work in domestic service roles. Often employed in larger houses with a team of staff, the young women would clean and tidy reception rooms, serve afternoon tea, dinner and answer room service bells as maids, scullery maids or the more senior parlour maids.

Diana Underwood was from a middle-class family; her father was a solicitor.[1] But in August 1930, when she was aged just 7, her mother died. A month later her father sent her away from home to boarding school.

She was from Deddington in Oxfordshire and was sent over 100 miles away to a school in Tunbridge Wells in Kent. After school, when Diana came home, her father, always 'careful' with money, thought she would be likely to get married quickly and there was no point in him paying for her to train as a secretary – knowing how to run a household would be more useful (for him and then any husband that came along). So she was sent to a domestic science college. She said, 'I wasn't very good at that. I wanted to do secretarial work, but Dad didn't agree.'

High Street

Barbara Beddow won a scholarship to study at grammar school but ended up working as a shop assistant:

> I grew up in a country village in the then West Riding of Yorkshire. I was an only child, quite bright, gained a scholarship to a grammar school and was academically inclined, but my father, who was an electrical engineer working with a firm of gas engineers, became a victim of the 1930s depression and at 14½ years, I left school and got a job in a rather upmarket shop – a children's outfitters. We catered for children going away to prep school and sold the local grammar school uniforms. Later I moved to a very select ladies' fashion shop.[2]

Other young women worked as secretaries, office clerks, sales assistants in shops, department stores and wholesalers. But as foreboding and fear spread across the country, Violet Parker's life in Cornwall had to change like many others:

> I grew up in Lostwithiel and went to school until I was 14 years old and then worked in a milk bar in town. We served milkshakes, coffees and made our own ice cream. I did that for four years until I was 18. It was very sociable and I enjoyed doing it. I just enjoyed every day and I wasn't frightened of anything. It was a lovely peaceful life. Everyone had boats and we went up and down the river. It was a peaceful and good life. It was a shock when the war came and my brother had to go when he was 18. It was terrible.

Dorothy Scott from Chesterfield, Derbyshire, was a ladies' hairdresser 'but the war changed all that. The call up papers landed on the doormat one morning and I had to report to the local Labour Exchange.'[3]

A Nation in Need

The imminent threat of the Second World War signalled great changes for the nation and people's lives. Little did these women know what lay ahead of them. But the nation was in need. On the eve of the Second World War, an article in *The Times* warned that, 'should this country be engaged in a major war in the next few years, she will be in a much less advantageous position for timber supplies than in 1914'.

The problem was that at the beginning of the war, Great Britain imported 96 per cent of its timber by ship from the Baltic States, Scandinavia and Canada.[4] It was the largest timber-importing nation in the world. With the risk that war could bring a stop to 'one of our bulkiest imports'[5], collieries, which needed pit wood to keep the mines open, were acutely worried.

The efforts by the Forestry Commission in the interwar period to replant woodlands that had been felled in the First World War were still too young to be used for pit props. The trees that should have been reaching maturity in 1939 had already been felled in the First World War, leaving only the poor quality wood behind. There were fears that there would not be anywhere near enough trees in Britain to fuel wartime industries in the Second World War.

Surprisingly, there was no provision to stockpile timber. There was just seven months' worth of pit props in reserve. So collieries made desperate pleas for more forestry workers, as the British timber trade only employed 14,000 people at the time.

Lady Gertrude Denman

Lady Gertrude Denman, otherwise known as Trudie, understood the needs of the nation at this time.[6] She was the only daughter of the wealthy industrialist Weetman Pearson, who later became Viscount Cowdray. Her father ran successful businesses in engineering, coal mining and newspaper publishing. He developed oilfields in Mexico, produced munitions in the First World War and built the Sennar Dam on the River Nile. He was a staunch Liberal who supported free trade, Irish Home Rule and Women's Suffrage. With this strong influence on Trudie, she learnt from her father's experiences and recognised the increasing industrial demands and domestic needs of war.

In addition, Trudie's mother, Annie Pearson (née Cass), the daughter of a farmer from Bradford in Yorkshire, was a strong woman, a feminist and active member of the executive of the Women's Liberation Federation. Trudie and her mother shared feminist values and the belief that women were equal to men. Trudie saw the opportunity for women during wartime: men were being conscripted and she believed that women could step into roles previously thought of as for men only, namely farming and perhaps more surprisingly forestry.

Trudie had experience of working for the Women's Liberal Federation, Women's Suffrage and had become chairman of the Women's Institute Sub-Committee of the Agricultural Organisation Society in 1917. She was instrumental in setting up the Women's Land Army in the First World War and so she was the 'go to' person for the Second World War.

On 9 April 1938, the Ministry of Agriculture called a meeting to discuss farm labour in England and Wales in the event of war and the establishment of a women's branch with Lady Gertrude Denman at the helm. Trudie knew her responsibility was to the nation at war, even though she had only just recovered from a very serious illness. She saw an opportunity in her role as head of the Women's Institute to facilitate the recruitment of women into the Land Army. County leaders and organisers could also be drawn from the ranks of the Women's Institute (WI).

But the government was slow to mobilise war preparations to step up production of home-grown food, and Trudie was anxious Women's Institute members would be recruited for other war work. At the beginning of 1939, Trudie urged that shadow County Chairmen should be allowed to find out which farmers would be willing to take on Land Girls, where billets would be found and that a decision on minimum wages should be made. 'Official cold water' was, however, firmly poured on her proposals, the Treasury writing to the Ministry that Lady Denman's ideas were a 'sledgehammer to crack a nut'. At the end of April, Trudie felt obliged to deliver an ultimatum that she would be forced to resign unless she was allowed to choose and appoint her headquarters staff. This produced the desired effect, the Permanent Secretary replying that he recognised that 'her request was completely reasonable'.

And so Trudie set up the Women's Land Army, and the Control Labour Officer for the government drew up a list of sources from which fresh supplies of workers could be recruited to replace the drift of men into the forces.[7] The government needed to increase the number of forestry workers and members of the Women's Land Army were added to the list. But not all welcomed the idea of women working in forestry.

3

Promise of 'A Healthy, Happy Job'

> Walking along Shandwick Place in Edinburgh one afternoon in June 1942, I saw photographs of the girls working in the woods in a shop window and thought 'That's for me!' They looked so happy and, as I was on the point of making up my mind about war service, it seemed to solve my problem.[1]

Young women like Marie Henderson were among those who were won over by the idyllic idea of working out in nature. A young woman wearing a green jersey, breeches, open-necked shirt, boots and an axe over her shoulder would have been an unusual sight. These young women would certainly never have heard of the Women's Timber Corps.

Posters of happy, smiling women advertising the beautiful world of trees and nature were very appealing, and key to the success of the Women's Land Army recruitment campaign led by Lady Gertrude Denman. Trudie had become director of the Westminster Press in 1933 (age 39), which published four morning papers, nine evening papers, over thirty weekly and sports papers and one Sunday newspaper.[2] The weekly circulation figures in total reached 6 million copies and they had 3,500 staff. She became an active board member supporting more liberal editorial content, including a better representation of Women's Institute activities. So she was all too familiar with the benefits of great publicity and understood which images, editorial and advertising content were appealing to young women.

Posters advertising working on the land or in forestry portrayed the job as more of a lifestyle choice, rather than something the women were conscripted to do, like working in munitions factories. One slogan read: 'For a healthy, happy job.'[3] The posters even today have a timeless quality and appeal to young women.

But Trudie did not stop there in her promotion of the cause. As a public figure from aristocracy and well used to making speeches, she toured the country to promote the organisation, talking at rallies to encourage more young women to take the opportunity to sign up.

In a letter signed G. Denman, Honorary Director, sent to all the Women's Land Army county secretaries and chairmen on 10 February 1942, she also mentions the 'Land Girl' film:

'LAND GIRL' FILM.

The Ministry of Information has arranged for the production of an eight-minute propaganda film about a member of the Women's Land Army employed in Scotland. The film is intended to illustrate the valuable part, which members of the Land Army can play on a farm. It will be generally released on Monday, February 23rd, and will be shown in cinemas as part of the normal programme during the following six weeks.[4]

Women's Land Army

Lady Denman was also acutely aware of the speed required to get the Women's Land Army and forestry section up and running, and her nationwide propaganda campaign to promote the cause was trailblazing at the time.

Based on the successes of the Women's Forestry Service in the First World War, she had a clear picture of what she needed to achieve, and equally what challenges she would face.

Trudie co-ordinated the re-establishment of the Women's Land Army in the Second World War in record time: 'never seen business despatched so quickly and speeches so relevant and short.'[5]

As a chairman Lady Denman excelled, her contemporaries praising her genius for organization and the impartiality, quick understanding, and sense of humour which enabled her to handle with success any meeting, however large or difficult. She could be formidable in opposition – which she enjoyed – but was fair and generous to those whose opinions differed from hers.[6]

Trudie's father had such great wealth that he gave his daughter a private estate for her 21st birthday, Balcombe Place in West Sussex, and 3,000 acres of land. Much of it was forest and it included 100 cottages, including part of Balcombe Village. Trudie became very attached to the property, the beautiful unspoiled land and she especially loved the woods. She was a Lumberjill at heart.

In February 1939, she proposed that she would use her home, Balcombe Place, as the Women's Land Army headquarters free of charge. At the end of July, the government gratefully accepted her offer. She was clear that even in wartime she wanted the WI to remain true to its purpose of improving the education and social life of countrywomen. During the war, WI members would help increase food and timber production and care for evacuated town dwellers.

So with just five days before the beginning of war, Trudie was ready. When the fifty staff members arrived at Balcombe Place, they were given cocktails while they waited for their rooms to be allocated. There were fourteen officers and thirty-five clerks and typists, mostly from the Ministry of Agriculture in London, under Trudie as Honorary Director and Mrs Inez Jenkins as Assistant Director.

The Timber Trade

In contrast to this slick operation mounted by Lady Denman, with a workforce poised and ready for action, there was chaos, conflict and confusion hampering the urgent need to increase the supply of timber in the Second World War. Civil servants, in consultation with the timber trade, had worked out a 'blueprint' for the production of timber during wartime, affectionately known as 'the Bible'.[7]

They sent all divisional officers of the Forest Service heavily sealed packages marked 'Secret: Not to be opened until the outbreak of war'. The package explained the split in the Forestry Commission to the Timber Production Department and the Forest Management Department.

It contained a long list of all the sawmills in each region of the country, many of which had gone out of business a long time ago, some that were furniture makers ill-equipped to deal with logwood. Many important sawmills were not listed at all. The acquisition of standing timber from private landowners became an urgent priority, as was the need to obtain suitable equipment and machinery to process the wood. Russell Meiggs laments that while the structure was clear and logical at HQ, the organisation of the Ministry of Supply and wartime timber production was politely 'less closely integrated' between the civil servants, private timber trade and the Forestry Commission:

> on 2nd September 1939 the Headquarters staff moved into temporary quarters at the Royal Hotel where for the first week they lived in a fever of secret documents, urgent instructions and increasing overcrowding as new staff [were] recruited. Heads of departments in vain sought a detached calm in odd corners; baths became waste paper baskets and rapidly overflowed; bewildered hotel residents found themselves driven from public rooms and retreating before a steadily mounting invasion.

The civil servants had perhaps not understood the importance of the issue, that timber was vital to the war effort. It was the number one commodity and resource upon which all other industries depended. Without timber, the coal mines would not be able to operate: there would be no pit props to hold coal seams open for miners to extract the coal. Without coal, the factories for wartime industries and ammunition production would not be powered.

Timber importers and private timber trade became protective of their own commercial interests and the Forestry Commission wanted to protect its conservation interests in the forest. There was also conflict over which organisation would retain power and control over timber supply during wartime.

It eventually comprised personnel from both the Forestry Commission and private timber trade to form the Home Timber Production Department of the Ministry of Supply. Although, according to Russell Meiggs, the 'organisation was neither simple nor static. It underwent three major changes and even in its final form was not readily understood by the interested public.'

Russell Meiggs says, '1940 was a difficult year for home production. The swiftly developing crisis in the war bred a natural and healthy spirit of impatience. While production was substantially increased it was difficult to match the need. The colliery owners showed acute anxiety over the forward supply of pitprops.'

Amidst these chaotic wartime preparations, the final straw was the suggestion that women should work in forestry too. This idea was received with hostility. Despite the urgent need for timber, and the rapidly dwindling supply of men, progress by Lady Denman was inhibited by prejudice and reluctance to employ women in forestry. All attempts were made to deny, ignore or limit the introduction of the women.

However, Lady Denman and her workforce at Balcombe Place took robust action to introduce women into forestry at the beginning of the Second World War. Despite reluctance from the all-male timber trade, small numbers of women from the Women's Land Army were trained to work in this field. Young women were transferred to the Home Timber Production Department of the Ministry of Supply or local timber merchants, when requested to work in forestry in 1939. But some thirty girls who were trained in Cheshire had to wait to be given work. Progress was slow.

Despite the reluctance to take on the women, Lady Denman was not dissuaded and found a way round this. She recruited women into the Women's Land Army and then assigned them to forestry. Some worked in farming before being selected, while others went directly into forestry. It is important to note that, as a result, the Women's Timber Corps did not exist in the early years of the war. Russell Meiggs said 'a separate, permanent women's service' would have improved cooperation between the exclusively male timber trade and women workers, but it was 'not acceptable to the authorities'. However, as the women were interviewed many decades later they refer to their time in the 'Timber Corps' even before it was established in April 1942.

Signing Up

With great enthusiasm, Olive Edgley remembered the time when she signed up:

> I joined the Women's Land Army and went straight into working in the Timber Corps in 1940 with my twin sister, Vera. We had the choice of joining the ATS, WRENS or the WRAF but one of Vera's friends said the Timber Corps was so fantastic that we decided to do that.

Teenage women were recruited from all over the country, from Cornwall and Kent in the south to Yorkshire and Northumberland in the north of England, from all over Wales and Scotland. Some 14-year-olds were said to have volunteered to work in forestry in Scotland. Many were recruited from big cities attracted by the outdoor life, with the promise of a new life in the countryside in the fresh air.

Enid Lenton worked in the railway office in Glasgow before signing up in 1940:

My father worked in the railways in Glasgow and had a good job. I went to school until I was 17 and then I had five years in the railway office, which I hated because it was indoors. Then I had a spell at home helping my mother. I was glad to get out of the railway office and forestry appealed to me being as it was outdoors. I wasn't worried, I looked forward to it and we had to do something because it was the war.

The young women seemed to have an exuberance and excitement when given the opportunity to work in forestry and do their bit for the war. Some girls were proud to be selected by the Women's Land Army to go into forestry because they were well educated or had secretarial skills.

Edna Holland went straight into forestry:

I joined when I was 17½ because at that age you could go where you wanted to go, at 18 they decided for you. They wanted people who were good at maths to measure the pit props for the coal mines and I had been very good at maths so that is what I decided to do.

Molly Paterson was recovering from illness at home in Scotland when a job became available nearby which involved working for the timber section of the Ministry of Supply in the surrounding Ardbrecknish Forest:

My mother knew the manager, Mr Dow and his wife Brenda. She worked in the office and was about to have a baby and so the vacancy became available. Although I had never worked in an office or done clerical work before they knew I was a capable girl and I got the job.

A few months later, ten girls from the Land Army were drafted in from Glasgow to join us in what was now called the Timber Corps and from there on they were known as the Lumberjills. Mr Dow and his wife were a lovely couple and he was one of the nicest bosses I have worked for. One day Mr Dow said to me, 'Molly, you may as well transfer from the Ministry of Supply to the Timber Corps as money is getting tight' and so I joined the Lumberjills.

The majority of the girls who volunteered to work in forestry were from towns and cities up and down the country. Lady Denman had the foresight to make it policy that women from countryside or farming backgrounds should not be eligible for recruitment into the Women's Land Army. So it became another form of 'evacuation' to protect young women, such as

Peggy Conway from Manchester and her friend Kathleen from Liverpool, during wartime bombing in the cities.

That is not to say that local women from forestry communities did not end up working in forestry. There were young women who preferred the comfort of their own homes and wanted to stay with family and friends they had grown up with. Often women found work in forestry through local connections, like the girls from Pickering, North Yorkshire. Hundreds of unofficial Lumberjills, like Frieda Ellerby, worked in forestry:

> There was an opportunity to join either the ATS or the WAF. But someone helped me to get the job. The Land Army wasn't being offered and I had a friend who said I'll see what I can do for you. It was through them you see, through the locals in 1939 to '40. It was like that you see. I wanted to stay local and be with my friends. It would be safer wouldn't it.

In the spring of 1942, Ernest Bevin, Minister of Labour and National Service in the War Cabinet, declared that 1 million wives were wanted for war work. Inconveniences, he said, would have to be suffered and younger women would have to leave their homes and go where their services were required. He asked a million women, either full-time or part-time, to work in munitions or in shops and offices in order to release younger, more mobile women to fill shells and make munitions. It would be better to suffer temporarily than to be in perpetual slavery to the Nazis. He said everyone would have to 'heave together'.

Having a Choice

In Scotland, working in munitions often meant young women had to move far from home to work in large factories in cities in England. Used to a more rural life, many women opted to work on the land in the Women's Land Army or Timber Corps, before they were conscripted on their 18th birthday. It was the same in England and was the push that the girls, like Joan Turner, needed to sign up: 'I joined the Lumberjills in September 1942 age 19 because we had a bomb factory near us and I did not want to be drafted there. I had to ask for permission to sign up and when I told my mum, she said, "What have you done?"'

Dorothy Swift felt the same way about working in the bomb factories:

When I volunteered to join the Women's Timber Corps in 1943 a few months before my 18th birthday I was living in Sheffield and only too aware that if I failed to opt for some kind of war work after reaching the age, I might well be conscripted to a munitions factory or any of the Armed Forces. Being an outdoor girl at heart I knew that by labouring in Britain's forests I could make a real contribution to the war effort.

Others joined the Timber section of the Land Army or Timber Corps as a way out of the Land Army because they did not like cows, picking vegetables out of the mud or did not want to be a rat-catcher. In those days agricultural work was regarded as the most menial of work, especially for women.

Just after Diana Underwood turned 18 in December 1940, she knew she had to decide what to do as she would be called up into the services: 'My cousin, Helena, knew someone who was organising girls into the Land Army, so she sent her to see us. Dad wasn't very keen on my doing farm work, so it was decided I should join the Timber Corps branch of the Land Army.'

Farming work was always regarded as a lowly profession and especially by the middle and upper classes. Forestry work suffered from the same attitude, especially from the wealthier families whose daughters volunteered to work in the Timber Corps. Edna Barton's first husband, who had passed away by the time she joined the Timber Corps, was a middle-class draughtsman, and wouldn't have been impressed that his wife was doing manual work: 'He wouldn't have liked it, I don't think. He would've thought it was common.'

And when grammar-school-educated shop assistant Barbara Beddow received her instructions and travel warrants to go to the Forestry Training College in the Forest of Dean, her 'mother was horrified' and forbade her 'ever to darken their doors again'.

Cornish Violet Parker, who had worked in a milk bar and had two brothers in the army, thought she should do something for the war:

> I did not want to work on a farm I wanted to go into the Lumberjills. It didn't interest me working on the farms. I was lucky enough to stay home every night. We had two sawmills in Lanhydrock, so I was lucky to work there, otherwise I could have been sent away.

Hazel Collins was resolutely averse to milking cows at 4.30 a.m.: 'So I went to see the Land Army woman in charge and I said, "Can I go into the WRNS?" and she said, "No you can't." She transferred me to North Devon in the Women's Timber Corp. I was very proud of myself.'

For some women, like Irene Snow, forestry was seen as an exciting, adventurous alternative to land work: 'We always thought it was a bit up from being a Land Army girl, working in the Timber Corps, as I didn't fancy being a rat-catcher.'

Other women were recommended to join the Land Army or Timber Corps because a life in the country was thought to be recuperative if the girls were recently bereaved. Edna Barton suffered personal tragedy when her 6-year-old sister died and six months later, newly married, her husband Edmund Packwood died too. He fell off a roof the day before her 21st birthday:

As my little sister and husband had both died within six months of each other, the family thought it would be good for me to go and work out in the country. I was not in Land Army for long before I asked if I could go in the Timber Corps as it interested me more.

But, for Mary Broadhead, joining the Women's Timber Corps was an opportunity to escape the gender stereotypes of the day and her incumbent child-rearing duties. Mary, like many others, saw it as an opportunity to leave home and gain some valuable independence and prove herself:

We had a big family. When the oldest had got married, that left me with all the young children to look after and I didn't want to be a mother all my life to young children. I thought they were old enough now to look after themselves a bit. And so I thought it was one way of getting away from family and finding my own feet and that is what I did. My mum and dad knew I was grown up and when I said I wanted to go they said, 'It's up to you.' My dad was quite proud of me. But my mum knew she was going to miss me and would rather I wasn't going.

One thing is for certain: many of the young women leaving home for the first time were fearful of living away from friends and family in a country at war, and worried about what life would entail. Hazel Collins said:

I always remember saying to my father I am going into the Land Army and he said, 'When?' and I said, 'As soon as you fill these forms in' because I was under age, only 17 and a bit. He said, 'The one thing you have got to promise me is you must not come home crying.' Oh I did so want to, so many times.

She continued:

When I first joined the Timber Corps in 1942, I was 17 and a quarter. I remember sitting in my bedroom in 1942, looking out of my bedroom window and I saw all this fire. It was London burning. It was London burning after one of the blitzes. It was like a sunset but in the north and you don't get that in the north. It was night, first it was yellow colour and then it was red. It was horrible it really was. I was quite worried.

Ode to the WTC

I heard the call of the ATS
I heard the call of the WAAF
The Wrens they made an urgent call
The NAAFI want more staff
I thought of each and everyone
But wanted something more
The 'whispering grass' it spoke to me
'Why not the Timber Corps'
So here I am in outfit green
Crossed axes and saw
Felling trees from morn till night
To help win this blinkin' war
I've been at it now a year or more
It's just the life for me
Until the bells of peace ring out
Up the WTC[8]

4

Green Beret, Tacketty Boots and Special Issue Undies

The Uniform

I was directed to a Women's Timber Corps training camp in Wetherby, West Yorkshire, having received in advance a large parcel containing my standard land army uniform. Consisting of two pairs of khaki dungarees, two working smocks of heavy drill, two cotton pique working shirts, one best cotton poplin shirt, a pair each of corduroy and gabardine breeches, one green woollen pullover and one three-quarter length khaki overcoat …

In addition, I found one pair of brown leather walking shoes, a pair of tough black working boots, one pair of wellingtons, one oil skin raincoat, three pairs of woolly knee-high socks, a massive sou' wester for stormy days ahead plus a bottle green beret worn to distinguish members of the Women's Timber Corps from those of the Women's Land Army, whose hats were trilby shaped and fawn. There were no man-made fabrics in those days, so our uniforms breathed naturally.

With help from my parents I took this equipment by bus to the railway station where my mum and dad said their tearful farewells. I felt like a fledgling flying its nest. The station platform was swarming with like-minded land girls in ill-fitting uniforms. I glanced at my reflection in a waiting room mirror to confirm that my own uniform fitted me well, although my hitherto unworn shoes were killing me. As our train steamed into the station it dawned on me that I had yet to pin brass-crossed axes to my overcoat sleeves, sew felt ones to my pullover and attach a Bakelite badge to my beret.

On the way to Wetherby I introduced myself to other raw recruits by my proper name, Dorothy Swift. While still in transit I palled up with two compatible 'fledglings', Muriel Cocker and Jean Mason, to whom I let it drop that my assumed name was Dot. We were to stick together for the next couple of years.[1]

For many of the girls receiving the Women's Land Army uniform, like Doreen Musson, it would have been the first time they had ever worn a pair of trousers. She said, '[It was] Very exciting receiving the uniform – khaki jodhpurs, green sweater, khaki overcoats, shirts, green beret, overalls, socks and shoes.'[2] The women received different items as part of their uniform, according to where they worked.

Identity

Women had such pride in this uniform and a sense of solidarity, which was so important for the girls when they were leaving home for the first time and taking a great stride in their jodhpurs into the unknown world of war work. It became part of their identity, as they entered a new world, where their uniform gave them the permission to work in a 'man's job' so they could do their bit for the war. It was both terrifying and exciting at the same time.

Dorothy Swift was one of the lucky ones to receive a full uniform for the Women's Timber Corps, which was the same as the Land Army uniform save for the bottle green beret.[3] This was thought to be more appropriate for forestry work and envied by the Land Girls.

But it was the item of clothing which caused the most problems for the Women's Timber Corps. There was much debate about how it should be worn, at a jaunty angle to the side or straight on, if at all. Joan Turner never wore the beret: 'I wore nothing on my head. The beret was just for dressing up.' Edna Holland was very proud of her beret, 'but we didn't wear it for working in because it was very impractical'.

The official badge was made from brown Bakelite and had a fir tree mounted on a royal crown. Fellers were issued with a brass badge of two crossed axes and were very highly prized by the girls, many of whom lost them at work in the forest. Coloured armbands designated women who had stayed within the service for two years or more and a red felt triangle badge was issued for every six months' service in the corps.

The iconic Lumberjill look you often see in photos or on parade was the brown shoes, long woollen socks, fawn-coloured gabardine jodhpurs, aertex shirt, Land Army tie, bottle green jumper and beret. The rest of the time the girls wore what was practical and comfortable out in the forest and made seasonal alterations to the uniform, if they even had one.

Borrowing Clothes

Wilma McLullich, like all trainees at Shandford, had no trouble being kitted out with uniform immediately on completing her training. But 'others were less fortunate and wore out their own clothing before receiving uniforms. They received neither compensation nor even clothing coupons, which was a great injustice.'[4]

Many women in Scotland, Yorkshire and Cornwall were never issued with a uniform, which made work less comfortable. Instead, they acquired suitable clothing as and when they needed it for changes in weather and season from brothers' wardrobes who were away fighting at war. It was over a year before Katie Ann Kennedy and her friends received uniforms: 'inferior to those worn by the Canadian Forestry Corps, which was a measure of our wartime restrictions. They were even given working gloves. I remember our reconditioned wellington boots leaking and our black boots resembling cardboard when they got wet.'[5]

It was very cold by the time winter had set in and Rose Simpson had to provide her own clothing:

> I was lucky: as my four brothers were away doing their service, I pinched their socks, jumpers, trousers, jackets and even my dad's long johns were cut down to size. Still we complained about wanting a 'walking out' uniform, so we were given a green drill suit along with a badge to sew onto the pocket. The badge was inscribed with WFS – Women's Forestry Service.[6]

Katie Dowson, who worked in Pickering, North Yorkshire, didn't have any uniform at all: 'We wore slacks. It was quite unusual in those days. It looked like I had shorts on but there were not such things as shorts, we rolled our dungarees up. In the winter we started wearing jodhpurs because they were warm.'

Just as unusual as it was to wear trousers, it was equally unladylike for the girls to wear boots, as Frieda Ellerby found when she went to the cinema:

> Sometimes we'd go to the pictures in the blackout in overalls. There was no point in changing during the blackout and they would say, 'Oh, here

they come in their boots. Clamp, clamp, no need to stamp.' 'Oh, we can't help it with our big boots on.' 'There's no need to stamp when you're coming down the road.'

But the unladylike appearance of the girls wearing slacks and boots was the least of their worries, as the new shoes and boots 'were a killer to wear', according to Joan Turner. 'The shoes were wicked you'd put fat on them to soften them, but they were for men.'

The heavy leather shoes with thick studded soles were called tacketty boots in Scotland because the studs are called tacketts. These shoes gave Molly Paterson 'terrible, painful blisters'. So many of the girls complained about the blisters. Some got so bad that they went septic and the girls couldn't work for days. Joan Turner explained that the boots had to be sturdy for work: 'We had to burn all the rubbish and I burnt my boots stamping out fire, luckily my father knew a boot factory.'

Alterations

Often the uniforms were ill-fitting, either too big or too small, so the girls who were good at needlework or sewing were relied upon to make do and mend like Joan Turner:

The uniform was big and bulky. I was good at sewing so used to try to make the uniforms fit. Gloves didn't last a minute on your hands, so you got blisters … We used to recycle material to make gloves and other clothes. Blankets into coats, everything out of rubbish, if you had an old jumper you would unpick and reknit it.

Working in winter, especially in Scotland, meant that the girls had a tough time and had to wear warm clothes to protect them from the bitter cold and snow. Molly Paterson, who worked in Argyll, was issued with gabardine trousers (not corduroy) which were made of very thick cloth: 'They were nice and warm on the very cold winter mornings but very hot in summer.'

Olive Edgley worked in the south-west and remembered the great coats with fondness:

Lovely, they were the warmest thick woollen coats if we were walking through a wood. It was different though if it was cold and you were just standing. In the really coldest weather, you are not very busy if you're the one doing the writing and it was freezing. But you had to carry on doing the work.

In the summer it was a completely different picture and one which the girls thoroughly took advantage of, working outdoors in often remote parts of the forest. Dorothy Swift replaced her dungarees with 'scanty shorts' and shedding 'as many clothes as possible during the summer seemed the most sensible thing to do'.

Special Issue Undies

Edna Holland rolled up her dungarees to make them into shorts: 'The dungarees did not stay like that for long as we cut them off into shorts. We were sent special issue undies, which didn't last long either as we cut those off into shorts too.' This item of underwear was probably ordered by men in charge of wartime uniforms in response to a demand by Dorothy Swift and her pals:

> I told Hammy, I had to think in terms of dancing when I use my clothing coupons, whereas she should think in terms of going to the pictures because she had two left feet. Neither of us wished to waste coupons on boring underwear, nor did the others when they thought about it. We petitioned successfully to have underwear listed under 'statutory requirements' in keeping with our uniforms. Laugh! We couldn't stop when our first batch of undies arrived. Each girl had been issued with two pairs of interlock, long legged knickerbockers with matching chin-high vests. We called them 'passion killers' but at least they kept us warm![7]

Part of the Control Labour's duties with the Board of Trade was to supply 'protective clothing' to be available to timber labourers who worked outside during bad weather.[8] Thus alongside thousands of pairs of rubber knee boots, working suits, overalls, waterproof capes and sou'westers was 'protective underwear'. The underwear caused much hilarity for the young women like Joan Turner: 'We were issued with underwear, woolly vest and on the bottom stamped war office and the knickers came down to your knees. At one concert, I did not dare turn around because you could see my underwear through the dress.'

It Felt Like Prison
on Training Camp

Joining up with the Women's Timber Corps, I was sent to the area of
Bury St Edmunds to a camp at Culford. When we arrived at Culford train
station there were about eighty girls that got off the train, all in uniform.
So many local people stopped to look. We were put on a bus, our luggage
was put on a truck, and we were taken to the camp. Oh it was when we
got to Culford, I thought it was like a prison camp to tell you the truth.

We were divided into groups, each group taken into a large wooden
hut, which became our sleeping quarters. My hut was number two. Then
we all had a talk on the rules of the camp and how we were expected to
behave. At 9 o'clock we could have a cup of cocoa to drink before bed-
time and at 10 o'clock the camp gates were closed. If you were late back,
you were taken to see the board of instructors to be told off and given
extra work to do. If a soldier walked a girl back to the camp he could
only go to the gates, then he had to leave and could not be seen hanging
around. On Sunday we were expected to go on church parade.

Mary Broadhead recalled her first night at camp:

The camp washrooms felt cold. The water we used was lukewarm and
the floor was made from concrete. Lots of the girls cried when they went
back to the huts that night. Some of them cried with homesickness and
just wouldn't stop. Oh I thought it was just like a prison camp.

For many of the new recruits like Mary Broadhead it was their first time
away from family. The training camp at Culford would be their new home
for the next four weeks. Previously used by refugees before the war, there
were no home comforts here. It became the biggest Women's Timber Corps
training camp in Britain, where thousands of girls were trained throughout

the war. Not far from Lakenfield airfield, Eileen Mark could hear the aircraft taking off day and night, which made her feel vulnerable, being so close to the dangers of war:

> We stayed in Nissen huts, which were like army barracks. The beds were like trestle tables with three sponge biscuits on top to lie on. When I first went I was homesick and worried when I saw all the planes going out, that was probably the lowest time for me.

The diverse backgrounds of the women often bemused the trainers on camp in Scotland. Bonny Macadam, a trainer at Shandford Lodge, near Brechin in Angus, recalled meeting new recruits as they stepped off the train at Brechin station. 'There were so many townies – shop assistants, hairdressers … you name them. They had high heels, hats with veils … absolutely incredible!'[1]

Women's Timber Corps

Lady Gertrude Denman (Trudie) declared that the greatest achievements of the Women's Institutes were that they were self-governing and all the jobs from making tea to stewarding meetings were shared by all members, not run by 'one or two super-women'.[2] She recognised the movement as a great opportunity for social reform, where the ordinary village woman could have a voice and a platform to represent the interests of all women through democracy. She wanted this vision to be shared by the Women's Land Army and Timber Corps too.

She provided the organisation with great leadership, courage, fairness, honesty and regarded everything with balance and objectivity, from an impersonal, disinterested way. 'This greatly helped to free the whole movement from personal issues.'[3] She was direct and to the point in meetings and expected others to be plain speaking too. She was good at knowing what ordinary people thought and felt, and so she would help simplify and clarify wording in reports too.

She was adventurous and sporty, a good horsewoman who rode side-saddle, and had a passion for hunting. In winter she played hockey, and in summer lawn tennis. An enthusiastic games player, she particularly enjoyed tennis and golf, and was president of the Ladies' Golf Union from 1932 to 1938 which she was very proud of. Sawing trees, chopping branches and making bonfires was a pursuit which Trudie also greatly enjoyed. So, there was no reason why she thought women could not be involved in the efforts to increase home-grown timber production.

In 1942, Britain's worst fears were met as timber imports from the Baltic were closed, Scandinavian countries were invaded, and ships could no longer be spared to bring large loads of timber from Canada.[4] At the same time, the demand for timber increased to build army camps, hostels, air stations, field telegraph poles, beach landing runways, ammunition boxes and field hospitals. But it was the supply of pit props which caused ministers within the Ministry of Supply the most anxiety. Pit props were essential in keeping the mines open and producing coal for wartime industries.

But the reluctance and prejudice that held back recruitment of women into forestry persisted, until the nation realised that timber was running desperately short and home-grown timber production needed to step up. On 4 November 1941 a letter from Inez Jenkins, to all the Women's Land Army Country Secretaries and Chairmen, stated:

Employment in Timber Production.

All employment by the Home Grown Timber Production Department of the Ministry of Supply is now scheduled under the Essential Works Order which means that no Land Army volunteer employed by this Department as a forester engaged in timber production – i.e. The lopping, felling, chopping, sawing or measuring of timber – is free to resign her employment without first obtaining permission to do so from the Ministry of Supply and the Ministry of Labour.

Women's Land Army volunteers may be offered employment as timber workers by their county office and the national need for increased timber production should be emphasised. At the same time the provision must be clearly explained so that volunteer realises that, if she accepts the offered employment, she will be entering the one branch of Land Army service in which she will be tied compulsorily to her job. If she refuses the offer of timber work, her refusal must not be recorded against her and an effort should be made to find her employment in agriculture or horticulture.[5]

Come 11 December 1941, in a letter from Inez Jenkins, Assistant Director, the idea of a 'separate Women's Timber Corps' is first mooted:

Employment in Timber Work.

Since I last wrote to you on the subject of the employment of members of the Women's Land Army in timber work, a scheme for the establishment of a separate Women's Timber Corps has been formulated by the Ministry of Supply and is now under consideration.

If this scheme is put into operation, the Women's Land Army will cease to be responsible for the supply of labour for timber work and volunteers who are already engaged in that type of employment will be offered a choice between remaining as timber workers and joining the Women's Timber Corps or remaining members of the Women's Land Army and transferring to some other branch of Land Army work.

I will of course let you know as soon as any final decision is reached on this matter. Meantime volunteers who offer service in the Women's Land Army and express a preference for forestry work may still be enrolled and placed in forestry or timber employment. No woman or girl however already engaged in timber work who is not a member of the Women's Land Army but now applies for enrolment should be accepted.

Yours sincerely,

INEZ M. JENKINS

Assistant Director.[6]

This Essential Work Order was one of the factors that made the members of the Women's Timber Corps feel more important and gave them a unique position and status. At this point there was a division of identity between the Women's Land Army and those working in forestry, which caused some conflict.

When the Battle of the Atlantic stopped timber imports to Britain completely, this marked a complete change in attitude and the Women's Timber Corps was officially formed in England in April 1942, and Scotland soon followed in May 1942.[7] By this time, women had made good progress in proving their worth in forestry, despite discouragement from the men and local communities in which they worked.

Women's Land Army
Balcome Place, Balcome
13th March 1942

Dear Miss Manley,

The new scheme for the formation of the W.L.A. Timber Corps is under consideration, whereby all timber workers who are going into employment with the Home Grown Timber Department of the Ministry of Supply will receive a month's training before being registered as a member of the Timber Corps. This will mean that in future large batches of trainees will be sent to Culford camp instead of small batches of volunteers for direct employment and it has been suggested that the first contingent of 100 volunteers should be sent to Culford about the middle of April.

The regulation with regard to the Essential Works Order will continue to be in force and the conditions of life in the camp will remain the same. The girls will go to Culford for one month's training and be subsequently employed by the Home Grown Timber Production Department wherever their services are required.

If you have any girls who are anxious to take up this type of work I should be glad to have their names and particulars as soon as possible in order to include them with the batch of volunteers I am collecting. The date on which they will be required has been given as April 13th, but I am not able to confirm this at the moment and would be glad if you would not allow any girls to give in their notice until I am able to give you definitive confirmation.

Yours sincerely,

Miss. C. Crozier[8]

All the women working in forestry at that date were absorbed into the Women's Timber Corps. The nickname the 'Lumberjills' was first coined on 18 April 1942 when the *Northern Daily Mail* reported on the 'First Lumber Jills', when '25 Lancashire girls between ages of 18 and 24, former clerical workers, typists, and hairdressers, leave Manchester for a timber training camp in South-East. They are the first contingent of girls of the Women's Land Army Timber Corps.'

Differences in pay, education and type of work divided the Women's Land Army from the Women's Timber Corps and created some hostility between the two, especially when the Lumberjills were routinely mistaken for Land Girls because they wore the same uniform, aside from the beret. The women who worked in forestry were in the minority, and so they developed a strong identity, regarding themselves as an elite workforce and expressing pride in their unique role.

All of the girls that volunteered for the Women's Timber Corps made a choice to work in forestry, not on farms. Being a Lumberjill could not be more different to milking cows, ploughing the fields and harvesting the vegetables. The Lumberjills worked with an axe and saw, felled 100-ft trees, lifted heavy timber with their bare hands, hauled tons of timber from forest to roads and made complex mathematical calculations based on cost of cubic volumes of wood.

They were not 'Land Girls,' they were 'Lumberjills' argued Mary Broadhead: 'I object to being called a farmer. I didn't want to be a farmer, I wanted to be a timber girl because they were tougher than farmers.'

Training

Recruitment increased dramatically with the establishment of four main training centres in England. By the end of the war, thousands of women were trained at Culford in Suffolk, Wetherby in Yorkshire, Hereford in Herefordshire and Lydney in the Forest of Dean, each of which could accommodate hundreds of women every month for training. The Royal Ordnance Factory hostel in Wetherby was used as a training centre for the Women's Timber Corps, but the other camps were purpose built with Nissen huts or based on timber-framed buildings.

In Scotland, while many girls were trained on the job out in the forest, one of the main training centres was Shandford Lodge, a shooting lodge with enough space to erect several army huts in the garden, 8 miles from Brechin. Some 120 girls arrived at the lodge every month and after five weeks' training they were sent to camps at Alness, Strachur, Innerleithen, Dumfries, Park House, Alyth, Ethie and to private firms and estates. The other main training centre in Scotland was Park House, Drum Oak in Aberdeenshire.[9]

The four-week training programme introduced them to four main areas of work: felling, sawmilling, measuring and haulage. They spent a week on each to help identify which girls would be most suitable for each type of work. They started with felling and sawmilling, then moved on to measuring and, for those over 21 years old, driving tractors and lorries for haulage. The training was hard, manual labour, which required lifting and carrying heavy tree trunks and branches in all areas of work. It also required learning how to identify the different species of trees through the changing seasons. Other jobs included burning branches that had been trimmed from the tree trunks, charcoal burning and fencing to protect newly planted trees.

After training, if they qualified, the women were enrolled into the Women's Timber Corps and directed into the area of work that they had either shown the most aptitude for or had the stature for, and sent to work for the Forestry Commission, Ministry of Supply or private timber merchants.

For some women, like Hilton Wood from *Meet the Members*, going away to training camp was a wonderful experience, stepping into the world of wartime work:

It's strange to look around the hut now, so bare and deserted. Soon another ten will be stuffing away their personal belongings and feeling just as lost and homesick as we did. I wonder if they'll be so happy as we have been. I wonder if they will grow to love the life as I have done. I shall never forget my first days.[10]

However, many thousands of women received no official training to prepare them for work in the forest. Instead, they were trained on the job.

Peggy Conway's first day on the job started at 8 a.m.:

my partner Jane was feeling unwell and decided to return by train to Liverpool (and was never seen again ...) So there I was 8 a.m. the next morning and an open-backed wagon arrived and tipped out a load of wild-looking men, who climbed over the fence with the axes and cross–cut saws, swearing vociferously. A bit of a shock to a nicely brought up Methodist girl!

When Joyce Earl was asked whether she got much training, she replied, 'You must be joking, we were shown the saw then just got on with it.'[11] One week she was called up for service, the next she was standing on Nottingham train station waiting to be transferred to her digs near Wimpole, Cambridgeshire, and she started work the same week, felling and trimming fir trees for pit props.

Enid Lenton lived outside Glasgow in Renfrewshire and worked near Blairgowie:

We received no training and had to learn the skills in a very short time ... There was one male forester who was older and didn't house at the camp. He lived in a house near the entrance to the estate. He told the girls what to do and we had to start from scratch, learn how to use the axes and saws.

Another member of the Scottish Women's Timber Corps, Chris Turner, who became a measurer, received one week of on-the-job training:

after interview, we had a brief medical and both of us were accepted as suitable 'timber fodder'. We spent approximately one week in the office discussing maps, how to work out the cubic contents of a tree and hence an area of standing timber. That was our sole office training.[12]

There was mixed reaction to whether the training of women for the Timber Corps had been adequate. Russell Meiggs suggested it might have been wiser to have adopted a stiffer physical standard for membership of the Women's Timber Corps.[13] But, he acknowledged, it was unlikely the Ministry of Defence would have agreed with large-scale rejections, especially after a month of training. He suggested it might have been better to reduce the number of recruits and take longer over training them in the early months – 'short term loss of production in favour of a long-term advantage'.

Regardless of how successful the training was thought to be to begin with, the women noticed how their bodies had changed with the work out in the forest. One month of fitness training and heavy manual work, wielding axes, handling 6ft crosscut saws and loading timber by hand, had a transformative effect on the women's bodies.

Eileen Mark said, 'we were butch in those days with muscles in the legs and arms.' Within a month, their bodies had changed to suit the type of work. Fellers wielded axes weighing 7 or 14lb, handled 6ft crosscut saws and loaded timber by hand. Some of the girls were referred to as Amazon women who could fell trees as well as the men, and you can certainly see from photos of the Women's Timber Corps how fit and strong the girls were. These women had a confidence in their strength and as the war progressed this new shape and physique became more acceptable in young women.

In the *Bury Free Press* on Saturday, 19 July 1941, it was reported that the girls participated in a tug-of-war competition at a fete held in the Abbey Gardens, Bury St Edmunds, and that 15,000 people attended:

A novelty of the tug-of-war competitions, which aroused much interest, was the section for the fairer sex. In this, the WAAF beat the ATS, and went on to score a victory over the Women's Land Army Forestry Section, in the final after a hard and long pull.

In Culford, one promising batch of newly trained members of the Women's Timber Corps was drafted in to help with one of the most successful responses to an emergency call for the clearing of trees during the war. In June 1943, the Home Timber Production Department was informed that 25 square miles, between Thetford and Watton, was required urgently by the War Office for battle training.

The area was well stocked with trees, so a large labour force had been in full production there for two and half years with four mills in operation. In October 1943, 428 male fellers were joined by a draft of 110 newly trained Lumberjills and 65 schoolboys for a week to try to clear 80 acres of land as quickly as possible. A grand total of nearly 200,000 cubic feet of wood was felled and removed during this week.

It wasn't just schoolboys that were recruited into the timber trade. In Scotland, girls of 16 years of age were in pre-service training from June 1942, and from autumn 1943 girls as young as 14 years of age were able to join the Girls' Training Corps. On 2 June 1943, *The Falkirk Herald* reported, 'Twelve Scottish voluntary organisations for girls have made arrangements to provide pre-Service training for girls between the ages of 14 and 16. Among these is the Scottish Girls' Training Corps, which has decided to form a Special Corps for the 14–16 age group.'

The 'organisations which offer opportunities for girls in the 14–16 age group' included the Girl Guides Association, the Girls' Guildry, the Scottish Association of Girls' Clubs, the Scottish Girls' Friendly Society, the YWCA of Great Britain (Scottish Division) and the YWCA of Scotland, Co-operative Youth Groups, the Girls' Association of the Church of Scotland, St Andrew's Ambulance Corps, the Scottish Association of Young Farmers' Clubs, and the Scottish Branch of the British Red Cross Society.

The report continues:

the Girl's Training Corps was formed with the assistance of the older girls' voluntary organisations to meet the needs of the 16–18 group prior to the first registration of young people. Its training programme was designed for this age group, and the Association has throughout the first twelve months of its existence resisted all suggestions to lower its age of entry. After careful consideration of all the factors, however, it has been decided to establish a corps for the 14–16 age group.

The Number of Lumberjills

The reports of the number of women working in forestry in the Second World War varies greatly and lacks consistency between sources. For instance, in *Meet the Members* it says that girls were recruited into the Women's Timber Corps until July 1943, at which point recruitment stopped and numbers were at their peak, with 3,900 in England and Wales and 1,000 in Scotland, totalling 4,900.

However, in *Home Timber Production*, Russell Meiggs says, 'By the middle of 1943, the Women's Timber Corps had over 6,000 members, engaged in every branch of production in woods and sawmills.' But later in the same book he states that in June 1943 the number of women working in forestry was in fact 8,500, considerably more than 6,000.

By December 1943, he mentions there were 8,500 women working in forestry, 3,100 working in the timber trade, 2,300 in England and Wales and 800 in Scotland, while 5,400 women worked for the Home Timber Production Department, 4,000 in England and Wales and 1,400 in Scotland.

However, in *Timber!*, the book about the Scottish Women's Timber Corps, it refers to the number of women enlisting as 1,100 in 1942, rising to 1,400 in 1943, 1,040 in 1944 and 450 in 1945. This totals 3,990 in Scotland alone, so there is some inconsistency with numbers.[14]

It is also not clear whether either of these sources include the number of women already working in the timber trade, as part of the Women's Land Army, prior to the formation of the Women's Timber Corps in 1942. In *Meet the Members* it quotes: 'Nearly 1,000 members of the Land Army in England and Wales were already working for the department, or the trade, and these seasoned pioneers became the foundation members of the Corps.'

In the *Agricultural History Review*, 'The Forgotten Army of the Woods: The Women's Timber Corps during the Second World War', Emma Vickers states: 'The nucleus of the Corps was formed by 1,200 women in England, Wales and Scotland who were already working for the Home Timber Production Department and for timber merchants under the auspices of the WLA.'

But Russell Meiggs stated that 3,800 women and girls (or juveniles) worked for the Home Timber Production Department prior to the Women's Timber Corps being officially set up, 2,200 in England and Wales and 1,600 in Scotland.

If we total these figures to get the number of women working in forestry, it makes between 7,700 in England and Wales and 5,590 for Scotland. This makes 13,290 female recruits working in forestry as Lumberjills, far more than cited in every other source. However, interviews with Lumberjills from Yorkshire suggest recruitment of women into forestry continued well after 1943, and even after the war had ended. For example, Mrs Joyce Earl was recruited just a year before the end of the war.[15] So the real number could be higher.

If numbers continued to grow in England and Wales after 1943 at the rate they continued in Scotland, by 159 per cent, my guess is that the real number of Lumberjills could be much higher. In addition, the number of unofficial recruits who received no training and no uniform suggest the number could be even higher. However, the lack of consistency or perhaps attention to the numbers of women working in forestry means we will probably never know exactly how many women worked in forestry. But it could be between 15,000 and 18,000.

Toughen Up!

There was an attitude that if the girls were to work in forestry they needed to toughen up, both emotionally and physically. There was no consideration given to their emotional well-being. The tear-stained cheeks and home-sickness that arrived with the girls was more reason to instil tougher rules and discipline. They had stepped into a man's job and the training and the treatment were the same. They just had to get on with it and any show of vulnerability was a sign of weakness. The training programme needed to get the girls ready for the basic living conditions and hard manual labour out in the forest, so to begin with they needed intensive physical fitness training to increase their stamina and strength.

Volunteers for the Timber Corps had to pass two medical examinations, the first with the Land Army and the second with the Timber Corps, because they had to be physically fit for the heavy work. Nonetheless, transforming from a childminder, hairdresser, shop assistant, office clerk or ballet dancer to the physical job of a Lumberjill demanded great strength and stamina. So, intensive physical training was standard at training centres, which took place at six o'clock every morning before breakfast. Photos in *Bon Accord* in May 1943 show the Women's Timber Corps girls 'doing "keep fit" exercises to help to toughen them up for their work in the woods'.[16]

There was a tough attitude towards training the women, whether in camp or on the job. On completion of training, there was a policy to send the women to work up and down the country as far away as possible from where their families lived. This was to minimise the number of girls returning home if they felt homesick or the demands of the job got too much for women like Hazel Collins: 'I remember hearing someone say: "Don't tell them where you have relatives." So when asked if I had any relatives in the West Country I said: "No!" But my Granny lived there in Ashsprington, near Totnes.'

Irene Snow grew up in a village called Wilsden, between Bradford and Bingley, West Yorkshire: 'I was sent straight into forestry to a place called Dulverton in Somerset, which I thought was the other end of the world. I had never been as far as that away from home before.'

Leaving training camp was when real life as a Lumberjill would begin, when the girls would have to fend for themselves out in the forest, doing arduous work in all weathers, and often facing pejorative treatment from the tough timber merchants. This policy and the remote locations of forests often meant that the girls were billeted in small cottages in remote villages miles away from family, friends and even the nearest cinema or entertainment. As a result, they could often feel quite isolated and alone.

Mary Broadhead was originally from West Clayton in Yorkshire, and after her one month of training she was destined to become a sawmill operator in Canterbury, otherwise known as bomb alley: 'We had to be up early to go to the next work placement, mine was in Chartham. At breakfast I was looking out for my sawing partner, who I worked with on the saw, but she was not there. She had just disappeared, and no one knew anything about it.' While the girls worked hidden from view by the tree canopy above, they heard the Luftwaffe, doodlebugs and bombs sailing overhead. 'So, when I left Culford camp, I felt so very much as if I was on my own.'

The Foresters

They're tramping through the forests,
They're trudging through the mire,
They're brushing past the undergrowth
They have but one desire
Their greatest thought, their highest aim,
To see, in England, Peace again.

They have no tanks or rifles,
They have no stripes or drill,
They have no ships or aeroplanes
But England needs them still.
They're fighting hard with axe and saw,
They're Britain's Women's Timber Corps.

They're proud of their profession,
Bad weather does not count,
They bring the tall trees crashing down,
The piles of pit props mount.
They're doing their bit to win the war,
This almost unknown Timber Corps.

By J.I. Melvin[17]

6

She Fells with Ease
10-Ton Trees

One warm and windy day in May, I was involved in setting up the filming of the Lumberjills story for BBC2's *Wartime Farm*. The most exciting part of the day was when my colleagues Jo Mason and Tracy Anderson were felling a tree. It was a glorious conifer tree standing alone in an opening of the forest, about 60ft tall and 3ft foot wide at the base of the trunk. After the wedge had been cut, the pair started to saw the tree with a crosscut saw. The girls were working hard, under the safe supervision of a forester, and I could see from a distance their faces were becoming quite pink with effort. Every now and again they would stop to wipe their brows.

We realised they were having difficulties because it was a windy day and the crown of the tree was blowing all over the place. Every time the tree rocked back and forth in the wind, it was pinching on to the blade of the saw. So they had to wait for the blade to free up again to continue sawing. While I watched, I started to feel nervous and realised that the Lumberjills must have had enormous courage to fell these trees, especially on a windy day.

When the blade was stuck fast, they tried to hammer metal wedges into the tree to try to free up the blade. The pair worked together but the wedge would not go in. The girls became hotter and hotter, working under pressure with a whole film crew and cameras rolling to catch the critical moment when the tree began to topple. It was so scary I was shaking as I watched the crown of the tree rolling around in the wind.

Jo Mason had felled a few trees before, so she knew the theory but had never used a crosscut saw. So she learnt on the spot and came into her own, as the women must have done in wartime. We let out a yell as the cloudy shape of the tree began to shift away from us. Slowly at first, and then with a creaking noise and a whoosh, the tree swung down through the canopy.

We felt the shock wave beneath our feet as it thumped down onto the earth 100 ft away and the trunk bounced and branches waved vigorously. I felt absolutely elated.

Jo and Tracey were glowing, cheeks flushed pink, perspiration shining on their faces. It really was a lovely feeling as we went over to the trunk to examine the angle of the rough toothy break, which formed the hinge of the tree when it fell to the ground. But my goodness, it made me realise just how dangerous it was for the Lumberjills during the war.

What a Novelty

We're the girls who fell for victory,
We're the girls who chop the trees,
Every time we swing our axes,
It's a stroke for victory.[1]

Deep in the forests across England during wartime you would hear the girls singing to keep up morale while felling trees for crown and country. There is a great British Pathé newsreel, so evocative of the era, that shows the girls hard at work while singing this song.

But when the Women's Land Army started work in forestry, the hullabaloo caused in the industry rippled out to local communities when they started to appear in forests up and down the country, armed with an axe and saw, wearing jodhpurs and gum boots. So extraordinary was the idea of the young women felling trees, that for some locals seeing was the only way of believing.

At Chopwell Wood, about 12 miles south-west of Newcastle upon Tyne, the locals would go to down to the woods to witness the spectacle as if it were part of a circus act or British wartime comedy show to keep up morale.

Frieda Ellerby had a great sense of humour and said she didn't mind all the jokes, because she liked the attention they got to begin with, and gave back as good as she got from the male foresters and locals: 'Women did not work in the forest before the Second World War. We were one big novelty we were. Never a day in life like it, we were alright you know.'

Precision Work

During wartime, British labour was always inevitably in short supply, and by the time priority industries had been served there were seldom any men left who were physically capable of handling timber.

Great skill, precision and physical strength were required for felling. The girls worked with axes weighing between 4½, 7 and 14lb. One hand either end of the handle, they raised the axe over their shoulder and then swung down, sliding the upper hand to meet the other.

When felling soft wood it was easier to sink the axe into the wood, but with hard wood the axe had to be swung with more force. So the stance was crucial, because a mis-swing or glancing blow off the wood could veer towards a leading leg. So, legs firmly planted square on to the wood, just more than shoulder width apart with knees slightly bent, provided optimum stability and safety.

The girls needed to decide which direction the tree would fall. So they cut a diamond shape or wedge on that side of the tree, just above the ground. They would then start work, chipping into the bark and then cutting more deeply into trunk. This was known as 'laying in' or 'dipping' the trees.

Becoming more accurate and proficient with the axe took time and practice. The axe is not something you want to be swinging around if you are losing focus or energy, as that's when mistakes happen. There's no doubt it was hard for the women to begin with, as it would have been for the men, but they built up skill and stamina quickly.

Butt of the Joke

But nonetheless, the women's felling skills were often a target for everything from harmless teasing to unkind ridicule. Mary Ralph started felling with only a quick lesson on how to do it:

One day just after we had started, the boss came to me and said, 'Were you visiting your relations on the other side of the woods last night, Mary?' I said that I had been, and he asked if I had seen any beavers. Of course, there were no beavers in our woods, so I just looked puzzled until he explained that something certainly had been gnawing at the trees.

Obviously, she didn't take it as a joke: 'As you can imagine, we made a mess of it at first but soon got in the way of it.' The girls were resolutely determined to prove they could do the job as well as the men and prove their worth, jokes aside.[2]

But sadly, even in the late 1960s, some twenty years later, the same jokes were still being made about the Lumberjills. No praise could be given without it immediately being taken back. A photo caption of a Lumberjill in the *Forestry Commission Journal 1968–69* read: 'Power saws and safety helmets were both unknown, but excellent work was done, even though the stump above recalls the work of beavers!'

The trees felled by the girls varied in all shapes and sizes, from the smaller young pine trees destined to become pit props to the 100-year-old great oak trees felled for railway sleepers or shipbuilding. The girls, like Edna Barton, worked in pairs once the dipping was done, one either end of a double-handed crosscut saw: 'You cut a wedge out of the tree first and then you saw through the trunk, give it a good push with your foot and shout "Timber!"'

But to begin, M.I. Chalker and L.M. Hurford in *Meet the Members* were not at all successful in their attempts to fell the trees: 'Our self-confidence received a check at our first attempt. The manager came along and found four of us pushing a tree and, when he asked us what we were doing, we said: "Trying to push it down." This amused him immensely.'[3]

Oftentimes the crosscut saw would get stuck in the tree. So they were taught to use a wedge and hammer to open the gap and free up the saw. The girls quickly learnt not to waste their energy on pushing a tree down before it was ready to fall.

Edna Holland was amazed to see how trees are felled more than half a century after the war on TV, by a big machine that grabs the trees, cuts them off at the bottom and runs up the trunk stripping all the branches off in one go, and then cuts it into lengths: 'It was very, very hard work for us. I sat there with my mouth open to see how they were felled by machines compared to how we did it.'

Deirdre MacKenzie explained how everything was done by hand back in the 1940s, and 'There was something very exciting about the moment when a tree was ready to fall; the cry of "Timber!", followed by the swish and thud of branches hitting the ground. Thirty, forty, fifty years of growth felled in five minutes.'[4]

Lighter Work

Some sources say there was great enthusiasm for this job at first, but the girls found it difficult to maintain the output of this heavy work. So the girls slowed down, and in some cases the foreman took them off felling because of their low output and left the men to do more of the heavy felling.

Irene Snow worked 8 a.m. till 5 p.m. most days: 'we had to be very fit, we helped with the horses, axed the trees and used a crosscut saw to fell them – not the great big ones – the men used to do those ones.'

Often the girls were left to concentrate on crosscutting and 'snedding' to trim the branches off the trunk and stacking, or clearing and burning, especially in those areas where the stands of timber were not easy. Mavis Williams remembered: 'This [snedding] was a very sticky job when the trees were newly felled because of the oozing resin, and a back-aching job if they had been left to weather.' Joan Turner got covered in sap from the trees: 'The Macs were so stiff they could stand up.'

For some of the young women, Forestry Commission lumberjacks did most of the felling. Eileen Mark and her friend Pauline followed behind, stripping the branches, clearing the ground:

> having good bonfires, catching ourselves alight, and then replanting the earth when it was cleared.
>
> They would take us to an open track in the morning, with sandwiches and tea. The ground was frosty, hard and snowy. We used to fell Norwegian Spruce, cut to size for pit props and trim off the branches. If they were tall enough they'd be used for telegraph poles. It was an experience, which I was glad I did. I wished I could do heavier felling work but it was really, really good.

Molly Paterson admitted she couldn't have done the heavier felling work even if she had wanted to:

> Some girls had very hard work to do with massive crosscut saws and axes. They would cut in with the axes at the bottom of the tree then they used the crosscut saw to complete the felling. I was 5 feet tall and weighed 6 stone and could never have done that sort of work.

But some of the stronger women were not put off by the size of the tree to be felled. With a strong Yorkshire accent, Mary Broadhead recalled,

'Oh there were a girl called Jackie from Scunthorpe and we went to fell this tree nobody else would touch. It was a big, strong thick tree, nearly 2 metres wide. There were just this one tree left on its own and so we got this crosscut and we cut the tree down.'

The felling and snedding was competitive between pairs, as Jessie Maclean explained:

the laying in was a work of art, which took long and patient practice. Even so, some of the girls never got the hang of it … It all seems picturesque and romantic, looking back, but it really was a 'jamboree', even then. We were always motivated to try harder. We considered ourselves far better than the few men working nearby, older woodsmen, who of course paid no attention to our superiority and foolish arrogance.[5]

Bella Nolan recalled:

On one occasion our foreman, Charles Stewart, expressed some doubt regarding the ability of girls to cope with tough work. The next day I volunteered to work a crosscut saw with him. During the day he kept asking me if I was tired and wanted to stop but I kept going despite being quite exhausted. At the end of the day we had cut down one hundred and twenty trees. Months later a new supervisor arrived and when I volunteered for a task he said 'It's okay I've read about you. Your record is in the office.'[6]

Mistakes

This number of trees could be felled more easily in a packed conifer forest in Scotland, where the trees had been planted for timber production in vast swathes. Meanwhile in England, the woodlands were smaller and had remained untouched for many centuries. These woodlands contained a variety of tree species, from large old deciduous trees to an understorey of bushes and younger saplings. As a result, in the summer, the speed and number of trees that could be felled in these forests was reduced dramatically. Margaret Finch was working in a wood in full foliage on the common near Chipperfield, Kings Langley, Hertfordshire, one scorching hot summer's day:

This was a huge forest and the trees were enormous and mostly oak, with lots of brambles, ivy and thorns completely covering the ground around the trees. We came to an enormous bush with this oak tree in the middle and there was the white spot indicating it was to be felled. The forest was in full foliage and after spending all afternoon getting through the undergrowth to the tree, we proceeded to fell it. As it came down we heard a lot of pinging noises. Then within another hour whilst trimming this large oak we realised we were surrounded by police.

It was a private wood, we were very hot, and we didn't expect to see anyone. So, we had stripped down to our cami-knickers, woollen socks and big leather boots swinging this 14-pound axe. Half-naked, we were marched off and arrested. It turned out we had brought down the telephone lines hidden in the foliage above. We never knew whether they were kidding or not, but the police said we had brought down the telephone lines to Churchill's war office and they suspected us of sabotage!

7

Danger, Dust and Noise in Sawmills

… A terrifying task, as anyone who had watched the great toothed circular saws whirring with murderous speed and sharpness will agree. It is
a task which requires extreme care, precision, and concentration, for the
saw which will travel with prolonged and undeviating ruthlessness up the
solid trunk of wood will slice in one second through the soft finger …
Men have been known to shake their heads and say no, it didn't take their
fancy; but the girls of the Timber Corps have done it …[1]

Vita Sackville-West, author of *The Land Girl* magazine and a history of the
Land Army, wanted to make sure people knew the risks these women were
taking in producing timber for the war effort.

Life in a Sawmill

Many girls worked in sawmills at some point during the war, both in
government-run and private firms. But handling heavy timber required
considerable strength to lever the logs into position on the saw-bench, so
the women often worked with the men. Provided they were not put onto
jobs which were too heavy for them, it was said they could maintain a good
level of output. They learnt to use the different types of saws and some
taught themselves to become saw doctors.

Otherwise, the girls worked on the smaller saws cutting timber for
firewood. Russell Meiggs suggests that it was a more effective use of the
women as 'auxiliaries' helping the men, 'acting as tailsmen on the benches
and stacking sawn timber'.[2]

Straight out of training at Wetherby, Margaret Finch's first post was to a
man called Mr Thorne who ran a sawmill in Kings Langley in Hertfordshire.

It was so noisy and dusty she was glad to be sent out into the forest to fell the trees rather than work in the sawmill. But if the weather was very bad, they were back in the sawmill: 'We worked on huge bandsaws, walking alongside the traverse, slicing these huge trees into planks.'

Mary Broadhead from Barnsley was trained at Culford and became a sawmill operator near Canterbury, until 1945. She volunteered to be a Red Cross ambulance driver by night after working in the sawmill by day, where she worked on a 28in saw cutting railway sleepers, pit props, planks and beams from the beginning of 1942:

> I think that they had been sent these girls and they didn't know what to do with them to begin with. But I were good at sawmilling and if they thought as though you could manage they didn't worry about it. They just let you get on with it, even though many times you didn't know what to do. We did the heavy lifting and oh we used to stack pit props and railway sleepers and how they were heavy, but we used to lift them just the same.
>
> To describe where I worked at the sawmill at Chartham you need to understand how the mill was set up. So, when you drove to the sawmill from Chartham, you drove through the forest. As you turned left, you would see that the location was set into a clearing into the forest. On the left nearest the road was the office, set further back on the left was a group of huts, which made up the mill.
>
> On the right-hand side of the track, which was made up of sawdust and other bits of timber, there were many stacks of timber and behind those stacks was another track, which was used by the tractor to haul timber from the forest to the sawmill skids. Beyond the track for hauling timber to sawmill skids was even more stacks of timber.
>
> The first hut [of the sawmill] was divided into two parts, one was for the saw doctor. His job was to sharpen the saws, set the angle on the teeth of the saw and sharpen the axes. The other part was for the steam engine.
>
> Next in line was the main part of the mill, which was open on all sides and this too was made from timber. The first saw nearest the steam engine was smaller (28-inch diameter) a bench saw, which I worked on a lot of the time. Then it was the middle-sized saw with a moving table, the table moved large trees into the big saw blade.
>
> At the rear of the mill was the skids, which took large trees from the tractor and trailer then moved them to the table of the saw for cutting. A flatbed trolley on four wheels and railway tracks ran from the side of the

shed out into the stockyard. It was used by the men to move the railway sleepers for stacking. The work I did the most was cutting planks on the smaller saw. The men usually used the big saw, with a moving table. The blade was about 3 feet in diameter cutting the tree into items such as railway sleepers, chocks and large planks.

Creating railway tracks was a widely used method of extracting timber from forests in remote areas direct to the nearest station or sawmill, and this was something which the women constructed with great success.

Danger!

But the reality of sawmilling was that it was one of the most dangerous jobs you could do. Accidents were routine and included amputation of fingers, bronchitis from dust inhalation and even broken legs, arms and other bones as a result of toppling timber or accidents with horses hauling the timber onto machines. Mary Broadhead had a serious injury one day:

I was on the machine and I had my hand on the piece of wood that I was cutting. Then a gust of wind blew straight across the mill and there was sawdust blowing all over and it blew in my face. I wanted to wipe it out of my face. But my fingers were near [the] saw and I didn't know what to do. Anyway, the wood clinched on the saw, the wood came up and my hand went into the gullet of the saw. When it got to the top guard, I couldn't go any further and it just chopped it off corner ways.

I went to Johnny the engineer and said, 'I've cut my thumb off.' He said, 'You couldn't stand there and tell me that,' and I said, 'Well I have, look.' He didn't stop for long and ran up the yard looking for Mr Wilson, the saw doctor, who came running back. But the lorry had gone down to the garage and there was nothing we could do but wait for the lorry to come back. So, I was sat by the stove in the hut and they made me a cup of tea. When the lorry returned two hours later, they took me down to the doctor and he said he couldn't do anything with it because the bone was splintered.

Sawmill Office

Diana Underwood worked in several sawmills in the New Forest:

There were seven or eight sawmills in various parts of the forest. We worked in the attached 'offices', which were small wooden huts, rather like present day garden sheds. They contained a bench, shelves, two stools, a telephone and a wood burning Tortoise stove which toasted our sandwiches, dried wet coats and kept us warm in winter.

We kept records of how much wood went into the sawmill and how much came out, the daily output of sawn timber, details of stock in hand and sizes required for which we received orders from the main office, Red Lodge in Lyndhurst. We passed on the sizes to the sawyer. He knew what he could produce from the round timber delivered and would tell the crosscutters the lengths he needed.

They handled the logs on the skids with a peevy, a long-handled implement with a rounded iron hook on the end. Bigger butts might yield railway crossings – 6ins × 12ins × 12ft long – or sleepers – 4ins × 8ins × 8ft 6ins long. The other sawyers cut appropriate sizes from the rest of the log. We checked the sawn timber onto lorries and ensured we had enough round timber on the skids to keep going and enough fuel for the engine.

We calculated the wages for the mill men, who worked piece work as a team and kept a close eye on the daily output figures, on which their bonus depended. If one of the team was away, we sometimes helped with stacking sawn timber or crosscutting. I spent several days on one end of a crosscut saw at various times.

Mobile Sawmills

Diana Underwood continued:

There were also a number of portable 'Forest Benches' consisting of one rack bench driven from the pulley of a stationary Fordson tractor. These cut four sides from the logs, thus making 'squared logs'. We sold the off-cut bark to local men as slab wood, by the lorry load. They sold it on for various building jobs or cut it up for firewood.

Most mills were driven by oil engines but the one at Lindford had a steam engine, the driver starting an hour earlier than the other men to get up steam. I spent half a day sawing up slab wood for the engine on a small saw bench when they were shorthanded.

The sawyers used plate saws and inserted tooth saws, these were sharpened every morning before work started and the sawdust was dug out and added to the pile outside. On the whole they cut the sizes that were asked of them, but some had a habit of keeping 'elbows' which had always been kept for boat building. Any large elm logs they would put to one side for coffin boards. We were told to discourage these practices.

8

Heave Ho, Haulage, Tractors and Transport

Trees were often felled in a remote location in the forest, on craggy ground, up a hill or near a body of water. So, removing the trees from the forest and transporting them to their destination by train to the dockyards or down the mines was a challenge.

Each tree could easily weigh upwards of one ton and so horses, tractors, lorries, boats and trains were required to move the heavy cargo. On training camps, only the girls over the age of 21 were allowed to drive lorries. But, as many of the girls had just turned 17, they missed out on vital training that would have served them well later, as once out in the forest they were expected to drive the timber trucks.

When it came to picking out those who would be learning to drive the haulage vehicles on training camp, much to her disappointment Mary Broadhead was not one of them: 'They sorted out the girls that had driving licences and those that hadn't got a licence couldn't go on it. I didn't get a chance to do the driving.'

As a result, many girls had to learn the perilous skills of hauling trees behind tractors and driving loaded lorries on the job without instruction. The roads they drove down, if there were roads at all, were often rutted and muddy forest tracks which required great skill and caution. The reliability of the motors in those days was often very poor. So the maintenance and mechanical repairs had to be done by the drivers, to keep the motors running and deliver the quotas of timber to the stations.

Horses

The girls also worked with horses to drag the felled trees from the forests, particularly when the ground was steep, rocky, uneven or remote and it was impossible to get a tractor or lorry near to the felling area. So, horses had chains on their hindquarters, which were used to drag the timber out. Edna Holland warned of the perils of working with horses:

> It wasn't easy especially when the horses were going uphill and my goodness you had to be careful that you were well out the way when the horses swung the trees round. The horses kept getting close to my feet, so I had to keep away and shook the chains at them to make sure they kept clear of me.

Often the girls became well accustomed to the horses and became close to their equine companions, acquiring the skills to care for the horses and understand their needs. But to begin with women, like Winnie Renshaw, lacked training and suffered the consequences of working with these at times stubborn creatures:

> It was my turn to take the horse. I was dropped off in an open topped lorry at West Week Farm. There was this huge black Clydesdale with a chain for dragging timber and a nosebag attached to the harness, but, I had no idea how to use it.
> However, I went into the wood and put the chains around the timber. The horse pulled the timber to the roadside and we worked hard all the morning when suddenly without warning the horse refused to move. I called to the men working nearby. They asked me if I had given him a drink and fed him his food in the nosebag? Well I knew nothing about this. I took off the headgear and led him to a pond. He knelt down and drank and drank until I thought he would burst. At last he got up again. I gave him his nose bag of food and from then on worked without a hitch until the end of the day.[1]

Joan Turner had her fair share of troubles: 'One time we were working with a horse that went mad and ended up in a bog. When I said, "Fetch a saw!" they thought I was going to saw its leg off.' She recalled another big shire horse, called Searchlight, which was 'a nasty piece of work'.

As the war progressed, tractors were favoured over horses for haulage, except for very steep terrain. Diana Underwood, New Forest measurer, recalled there was only one haulier family that used horses for hauling timber from the woods in the New Forest by the time she had finished working there in 1943.

Tractors

Tractors were used in the same way as the horses to extract the timber from the depths of the forest to the roadside, and weren't on the whole more reliable than horses or less temperamental. As Dorothy Swift observed, they still weren't as reliable as the Lumberjills or the foresters would have liked:

> I shall never forget the frustrated tractor driver who flew into an uncontrolled rage when his old Fordson Major refused to start up. He thumped, kicked and swore at it. Then he bashed his bloody machine and his mate's head with a spanner. The tractor still wouldn't work – nor would his mate.[2]

The girls didn't need a licence to drive a tractor unless it was going on the main roads, so often with little training they learnt to drive on forest tracks. The fallen trees were coupled to the tractor and dragged out by chains. But the girls had to be careful not to catch the timber on stumps or uneven ground or risk being thrown off the tractor by an abrupt stop.

There was also a limit to the size of tree an ordinary farm tractor could pull. If it was too heavy a typical Fordson Major tractor would pull a wheelie up on its two back tyres. If the ground was uneven or on a slope, the tractors could topple over onto the driver, causing serious injury or death. But if caught before the tipping point, the tractor could skilfully be brought back down by the foot brake. Otherwise it would remain in a vertical position.

According to Dorothy Swift, 'Corrective manipulation depended more on the luck than skill. I cannot believe we dared to do it.' The tractor driver she worked with, from a well-off family, made a mistake one day when it turned over and broke her back. She was hospitalised at first but was later allowed to return to work, 'but could only walk on the flat, no hills.'

Caterpillar tractors were more stable and had more power. They were able to drag heavier trees over more uneven ground. Diana Underwood recalls, 'Most of the felled round timber was hauled by Caterpillar D2 tractors from the woods to nearby sawmills or to the roadside to be collected by road-going timber carriages. All the machinery was repaired from the main workshop by Lyndhurst Road station.'

Edna Holland, however, had to teach herself how to maintain and drive a Caterpillar tractor, which she christened 'Hellzapoppin', with a group of four girls she worked with:

It's 7.30 a.m. and the great day starts. We all take our turns at winding Hellzapoppin up, she not being one of these modern lorries [*sic* – actually tractors] which boast a self starter. Eventually she starts up and off we go, first to take the other girls to the different woods, then to take loads of various sized pit props to the station to be despatched to the pits.

We usually sing as we go. We each chose a song, then the four of us sing it, and for a while we'll go sailing along on an almost deserted road. Suddenly Hellzapoppin begins to make suspicious noises under her bonnet. She splutters a bit, changes her mind, then starts to complain again. Without losing a precious minute, we plead with her:

'Please Hellzapoppin, don't fade out again!' Just when we think she's heard, being somewhat contrary, she fades out altogether. Then we say, 'Damn you!' and clamber out to poke about in her bonnet and turn and crank, and crank and turn, and with every turn our language gets stronger. After a lot of persuasion, she decides to go, and we finish the load.[3]

If Hellzapoppin behaved they could get three loads done in a day before heading back. But other times they would have to abandon her and walk home feeling tired, dirty and cross at the end of the day.

Loading and Stacking

The timber had to be transported between forest and tractor to lorry and train, so all members of the Women's Timber Corps would be involved with stacking and loading pit props and sawn timber from one vehicle to another. No Lumberjill regarded it with equal value, some disliked this heavy, demanding work while others enjoyed the camaraderie and team-work required.

Before Olive Edgley joined the acquisition team she was measuring fallen timber at the Bow Wood Estate, where there were quite a few of the Women's Timber Corps loading timber from the mill to the trucks:

The worst thing was loading, lifting them onto the backs of the trucks and I hated it. We did it in twos or threes. The lorry would back up and we'd load them up. We developed muscles that are with you for the rest of your life.

Violet Parker and three others worked on one lorry together:

We used to have to stack the timber, two up on the stack and two in the lorry, then take it down to the station to stack the timber into the wagons. All of it had to be done manually and we loaded and unloaded three or four lorry loads a day. We were very strong.

Dorothy Swift loved the challenge, risks and excitement of loading timber onto trucks:

Our favourite job was to stack pit props on to a wagon, then ride with the driver to the railway station where we unloaded them into a waiting truck. Larger and heavier timber was loaded with a special pulley fixed to a tripod worked by a tractor. This winching was hard and dangerous, and it was during those loading sessions that I learned lots of new swear words.[4]

Edna Holland also enjoyed the heavy work of loading and hauling:

We were taught how to load them up onto the lorries, being taught how to pick them up in twos and throw them onto the lorry. We'd say '1, 2, 3.' Then from there we would go in the lorry to the station and throw them onto the station wagons. My goodness we got muscles everywhere, but it made us feel really good.

Lorries and Trucks

Enid Lenton had been driving for four years when she signed up: 'During the winter when the road was icebound, I drove a small truck with all girls in it from camp to Aylth. It was just a small track, so we had to be very careful on that icy road in the dark.'

However, driving the timber haulage trucks required even greater skill to manoeuvre when fully loaded with timber to take down to the station. Katie Dowson used to take the timber down to the railway at Pickering station via forest tracks and roads, which were often rutted, uneven and deep in mud, making driving even more difficult:

Have you been to Low Muffles? It wasn't even a road and didn't have a surface at all. We'd load the lorry with pit props and climb on. We were frightened to death. We were all on the lorry with the pit props, with

Campy and Fred and Jings. It was so stupid because he could have killed the load of us.

Many of the girls like Frieda Ellerby said they often rode on the flatbed of the open truck, sitting on top of the timber as it was transported to the station: 'We loaded the pits props into trailers for the Bevin Boys in Durham and then I used to sit on top all the way to Thorntonly Dale station.'

There were numerous serious accidents that occurred during haulage, some with fatal consequences because the correct training had not been given and there was little consideration given to health and safety. Diana Underwood knew of the dangers, but it was obviously a common practice: 'We weren't supposed to go on the back of the lorries, but unofficially we did.'

The lack of training, rules or adherence to health and safety around driving haulage trucks was astounding back in the 1940s. Margaret Finch was working in Epping Green, Hertfordshire, when her foreman turned up with a 55ft articulated lorry. He gave her the keys and a letter, with instructions to deliver the trees to Welwyn Garden City railway station (about 7 miles away):

Jean couldn't even ride a bike and I didn't know anything about lorries or cars come to that. So, she insisted I had to drive it because I could ride a bike. Then the fun began, as we didn't know what this stick was in the middle of the cab. We had a vague idea it had something to do with the engine and off we went. When we got to a corner I stepped on the brake and Jean moved this stick and it made an almighty screeching noise.

Anyway, we made it to Welwyn Garden City, only a very small town, and were going down this street when a policeman stepped into the road in front of us. We were only doing about 5 miles an hour, but we were so frightened of stopping this lorry in time, not forgetting we had a 55-foot wagon loaded with trees behind us. We stopped with a screech, as we assumed we had to move this stick to stop the lorry as well as using brakes.

Anyway, he asked us where we were going, and we said the station. Then he said, 'No I didn't mean that, I meant this is a one-way street and you are going the wrong way. So be good girls and reverse back to the turning.' Well we looked at each other and laughed and then said, 'We don't know how to reverse we only know how to go forward.' He said, 'For God's sake what are we coming to, and what is that awful noise and have you got a driving licence?' We said, 'No,' so he got in and reversed back for us and said with a very loud gasp, 'No driving licence and you don't know how to drive or reverse, God help us.'

Eventually we got to the station, don't ask me how. So then we had to go on the weighing bridge for it to be weighed, then we were asked, 'What is the weight of the wagon empty?' We looked at each other and started to laugh. The railway clerk on the weighing bridge said, 'Oh go on, do what you have to and then when it's empty come back here to weigh up.'

After loading the trees on the railway wagon, we looked like as if we had been down a coal mine. Innocent like, we reported to the weighing clerk and he said, 'Where is the wagon?' 'By the train,' said Jean. 'Well you need it to weigh against when you came in loaded.' So we then had to admit we didn't know how to turn it round to get out of the station yard and the pantomime started all over again.

He didn't know how to drive either so then he had to go and search for someone who knew how to drive an artic. Eventually someone came and gave us basic lessons on how to drive, put this pedal down when you move 'the stick' and then pointed us in the direction of the police station to get a driving licence. So off we went again and found the police station and who should be behind the desk? Yes, that policeman, anyway he gave me the driving licence and said to Jean 'I don't think you better have one, do you' and we all laughed. Don't forget there wasn't much traffic about then, lucky for us, and hardly any traffic lights.

Alternative methods of haulage were sometimes required when water, not land, had to be crossed to extract timber from the forests by boat. This is what the Women's Timber Corps were doing in Scotland to transport the timber across the lochs.

Rafting

After hearing about the life of the Lumberjills in Ardbrecknish, Argyll, from Molly Paterson, I felt compelled to make a visit. She spoke of the clouds rising above the loch and how the women did timber rafting using motor-boats. When I read more about this in *Timber!* I knew I had to retrace their footsteps. The first time I passed by Loch Awe by train I thought it was one of the most amazing places. So, one warm and sunny February I spent an idyllic four days living by the banks of Loch Awe.

I wanted to make the most of my visit, so I hired a motorboat and with little explanation other than 'this is the throttle' the boat owner, Donald, pushed me out into the loch and waved me off. I took off up the loch alone, heading straight into the wind, which was strong in places. The last time I drove a boat I was the same age as the Lumberjills, so I was nervous at first. But soon I gained my confidence – it was magnificent, and I couldn't believe I was getting a taste of what the Lumberjills had experienced.

It was so lovely, such a beautiful and sunny day, blue sky, snow-capped mountains on Ben Cruachan opposite. Just me, a noisy engine and the boat in the middle of the loch. There was not another boat in sight, so I let out an excited 'yahoo'. It felt so good. Right at the top of the loch, 7 miles to the north shore – did I really go that far? – I saw Kilchrenan Castle and opposite on the hillsides of Ben Cruachan the vegetation was burning. It was quite impressive to watch, the way it tore up the hill in two diagonal lines of orange flames, other times it was very smoky and left a lovely smell in the air.

I had thought that I was not going to land on the islands on the way out because I was nervous. But as I became more relaxed with the boat handling my excitement took over, and I pulled in to the smaller island and its shores below the ruined abbey, and enjoyed a picnic looking out to the vast forests the Lumberjills worked in wartime.

I then visited Inishail Island. The Lumberjills were right, it was such a peaceful and beautiful place. There were some huge old trees on the island that circled a graveyard and the ruins of an old monastery. The Duke of Argyll and the Campbell family, landowners over the last few hundred years or more, are all buried there, even until recently. Newer gravestones from 2008 and 2009 stood amongst ancient tombstones now so ruined that you could barely read their inscriptions. I sat down in this special place and imagined the stories of the women who worked here.

The women worked here on the island felling trees and extracting them to the loch with horses, which I could hardly believe swam across the loch to the island. I verified this with a friendly elderly local man who confirmed that's what they used to do, as it was easier than transferring the animals by boat. Other livestock, including sheep and cattle, were also swum across the loch in the past. The women spoke about how the horses loved the island and unlike other places, where they grazed, here they would play. They said there was a tranquillity on the island, : 'everyone felt it, even the men, though some of them would have laughed at the idea if you suggested that they were sensitive to the atmosphere.' I certainly felt it too.

Sandra Manson was among those lucky ones to work on Loch Awe:

No explanation was given. Mr. Dow, the forester, met me at the station and we proceeded to Ardbrecknish Manse, where the timber corps girls were billeted. During the course of our journey he persisted in asking me about my experience with boats to which I could only reply that it was very little. The next question was 'Can you swim?' I said that I could but still no explanation was given to these strange questions.

Instead of going to the billet we went straight to the jetty, bag and baggage, where I met the travelling mechanic from Alexandria. He was working on an ex-Navy liberty boat which required a new clutch. So the mechanic and I spent an exhausting day fitting the new clutch. I had no mechanical experience before I started but just followed instructions and, by the end of the day, we were in business again. Donny took me out to show me how to operate the engine and then left me to get on with it. I felt very proud that first evening when I took the men up Loch Awe without mishap.

On the steep sides of the lochs it was easier to extract the logs by forming a 'raft' and towing them along the loch from a 'rafting bay' to a suitable loading point where they were transferred to a lorry for transport to the station.

I remember it was a glorious summer morning when we started 'rafting', with the loch like a sheet of glass but, in spite of such favourable conditions, I felt quite apprehensive about the day of rafting which lay ahead. Would I be able to manage? However, as I set off for the rafting bay I felt my confidence return.

Horses dragged the timber to the water's edge where two WTC members, complete with waders, were waiting to unchain the logs. One girl then floated the logs and held them in position, while the other fastened them together with 'dogs', a metal ring with sharp spikes sticking out of them, placed at intervals along a chain, and hammered firmly into place in the butt end of the trees. A strong rope was then tied to the centre log of the raft and other end passed to me on the boat. This end was secured to an iron too, fitted in the stern and then I was ready to set off with my raft.

On a fine day, about two hundred trees were extracted by this method. As we were rafting at the narrowest point of Loch Awe, it could be quite stormy and in strong wind we had to abandon rafting but only once was I caught in the middle of the loch, quite unable to make headway. I was blown off course, drifting in the mist, to the opposite end of the loch, so I cut the engine and tried to steer nearer the shore. It was with relief that I caught sight of the old pier, so I made for it to obtain some shelter, remaining there till I felt it safe to go and collect the workers.[5]

Molly Paterson also worked in Arbrecknish, but worked in the office: 'There were no tractors to pull the tree trunks, as the ground was so difficult and hilly. All the timber was pulled out of the forests by horses with chains and dragged to the roads or the loch side; it could be very dangerous work.'

Margaret Grant, *Timber!*, also worked on rafting at Loch Awe, where she stood in the water wearing waders with a big hammer in her belt, the chain from the raft over her shoulder. She attached trees together using 'dogs' rings with spikes on them. From experience, I can tell you the water in the loch is icy – it's not the place to go for a swim, even in the summer, and makes you lose your breath. There's no way you could stay in the water for more than a few minutes.

'One of these times' Margaret Grant was rafting when:

a fellow had just unloosened his load and floated it towards me and his horse had started off to go up the track again. He didn't notice that the hook on the swing tree had caught onto the chain, just under the water, which was over my shoulder and, as the horse walked away, this whole thing tightened, and the load came towards me. When you are under water, with timber above your head, you suddenly lose your sense of place, which way is up and which was is out. However, the next man coming down hauled me out.

I could have drowned quite easily, if he had not been coming down. I can swim but I was struggling under there losing my sense of direction. I was worried about the chain but there was no terrible sense of panic. Maybe drowning is not as bad as you think. The next thing I was aware of, was being battered on the back by a couple of men and lying sodden beside a fire on the shore.[6]

Audrey Broad.

Edna Holland.

Violet Parker.

Joan Turner.

Joyce Elizabeth Gaster.

Enid Lenton.

Ethel Oliver.

Evelyn Taylor's brother was in the army in the
Second World War and this photo of his sister
was in his top pocket behind a tobacco tin.
A bullet hit the tin and saved his life but left
brown marks on the photo.

Lumberjills wore a mix of uniform and their own clothes – Joyce Elizabeth Gaster.

Special issue undies. (*Best of British* magazine)

Bakelite Women's Timber Corps badge. (Illustration by Joanna Foat)

Crossed brass axes badge. (Illustration by Joanna Foat)

(Above and left) Edna Barton, 1942, at Culford training camp, Bury St Edmunds, Suffolk.

(Left) Eileen Mark.

(Below) Edna Holland and friends on training camp in Wetherby.

(Above) A Lumberjill of the Women's Timber Corps. (© Crown Copyright, courtesy of Forestry Commission)

(Left) Timber! (Forestry Commission archives at Kielder Castle.)

Lilian Crampton, front left, felling at Grantham Wood.

Women's Timber Corps using a mobile sawbench, 1945. (© Crown Copyright, courtesy of Forestry Commission)

Stripping pit props. From left to right: Myra Turley, Gwen Murral, Kitty Byett and Edith Robothan.

Violet Parker, Lanhydrock Sawmill, Cornwall.

Brenda and Nancy Harrison on top of stack of wood at sawmill (Nancy at top, Brenda next to her).

(Left) Joyce Elizabeth Gaster on a horse.

(Below) Lilian Crampton riding a horse at Grantham Wood.

(Above) Joyce Elizabeth Gaster on a Caterpillar tractor.

(Left) Joyce Elizabeth Gaster on top of a haulage truck.

Joyce Elizabeth Gaster extracting timber
on wagons.

Irene Snow.

Joan Turner on haulage.

Hazel Collins, measurer with notebook, in Holsworthy, North Devon.

Winnie Catterell, measurer, in South Water.

(Above and opposite top) Eileen Mark burning brushwood.

(Below and overleaf) Ann Moffat sitting around a smoky campfire with other Lumberjills on the Isle of Wight.

Notebook, Measuring Tape and Mathematics

Mathematics

To join the WLA I had to go to Chester to be interviewed by two rather posh county ladies! Surprisingly I was asked 'Are you good at maths?' I replied that I had done maths for school certificate. It seemed a strange requirement for someone expecting to work on a farm. 'There is a need for timber measurers,' I was told.

Training of women measurers began soon after outbreak of war. They were regarded as the 'brains of the outfit'. Peggy Conway was among the first cohort to be trained when the Forestry Commission realised it was desperately short of timber measurers right from the start of the war in 1939.

The women who were first recruited into forestry in the early 1940s would today most likely be the girls who are encouraged into the Science, Technology, Engineering and Maths (STEM) careers. Initially, it was only acceptable to the timber trade to recruit women for 'lighter forestry duties', such as timber measuring. This involved measuring the cubic quantity of wood in a single tree and the volume of wood in an area of forest. However, there was some elitism about the Forestry Commission and timber trade's selection of women, as only the most academic women were chosen. Often these girls came from wealthier backgrounds, as their families had been able to afford to keep them in education.

In a letter from the Women's Land Army Head Quarters on 5 January 1940, it confirmed that: 'The Forestry Measurers are drawn from a different type of girl altogether. They must, as Mr. Propert says, have a higher education, possess some mathematical aptitude and have either been to a University or have had previous experience of figure calculation.'[1]

Ten days later, on 15 January 1940, a large draft of well-educated women arrived at Lydney station to start their training as timber measurers.

The Home Timber Production Department urgently requested more volunteers from the Women's Land Army for three- to four-week training at Parkend in the Forest of Dean to become timber measurers. Mrs Inez Jenkins advised in her letter of 15 March 1940 to Miss Rennards that 'Previous experience involving figure work or school certificate standard in mathematics is the sort of qualification that is required'. The Women's Land Army was setting a more appropriate experience level for the job.

And yet, even though being employed for so called 'lighter forestry duties' of timber measuring, the Forestry Commission also requested that the women also had to 'be of good physique'. In a letter dated 26 March 1940 to Miss Rennards about timber measurers at Parkend, it says, 'Miss Faulkner sounds a very suitable trainee as far as qualifications go and if you have interviewed her and approved her as being of sufficiently good physique for timber work I would be perfectly prepared to accept her as a trainee.'

One later applicant, Miss Prentice, reached matriculation standard in mathematics and had taken one year's science course at Liverpool University. In a letter from the county secretary for Oxfordshire on 10 April 1940, she assures Miss Brew at Balcombe Place that 'Miss Jean Prentice appears to be quite strong enough for timber measuring work'.

It appears the Forestry Commission wanted to make sure that the women were both highly educated enough and physically strong enough to work in forestry. But seemed to doubt whether women could be both intelligent and strong? I wonder if the same high standard was set for the men? Nonetheless, once the initial prejudice of introducing women into forestry had been overcome, the entry level requirements for measurers became more realistic.

Peggy Conway had a great love for trees and the countryside, so going to work in the forests seemed to be an appealing suggestion:

I enjoyed my training at Park End very much. It took place in a Forestry Commission training place housed in wooden buildings.

We learnt to use bush saws, axes, crosscut saws and bark scrapers. Our measuring kit consisted of a 60-foot-long tape in a wind-up leather case, a 6-foot girth tape, 'chalk,' a thick blue wax crayon, a scribe and a 'Hoppus' book calculator for working out cubic content. At the end of the fortnight we were sent off in pairs to timber operation sites.

The role involved measuring standing timber, felled and sawn timber, and calculating the cubic quantity of timber produced, piecework pay for the fellers and income tax records for the timber merchants.

Diana Underwood went to the Forest Training School at Parkend in the Forest of Dean:

> It was hostel type accommodation. We spent the first day indoors, learning about measuring timber and the importance of accuracy as the fellers' wages (they were paid piece work) and the amount paid by the Ministry of Supply for all the timber bought all over the country would depend on our figures.
>
> Out in the woods, with notebooks, 100-foot tape measures, and a quarter girth tapes, we learned the difference between hardwoods, oak and sweet chestnut, and softwoods, larch and pine. We were shown how to measure the felled and cleaned trees (butts) and number the base if the cutters had not already done so, using blue-waxed chalk. We had to record the cordwood (branches cut into 4-foot lengths and stacked 4ft × 4ft × 8ft) and the part cords. The brushwood was burned. Some softwoods yielded pit props of a certain length, which we also had to record. We were later able to work out the cubic capacity of each numbered butt with the help of a small calculator book, a Hoppus.
>
> Occasionally two of us were taken to a softwood plantation to mark straight trees for telegraph poles. However straight they appeared from all angles, while standing, when they were felled and laid out on skids, they seemed to twist all ways. The G.P.O. Buyer always complained about them, they were not as good as the ones he used to get from Norway, but he had to take the best ones. His 'rejects' went for Air Ministry or Admiralty poles.

With practice, each tree could be measured for its cubic capacity by sight with the aid of a Hoppus Ready Reckoner. This was a quick reference guide, which calculated the cubic quantity of wood in any tree, based on the measurement of girth and length of a tree felled. It also provided the cubic quantity for round wood and sawn timber. The book would enable quick calculations to be made to convert the amount of wood into wages or cost to a purchaser and producer. But often the girls needed to measure fallen timber with their tape measure. This was not always easy, with dense undergrowth of bracken and brambles to get through to reach the bottom of a tree.

While measuring involved more mental work than physical work, it was not free from the hardships of working in a rugged environment once the trees were on the ground. Molly Paterson explained: 'As timber measurers, some of the girls had to crawl around in the mud under the trees to do the measuring. During the winter it was very cold work sometimes with snow and ice and often in the rain.'

The measurers helped identify potential felling sites, they assessed for volume, advised on extraction routes and stacking grounds and calculated the rates of pay for the fellers based upon the amount of timber they had felled. This gave the measurers power and often the male fellers resented their position.

Ethel Oliver, from Whitburn, was a Chopwell Lumberjill, spending nine months in the 360-hectare (900-acre) beauty spot, responsible for measuring the length and girth of trees after gangs of men had felled them. The lads were always trying to get one over on her, as her measurements helped determine their pay packet based on volume of timber felled.

Dorothy Swift was a measurer and took pride in the importance of her job:

Measurers with a mathematical ability had an onus to be fair and earned a wage in keeping with their responsibilities. Girls who qualified as measurers had to prove that, if necessary, they could work out in their heads the cubic capacity of a tree. Even so, each was issued with a Ready Reckoner in book form to speed things up a bit as electronic calculators were things of the future.[2]

A Cut Above the Rest

Measurers were perceived to be different to the other girls, not only in the basis of class and education but also because they were paid more.[3] This created conflict between the girls and Eileen Marsden found some of the measurers snooty: 'I always remember meeting another member of the WTC and asking what she did, and she said [imitates a middle-class accent] "Oh, I'm a measurer."' Working alongside women from different social classes for the first time, Pat Rouse couldn't help but notice the differences: 'Oh they were toffee-nosed, weren't they? I shouldn't say this, but they were people that came from universities.'

Hazel Collins was a well-educated Lumberjill who sat an entrance exam, won a scholarship and went to grammar school until she joined the Land

Army: 'I was always good at arithmetic. When the new boss, Teddy Gibbs said "Any of you good at maths?" I said, "I am good at maths," and so he said, "You can be the lady measurer then," and I got more money than the other girls.'

What made the Women's Timber Corps unique was the eclectic mix of women from town and countryside, all areas up and down the country, different classes, work experience and educational standards. But when these women came together, the essential work order, uniform, recognition of mathematical ability, physical strength and higher pay packets for measurers gave the corps a strong sense of identity. Even though the well-educated women appeared to be worlds apart from the girls who came from the woollen mills in Yorkshire or factories in the south. As a group they were very diverse, and stronger for their diversity as a workforce. However, this confused people who wanted to pigeonhole the women into sections of society. People did not understand forestry or the nuances of the job, so they were criticised for being both too working class, having manual jobs and for being too well educated.

Farming work was always regarded as a lowly profession, especially by the middle and upper classes. Forestry work suffered from the same attitude, especially from the wealthier families whose daughters volunteered to work in the Women's Timber Corps as measurers.

Eileen Mark, a working-class girl who became a measurer, was rather amused by the reputation, which she may not have felt she deserved having worked in a glass bottle factory before signing up: 'We were fondly known as the snotty lot. Our nickname was the Airborne Land Army because we were above the rest.' Others regarded it as the Rolls-Royce of the Women's Land Army, because a higher academic level was required.

Regardless of what others thought, measurers like Audrey Broad developed a sense of pride in their mathematical skills and were keen to be promoted to the more senior roles of supervisor and forewoman in recognition of their abilities:

> I was chief measurer. We used to measure the butt to break, break to end, and then calculate the cubic quantity from the quarter girth measure at the centre of the trunk. I used the Hoppus Measurer book to look up the length and quarter girth and that gives you a table with how many cubic metres there were in that tree.

Others, like Molly Paterson, were confident in their day-to-day work and knew how invaluable they were to timber production:

It was only me in the office for a time and I did all the wages, converted all the lengths and girths of the tree trunks into cubic feet of timber and prepared dockets for the stationmaster. I would organise the transport for all the pit props, which were to be sent to the coal mines. They were taken to the station by lorry 7 miles away at Dalmally.

On arrival they were loaded onto the railway wagons. All the loading and unloading had to be done by hand and it was very hard work. Sometimes I would go with the wood to help with the loading work at the station. At one time, I knew the name of every colliery in Scotland and the North of England because I did the docketing for the pit props. Some timber would go for coffins and the big stuff went for telegraph poles.

There was no doubt the measurers, like Dorothy Swift, felt a sense of achievement and were extremely proud that they had met the challenge of working in a well-paid and respected job: 'I came into my own as a timber measurer, when my training was put to the test at Bishops Wood. I had made it.'

By August 1941, when the school at Parkend closed, some 400 girls had been trained as measurers. While I was at the Forestry Commission, I worked with the BBC to film a special Remembrance Day *Countryfile* programme dedicated to the Lumberjills at the Forest of Dean, as it was such a significant location in the history of the Women's Timber Corps. Three Lumberjills were interviewed: two measurers, Olive Edgley and Eileen Mark; and one feller, Irene Snow. It was a wonderful occasion.

After the filming, I stayed in the Forest of Dean to meet up with more Lumberjills and explore the forest on foot and by bicycle, where so many of the women had lived and been trained. It is a vast forest, so incredibly beautiful, and is inhabited by a few charging, snorting wild boar, which made me jump out of my skin on one occasion. The building at Parkend still stands and was very beautiful, covered in autumn-coloured leaves from red to yellow and green. I can only imagine the pride these women had when they started their training, feeling valued for their intellect and empowered to work in a role of great responsibility during the war. I was delighted that a memory of the Lumberjills is still preserved in the Forest of Dean and its Heritage Centre.

Put in Charge

Mavis Williams moved to a new camp in Cornwall, where she was working with civilian workers of both sexes and members of the Women's Timber Corps.[4] The work on camp included felling for pit props, charcoal making, logs for firewood, loading railway trucks, hauling by horse, clearing and replanting. She was shortly promoted to forewoman, even though she was concerned she had never done charcoal making before:

Now the prospect was daunting. In charge of the 'whole works', I had to learn fast. I was fortunate in having the help of a well-educated man who had fallen on hard times. He was very patient and proud of his ability to make good charcoal.

The civvy women were the toughest bunch I had ever met, their language making my hair stand on end. I was soon to realise however that they had hearts of gold, if accepted for what they were. They would bring food for the Timber Corps girls whose digs were not too good, give pocket money to the younger girls who found it difficult to manage, [and] help anyone who was in trouble[,] such as paying the fines of two girls who had been caught riding without lights. Their language may have been colourful, but the standard of honour was high.

A measurer arrived, and shortly another ganger, twice my size in every dimension, but very efficient. Women worked besides men – felling, sawing, stacking, cutting logs by hand on the Porta-saws, packing kilns, and hauling wood to the sawing ramps. Some of the finest workers were the gypsies, who brought their horses for hauling, staying till one job was finished then moving on.

Enid Lenton received little training to help take on her promotion, she was simply left to get on with it: 'I was made a supervisor and put in charge of forty girls altogether.'

Often the women who had been trained as measurers were promoted, above the men, and put in charge of the economic resources of timber production too. Barbara Beddow had responsibility for wages and accounts and more authority than many of the male forestry workers:

On the move again, to Carlton, near Selby. My supervisor, a Yorkshire cricketer, called Frank Dennis, asked me if I would be a forewoman in charge of operations, and as it meant better pay and a new challenge I accepted.

I am sure we had no idea of the variety of jobs that the Timber Corps girls were doing, and we had none of the referred to training. I was made a forewoman when I went from Middleham to Carlton, [correspondence was] mostly by postal communication. If I had any real problems, I could contact the supervisors, but one lived in the Midlands, another up North and they seldom visited, just as long as my weekly returns were correct, and my accounts were paid and the tree fellers, who were on piecework, (some of them could not read or write, but knew their earnings to a penny), did their jobs … Again, I had not done any office work or dealt with finance in any way. I indented for the money I would need; it came through the Post Office – then I placed it in a Bank Account.[5]

Buying Up Forests

Purchasing woods for timber was a vital part of the job for Olive Edgley and other measurers working in acquisitions, as some 90 per cent of wood came from the private landowners, rather than the Forestry Commission estate. Quantities of timber to be felled and the price would need to be negotiated, and this was a challenging aspect of the job. Tact and diplomacy were needed, as was an ability to communicate with people from a different class and background, who may have been prejudiced against the young women.

So, Vera, my twin sister, Tessa Lockey and I went to Minety, a little village in Wiltshire, working in acquisitions in a threesome. We had to find our own lodging and HQ so that instructions could be sent to one location. So, we found digs in Chippenham with a lady called Joan Stockford-Beale, who was a bit posh. We took two rooms, and used it as our HQ to store clothes, bicycles, measuring equipment and tools.

We only ever dealt with people from the Forestry Commission and received instruction by telegram and then proceeded to contact the estate managers. We were part of the acquisitions team, so we had to go to negotiate woodlands to be felled for pit props. Sometimes we'd do as we were told by the estate managers and other times we would pinch a bit more.

We would ask what they would let us have; we needed a lot of softwood stands for pit props. Then we'd ask what else have you got? If they were mean, they would not let us have much, so we always tried to pinch a bit more. If they were really nasty we said, 'We have to take it anyway'. Sometimes we would have to contact Captain Blunt and he would have a talk with them.

Captain Blunt was in charge of buying and was in touch with the major estate owners. I remember being in his office once and he asked me to find a little village and I couldn't find it and was getting into a hot sweat, but when he came to look he couldn't find it either. They did ask us if I could read an Ordnance Survey Map and that is probably how I got to be a measurer.

Measuring was an exacting job; softwoods were easier but hard woods were different, more difficult to measure the cubic girth. When thinning trees, you looked at the top, so you went home at the end of the day you had a crick in your neck like nobody's business. In between we'd have a lot of paperwork to do and we had to work out the nearest station for the wood to be dispatched. We had a quarter girth tape and scribe knife to make a mark in the bark of the tree.

With softwoods you would give the average height of the stand, 18–20 feet and read the girth size. We got really good at estimating the girth size, two and a half, three and a quarter or five assessing hundreds of trees at a time. We would walk through the wood, see a mass of trees ahead and take a section each and the one in the middle would write everything down. At the end of a job or if the weather was very bad you would go back to Chippenham and catch up on all the paperwork.

Anstace Goodheart from the acquisitions team in *Meet the Members*, laden with tools, pots of paint and brushes, worked in twos or threes and took it in turns to measure and mark every oak tree, say over 14in quarter girth with white paint. But as she explained, it was no easy task when the woodland had not seen an axe or saw for more than 100 years and the paths were a mass of brambles and briars:

I crawl on my hands and knees with a paint brush between my teeth as it's the only way to get to some of the trees to measure and mark them up. Once we get into our stride where the forest floor is easier to traverse, we shout out sixteen and a quarter, seventeen and half. I love it. It sounds like I know just what I am doing. The softwoods are easier to identify and to measure but we need the oaks for shipbuilding and sawn timber for the mines and these are more difficult to measure but soon we find it easy to guess with accuracy the size of the girth.

We had to carry out a census of woodlands in the county, to work out what they could get. The problem being there are lots of smaller privately-owned woods and many times we do not know who owns them. We have to work out what they've got and how much we can get our hands on.[6]

Aside from these difficulties there were many competing demands on woodlands in the Second World War. The forests were not only needed for timber, but also by the services for building aerodromes, battlefields for training and army camps, and for storing vehicles and ammunition stockpiles. The forests needed to be both cleared of timber while also having the added advantage of providing shelter, cover and camouflage for these facilities.

Sometimes the felling of areas of woodland was required at very short notice for the construction of aerodromes and defence lines.[7] In the first two years of war, the conflict of interest was less of a problem. But by 1942 reserves of ammunition and vehicles required more shelter, and by 1942 and 1943 there was a feverish race against time to build aerodromes. In the urgency, some bases used explosives to clear the land, which was a terrible waste when high-quality oak, a good-quality timber which was so urgently needed for pit props, was ruined.

In addition, large stocks of ammunition, vehicles and supplies had to be built up along the main roads leading to the south coast. So in these areas no fellings were ordered within 10 miles of the coast, and permission had to be sought for any fellings of 5 acres and upwards by both the services and the Home Timber Production department.

The Women's Timber Corps found it hard to acquire trees which it would be perceived to be in the public interest to preserve, such as landmarks and beauty spots where trees were essential to the character of the landscape. In theory, the divisional officer could have refused a licence for any of these trees. In the end it came down to public spirit and the personal judgement of the buyer and seller.

Not such a problem for the private seller, whose view of the local village was of less concern than the income he generated from the sale of timber. However, sentimentalism came into play towards the end of the war, when wood stocks were depleted. Some 50 per cent of the New Forest was felled, yet the casual visitor would see no sign of wholesale desolation because belts of trees were left to screen the felled areas along roadsides.

Anstace Goodheart from *Meet the Members* explained that one needed almost magical powers of persuasion at times in acquisition:

Sometimes it was very hard to be firm when old ladies told you, with tears in their eyes, that their wood had been planted by brother Richard in 1880, and that they had watched the trees grow from day to day, or that it was their favourite walk on a summer Sunday evening, and where would all the dear little red squirrels go?[8]

Finding the Best Trees

Martha L. Grant was part of the census team: 'Census work could be very frustrating. A flying census had been taken in Scotland in 1941 of woods over five acres but now all the green patches on our map had to be visited and surveyed.'[9]

While a census of British woodlands had been made in 1924, it had never been very accurate and was now out of date. A new census began in 1934 with a team of twenty-five people assessing every parcel of woodland of 5 acres or more. But by the middle of 1939, only 18 per cent of the country had been covered. So, the rest of the census was completed with urgency in flying surveys. At last some good news, this gave the Forestry Commission the exact location of large stands of wood so vitally needed for war.

At the beginning of the war, stocks of timber were desperately low with just seven months' worth of pit props left in reserve. However, the nation relied on imported timber from overseas until the German U-boats threatened supplies. By late 1941, there was an urgent need to carry out a census of British forests, to identify how much timber was available and where the trees could be found. This exercise was carried out across England, Wales and Scotland, in part by the Women's Timber Corps.

It was physically impossible to visit and measure every wood, so a sampling method was used. Measurers from the Women's Timber Corps were drafted in to assess how much timber was still available. The job was very demanding, requiring hundreds of miles to be travelled, often with little reward. It was not uncommon for them to travel for 10 to 20 miles, if they were lucky by car, but usually by train, bicycle and often the final few miles on foot over rugged terrain. The girls would arrive hours later at a green patch on the map that had been identified from the flying census to see whether their journey had been successful.

Figures were required within the first three months of 1942 and the girls needed to sample 5 per cent of the forests, by selecting one in twenty of the green patches marked on the Ordnance Survey maps, uniformly distributed over a county.

Miss MacGregor remembered: 'Squashed into a Morris 8, we did Cornwall in a fortnight, and emerged completely breathless and very dazed. Most of the country was blanketed in snow in January 1942 but in Cornwall we were engulfed in pouring icy rain.'[10]

The Blitz slowed down progress, so 5 per cent could not be reported within three months, so they surveyed only 2½ per cent and the fieldwork for the sampling was complete in March. They then had to start again to survey the remaining 2½ per cent. By the end of 1942, sampling a further 5 per cent had been requested to act as a check on the first 5 per cent to make a census of 10 per cent of the forests complete.

The census team moved across the country from Cornwall to Yorkshire. By now, the census unit had dwindled to just three pairs of girls in the Women's Timber Corps. Working alone, their final aim was to sample 20 per cent of the forests.

Miss MacGregor recalled one of her most memorable days on the census team in Scotland: 'Let me tell you about a day in June, a very hot day it turned out to be though we left in the cool of the morning.'

Miss MacGregor and her fellow Lumberjill set off to find green patches of forest that had been identified on the map from the flying census of the area in the Highlands. They cycled 10 miles to the first patch of forest and then spent two hours surveying the Scots pine, European larch and Norway spruce and assessing the volume of timber available:

> It is not possible to cycle beyond the head keeper's house, about half a mile down from Glen Feshie Lodge. Several deer grazed with the cows at the keeper's house; they are not in the least timid and are there all year. In front of the house a beautiful red fox and three cubs were stretched out, only caught that morning. The walls of the stables are literally covered in antlers of all shapes and sizes. It is a temptation to linger, but we must go on as the longest walk is yet to come.

The pair continued in the heat of the midday sun across a bridge over the Feshie River, fought their way through juniper bushes, past the remains of an old church and holding. Where once the glen and hillsides were inhabited, the women passed tumbledown stone walls and a rowan tree, which used to be thought to ward off evil spirits. Then they entered the remains of the old Caledonian Forest with scattered pine trees and 'high precipitous rocks rising' from the edge of the plain:

> We have not been speaking or making a noise but in the distance, we see a herd of deer, about a hundred, and the leader's head is raised as he sniffs, tilting his antlered head this way and that. All is not well, and he leads the herd away, a sight never to be forgotten, and as they wend their way up the hillside a golden eagle soars silently above the rocks, keeping guard on his young, and ever watchful for prey. For 4 miles we pick our way along the glen narrowing at times till we have almost to walk at the river's edge. Our green patch is just around the next corner; we will have a rest there before doing any measuring.

But alas, when the girls reached the next corner their hearts sank. The trees had been felled years ago, perhaps in the First World War, and now only a few small stunted trees could be found. This was typical in census work and a whole day could be wasted without finding a single tree for timber production: 'Our long walk in the scorching heat was of no avail, so after a rest, we turn and retrace our steps, thinking lovingly of our bicycles down at the keeper's.'

Despite many unsuccessful days' work, finding little suitable timber, the good days outweighed the bad and the census of 1942, carried out by the Women's Timber Corps, revealed where a high quantity of coniferous woods could be found and turned into pit props.

10

Bonfires, Charcoal Burning and Planting

Bonfires

Our main job at this place was to burn the brushwood brought to us by fallers, whose lunches we might have swallowed. Even today the smell of a wood fire makes me feel nostalgic. In wartime our bonfires emitted a magnificent aroma from burning pine needles, which we spontaneously inhaled. We burned left-over twigs and leaves using our bonfires to toast bread, melt cheese and brew our 'cuppas'.[1]

Like Dorothy Swift, many of the women's fondest memories of working in the Women's Timber Corps are captured by the photos of young women sitting round a smoky campfire, chatting and sipping tea from enamel mugs. However, the idyll of a forest fire surrounded with happy, smiling faces was not a luxury but an essential part of the job.

After the trees had been felled and branches removed, the trees would be cut to size for pit props and there was a lot of brushwood left behind. The branches from twenty to a hundred trees would leave a lot of debris. While this could be left in bundles to compost and decay, common forestry practice during wartime was to replant the area that had been felled. So heaps of smaller branches, from broadleaves or conifer trees, called brushwood, would be piled onto fires and burned. The pine needles were highly combustive and would crackle and fizz like fireworks as they were thrown on top, releasing plumes of smoke. Once burnt, the earth could be cleared and would be ready for replanting. Generally seen to be one of the lighter forestry duties, more often than not the women were asked to clear up the brushwood left behind by the men.

After Christmas one year, Eileen Mark was reassigned to the Watergate Estate in Sussex, which belonged to G-Plan furniture makers, and Gommes Estate where there was farming too:

There were a lot of Forestry Commission chaps there who did most of the felling and me and my friend Pauline followed behind, stripping the branches, clearing the ground, having good bonfires, catching ourselves alight and then replanting the earth when it was cleared.

In the colder days, Mary Broadhead would long for enough brushwood to start a fire to keep them warm and to keep up morale during the long cold winter: 'Into the cool weather of winter, it would be very nice to have a fire going in the woods to help keep warm – for it was no picnic.'

But in the warmer days it was a completely different story. The risks of a forest fire increased dramatically on a hot summer's day, when all the trees are tinder dry and the autumn leaves could catch light with the smallest spark. Frieda Ellerby loved clearing all the brash (removed branches), after she had felled the trees: 'We made great big bonfires and burnt the lot. But in summer it was roasting. We just stopped by them because we had to stay with it until it had burnt right down and made sure it was out.'

A potential disaster arose when flames from a bonfire spread to the forest's peat floor where Dorothy Swift was working one day:

and travelled some distance to break out more fiercely on the other side. When this had been extinguished, we land girls were ordered by our fore-man to stay in the site hut all night to fire watch. We had to be ready to beat out any recurring flames, though goodness knows what would have happened if fire we could not control should have sprung back into life.

No help was at hand. No houses around the corner, nor was there a vehicle standing by to dash us to a telephone box. We were on duty four nights on the run, having been told to stay in bed all day. It was a hot July, so we were not cold at night, but we were very scared. We hid our fear by singing funny songs.[2]

Brashing

'Brashing' was the name given to removing branches from standing trees, taking off the lower branches and leaving the upper branches intact. 'Snedding' refers to the branches being removed from a felled tree. In both cases, branches are removed from the trunk of a tree with a billhook, axe or bow saw. The stripped branches would sometimes be referred to as brash and would also be burned to clear the woodland area afterwards.

But how do you remove branches from standing trees? Well, one Lumberjill found out. Lillian Veitch worked on a 4,000-acre estate in Scotland, near Penrin, doing brashing. They were 5 miles from the border near Coldstream in Northumberland, and 14 from Berwick. She worked on Palents Verney Estate in the Land Army and was plunged in at the deep end with no training:

We spent six weeks on one wood, and we had to climb the trees and prune the branches off the trees which were used for pit props for the mines. The estate owner couldn't bear anything happening to his trees. He loved his trees and had shares in the coalmines, so he used his woods for pit props.

Brashing was a popular practice for producing good-quality timber growth, encouraging the pine trees to grow straight and tall. This would allow the best price for the timber, making the trees most suitable for pit props, telegraph poles and other higher value timber products. This was often practised by private landowners who cultivated trees as an investment opportunity and commodity.

Lilian Veitch continued:

We had to prune all the branches that were dead up to very top, not touch the green ones. We had a 7-foot ladder and sawed-off branches, keeping gaps to step on the way up and back down. One of my friends sawed off the branch she was sitting on!

Although Lillian's friend fell from high up the tree, luckily she had a softened landing on all the branches that had been piled up below. Her moment of peril came when she was momentarily distracted while talking with great excitement about the dance she'd been to the night before.

Peeling and Stripping

For the past five months I have been working at a colliery, the sole representative of the WTC. My Welfare Officer tells me that I am the only member of the Division who works at a colliery, so fellow members, pin back your ears and listen to what it feels like to be working along with five thousand husky colliers. Or at least I shouldn't say working with them, for obviously I am not down the pit. My work consists of scraping bark off the pit props in preparation for drying before going down the pit to be used.

I remember so well that at Wetherby, during training, it was always impressed on us that we must leave no branches, arms, etc. on trees intended for pit props. Now, only too well, do I realise how important this is, mainly for the safety of the miner, but also to help us poor lassies who have to peel them.

To do this work a prop is placed on two trestle tables with slots to hold in position. Using a sharp bladed knife and downward sweeps, light work is soon made of the business. The knife, weighing about ten to twelve ounces, measurers approximately one foot wide, the blade three inches deep. Two supporting handles help to give a better pull on the knife.

On the whole the work is very simple, but none the less interesting. We, meaning the civilian girls and myself, work the usual hours with Saturday half day. It was a little embarrassing at first, when all the miners on seeing me in my uniform, declared in loud Yorkshire accents: 'By gum, its comin' to summit, when Land Army Lassies are at pit.' However, they have grown quite used to me by now, and look on me as part and parcel.[3]

K. Stenton's account from *Meet the Members* shows that softwood trees destined for use as pit props or telegraph poles were stripped of their bark. In peacetime, removing the bark from the pit props was intended to speed up the drying process, make the timber lighter for transporting by lorry and easier to handle down the mines.[4] It was also said to last longer underground. So it was common practice to carry out peeling in the woods, and there are iconic pictures of the Lumberjills showing them doing this work.

However, there was a change of opinion during wartime as to whether the extra work required in stripping the wood was worth it for the reduction in drying time. The increase in demand for timber production during wartime meant that from 1942 it was no longer compulsory to peel props and so from this time it declined, and was later abandoned due to the shortage of labour and time required to strip each tree.

While Dorothy Scott was working in Leicestershire, she was invited to go down a local mine to see what they did with the pit props the women supplied: 'It was a real eye opener and goodness knows how the men coped with the cramped conditions and the heat. We could hear the roof cracking over our heads!'

Wanting to see what the Lumberjills might have experienced, I took a trip down the mines to Caphouse Colliery, the deepest mineshaft in Yorkshire.[5]

111

It revealed the dangerous and squalid working conditions for the miners. A queue of thirty or forty miners, armed with a hard hat, brass lamp and pickaxe, would squeeze into the mine shaft; tightly packed, the door clangs shut and the operator shouts, 'Below.' The lift travels 150 yards in less than ten seconds and there's a sudden jolt at the bottom.

Down the mines there would have been a revolting mix of hot odours, from coal and human faeces, to sweat and lingering fumes of gunshot, as well as urine. 'The toilets were called the shovel because they forgot to build toilets down the mines,' the operator and tour guide says with a chuckle. But there would be a gentle circulation of air around the mine corridors to prevent build-up of methane gas or carbon monoxide, which could poison the miners within seconds. Each morning, a man travelled the mines with a canary to pick up any signs of gas. If the bird passed out, they knew there was a problem.

At the bottom I could see the pit props in action, some very small ones holding up whole seams of coal barely 3ft high. There would have been twenty or thirty pit props holding up a whole ceiling as men sat underneath on their knees or backsides, picking away at the walls. In the narrowest seams, the men would work on their bellies. It's so dark you can see nothing but blackness without the light of the lamp. I was pleased to be back above ground and to see daylight again after my visit.

Olive Edgley was mindful of the dangers the miners faced when preparing pit props:

> Did you know that softwood creaks and that is why it is used for pit props because before it snaps it creaks and groans and the hard wood doesn't. So we were told. It gives the miners a chance to get out before the seam collapses in on them.

For Edna Holland, the safety and suitability of the pit props they made was at the front of her mind because her father, who worked at Armthorpe Pits in Doncaster, unforgivingly criticised the props they had despatched to his mine:

> He only ever wrote to me once. He said, 'You're not measuring the pit props properly and they are not straight enough.' It made me think if I ever had a son I wouldn't have them working down there in the pits on their belly like my Dad did.

Charcoal

From coal to charcoal, the Women's Timber Corps became involved in more specialist areas of forestry during wartime. Charcoal was an essential product, which was used in gas mask filters following the gas attacks on soldiers in the First World War. Mustard gas, which was almost odourless, was so powerful that only small amounts were needed to be added to high-explosive weapons like shells to have devastating effects. The fear was that chemical weapons would be used against British civilians, so gas masks were distributed to everyone.

Audrey Broad recalled that some of the girls made cordwood, the name given to smaller pieces of cut branches, which were stacked up and taken away to make charcoal: 'Some girls worked on the charcoal burners. They had to weigh the charcoal and got blackened from head to toe because there was so much smoke.'

Ann Moffat was one of those women who joined the Women's Land Army and ending up working on the charcoal kilns. She would saw up cordwood into lengths before it was drawn into charcoal kilns, where an older man put lids on the burners and set light to it. They used to burn for twenty-four hours, and it took twenty-four hours to cool down.

Another essential job for the Women's Timber Corps was to find and prepare alder buckthorn during wartime, which was used to create a very special charcoal used in high explosives. It is a bushy deciduous shrub, which grows in small quantities in the most awkward places, entwined with brambles and in the thickest undergrowth. So it was a hard job for the women like Barbara Beddow to identify the small branches and prepare it for use in munitions:

I learnt that the gypsies worked this alder buckthorn in peacetime … I was issued with a hut for an office, and an open sided shelter for the girls to work in, some bushman saws to cut out the branches. We bought a set of cobbler's knives – we chose to erect the huts on the bank of a stream on the edge of one wood. We soaked the branches in the water, then scraped off the bark.

I managed to beg from a local farmer, some sheets of corrugated iron, which we laid over stakes in the ground. We lit fires underneath and dried the bark, then filled the sacks with the end result and sent them off to be turned into *cascara segrada*. The sticks were cut into equal lengths, labelled and bundled and sent to be used in high precision work in the making of ammunition.[6]

M.E. Reyer in *Meet the Members* worked on alder buckthorn, and wrote:

> One of our most amusing experiences during this job occurred when we had almost finished a wood which had been particularly difficult from the beginning. We had three or four good stacks of bundles all neatly tied and compact. One morning a villager came up to us and asked if we knew that our wood was being sold in the village as 'firewood.'
>
> Our mortification was complete when we discovered that the culprit was a small boy who enthusiastically helped us to convey our bundles to the stacks, with a small cart. When we had gone home tired and hungry he had calmly trundled along, collected one or two bundles and set up to supplement his 'Saturday's penny.'
>
> A porter at the station at which we were loading, put his thoughts very neatly into words. We were throwing bundle after bundle of sticks into the truck, while he stood silently watching us. Then he pushed his hat back, scratched his head, and said in a very sarcastic voice: 'Why need England tremble?'[7]

Little did he know that the small twigs were worth all the effort, as they were going to be used in precision bomb detonation. It had a more predictable burn rate than other charcoals, so it was ideal for fuses where timing was important for blowing up bridges or to create smoke screens, under which the Allies were able to cross the Rhine in 1945.[8]

D-Day Landings

Rose Burton worked at Stansted Park, part of the Earl of Bessborough's estate:

> Here we chopped down a young chestnut which we bundled together. It then went down the road to a joinery firm to be wired together to make D-Day trackway, which the troops used to land on the Normandy beaches with their tanks and lorries.

With great pride, Eileen Mark recalled making D-Day landing tracks and demonstrated the repetitive process with her hands as if working on the machine: 'If it was raining I would go to the barn and using chestnut palings we'd put them on a machine and then made tracks for D-Day landings.'

Creosoting

Margaret Finch was among many girls who worked on the creosote dipping tanks:

> We came back to Thorne's Mill in Kings Langley and worked in the mill. Then sometimes we had to go on the creosote tanks. We hated that job, dipping the cross bars that go on top of telegraph poles into the creosote tanks. Oh, we stank like hell, no matter how many baths we had.
>
> There used to be a dance held at the town hall in Watford about 4 or 5 miles away. But when we had been on the creosote tanks, oh dear, they eventually asked us not to come, as we smelt the place out. Oh we really did smell when it got warm.

Replanting

The drive to continue planting trees in the Second World War was ever present; all the while, thousands of trees were being stripped from Britain's forests. On Friday, 29 March 1940, the *Western Mail* reported:

> Girls who had taken up forestry were doing excellent work in helping the Forestry Commission to plant new trees to replace the timber which was now being cut for war purposes.
>
> In Glamorgan nearly 100 girls were working against time hoping to plant 3,500,000 trees before the end of April, having begun this huge task only in December. The weather had been their greatest enemy in this race against time, for the young trees could not be planted in a severe frost.

Other Land Girls were doing afforestation work in the New Forest, the Forest of Dean and in Sussex, also in Suffolk forests near Bury St Edmunds and across the North York Moors. While half of Great Britain's trees were being felled during the Second World War, licensing for timber felling was introduced and retained afterwards as a conservation measure. A very large effort went into planting new trees throughout the war, over 100,000 acres were planted during the war years, and much of this was done by the Women's Timber Corps.

Doreen Musson remembered: 'Those assigned to the Timber Corps felled trees, trimmed and cut them to length, drove tractors and heavy horses and ensured the cleared areas were left neat and tidy for prospective replanting.'

Before the war in the north of England there were just a few small woods in Kielder. Planting only began in 1933, but it is now the largest forest in England and the powerhouse of timber production across the country. The small operation of male tree planters were called up to fight, and so a group of twelve girls from the Women's Land Army arrived in 1941 to replace them.

Alfie Weir was 6 when his family came up to Kielder and moved into the coach house next to the viaduct. His father had worked in forestry, in the private sector, in the supply of pit wood in Wales. In 1926, Alfie's father started working for the Forestry Commission and eventually managed timber production for the north of England:

They found the girls were able to match the 2,000 trees the men planted per day but were criticised at first for planting the trees too close together. So after that they needed to be supervised to space the trees out. They planted Norway Spruce and Douglas Fir trees in the winter and did weeding and nursery work in the summers.

Eileen Mark was planting trees in Sussex:

There was a yardstick that we used to plant the trees at correct spacing and once I had to plant up a hill. This was not an easy task and so the lines of trees where all cock-eyed. Many years later the storms of 1978 brought down many of the trees I planted back in the wartime.

The change from domestic work to forestry was quite a shock for Katie Dowson:

It was cold outside, and we had no shelter near the nursery where we planted the trees. There was a little hut there and we used to count and plant trees and grade them into hundreds and pile them into little bundles.

That [was at] Low Muffles and then there was High Muffles. I went with a gang of men to plant trees. We had to have them in a mailbag. You set off with one hundred in a bag and they did weigh a lot. The ones like they would grow in the nursery. We went around after they felled and planted the new trees.

When we planted trees, we paced it out. I used an ordinary spade and you put it behind the spade and cut a piece, popped your tree in the point. I think where deers had been, bark was off the trees. We didn't used to know what was happening, but the forester found out.

Young trees are most vulnerable to predators, such as deer and rabbits, who like to eat the fresh shoots and bark. So, some of the girls, like Joan Turner, were tasked with fencing the newly planted trees to protect them:

We were doing fencing to protect the new trees and we had ferrets to kill the rabbits where we were going to plant them. I took one ferret from a box on a lead and it got out and got inside my trousers and they are dangerous. Then German prisoners of war arrived, and we were left with them, doing fencing with barbed wire, would you believe?

11

Thirty-Two Shillings a Week or Less

Better Pay

By 1942, a wartime career in forestry proved to be appealing for many women. The promise of travel, better hours than the Land Army and a more generous pay scale including piecework, where they were paid for how much timber they produced, meant that it was a popular choice among the girls. Around 250 women a month between the ages of 18 and 35 volunteered for the corps. Although, pay packets may not have reflected official rates of pay.

The terms of employment sounded good as they were similar to the Women's Land Army, including two free travel warrants a year.[1] Members were entitled to one week's paid annual leave, exclusive of public holidays, from the date on which their employment commenced. If off sick, they received one week's full pay and received payment towards their board and lodging for the remainder of illness.

But there seems to be some discrepancy, because while the Women's Land Army recruited women for forestry work through the county secretaries and provided welfare officers, the Home Timber Production department had overall responsibility for pay. It was based on rates laid down for timber production, minus 2s per week (reduced in 1945 to 6d per week) to offset the privileges and the cost of the uniform.

Officially, the girls in the Women's Timber Corps had a sliding rate of pay according to age and position. However, it is clear, that in some instances the official rates of minimum pay were ignored. On 13 June 1940, a letter was sent to G. W. Jones Esq., Linmere, Delamere, Nr Northwich, from the county secretary:

Dear Sir,

Miss Estelle Matthews, one of the Women's Land Army workers now at Delamere Forest, came into see me on Monday, and said that she had only received 13/5d. in wages for the past week. I am at a loss to understand this, as you are, I know, aware that the minimum wage for workers under 18 years of age is 22/6d. per 48-hour week, plus 6d. per hour overtime.

Perhaps you will kindly look into this matter and let me know the position? Miss Matthews also tells me that Miss Violet Smith and Miss Muriel Simon are leaving you today and going to a farm. Would you very kindly ask them to let me know where they are going, and why they are leaving Delamere.[2]

Minimum Rates

By early 1942, it was clear that the position regarding pay had to be revised and new age-related pay brackets were introduced, increasing the minimum wage for the women who worked in forestry. On 10 February 1942, Lady Denman sent a letter to all Women's Land Army county secretaries:

Timber Work
New wage rates for women engaged in timber production work have now been fixed and will apply, where these are higher than Land Army minimum rates, to members of the Women's Land Army in the employment of the Home Grown Timber Production Department of the Ministry of Supply.

The new gross wage of 48/- fixed for women timber workers of 19 and over is considerably above the Land Army minimum. The gross wage rates for women timber workers of 17 to 18 and 18 to 19 are however below Land Army minimum rates for these age groups and Land Army minimum rates must therefore be applied.[3]

In 1942, the English Women's Timber Corps and Women's Land Army paid their 17- and 18-year-old recruits the same rate of pay, 32s and 38s per week respectively. In Scotland, the wages were slightly higher at 35s for 17-year-olds and 41s 6d for 18-year-olds.[4] The money had to cover the cost of billets, food, income tax, personal expenditure and in many cases contributions to a home. The Lumberjills, such as Mavis Williams, reported that the younger girls on lower wages 'found it difficult to manage'.

There were guidelines that wages should be increased where necessary to provide 14–18s clear over and above the cost of board and lodging. However, this was not always followed. A Land Army Benevolent Fund was set up to assist in 1942, with a treasury grant to help women in England and Scotland, which was supplemented by subscriptions, donations and fund-raising events. The money was distributed in grants for those requiring medical assistance, education, training, resettlement or those on lower incomes with high expenditure.

Specialist Roles

Once the Women's Timber Corps recruits reached the age of 19 or took on more specialist roles, their pay exceeded the Land Army Minimum rates, starting at 46s in Scotland and 48–50s a week in England. They were also able to work overtime, at time and a quarter, over forty-seven hours per week.

Measurers were paid 55s as a minimum, but they were not paid overtime unless they worked between 4 p.m. on Saturday and 5 a.m. on Monday, when they were paid time and a half. Tractor and lorry drivers and gangers were also paid 55s as a minimum before overtime rates kicked in.

Girls working a forty-eight-hour week in sawmills received the same as forest workers, except those working on machines. In these cases the rates of pay were higher, starting at 62s and increasing to 72s, more than double those starting out in the Timber Corps aged 17.

Piecework

Katie Ann Kennedy was given the opportunity to be paid on piecework, like the men, paid on the amount of timber she felled: 'Two of us on piecework could fell one hundred trees a day, snedding and sawing them into Millwood, pit props and pulp. We were paid one shilling for each tree. It proved to be too hard for girls.'[5] Neither women nor men would have been able to keep up this pace of felling, as the number of trees they felled may well have depended on the size and ease of access to trees. This model of piecework would only have worked in Scotland in purely conifer tree forests, where the trees were of a standard size.

In England, where forests were mixed with different size and species of tree including larger broad leaf trees, it was more appropriate to calculate the rates of pay for the fellers based upon the amount of timber they had felled. There may have been some women who benefitted from this method of calculating wages.

However, payment on piecework would not have been the norm for Women's Timber Corps and many had little spare money to spend.

The local officer, responsible for finding the girls billets, met Diana Underwood at Southampton station and was supposed to check the digs before they moved in. But she rarely did, and so the girls were better off looking themselves:

> We were sometimes able to find our own digs, but it was never an easy job. Workmen were building an airfield for the Americans at Stoney Cross and they were able to pay more for digs so we were unable to get in anywhere for the recommended one pound a week and usually had to pay 25 shillings, sometimes 30 shillings.

Pay Gap

Home Timber Production by Russell Meiggs shows the disparity between wages for men and women working in forestry.[6] In June 1944, males classified as 'General Labourers' earned 72*s* per week, up to 29 per cent more than women over 19 years of age classified as 'Labourers', who earned 56*s* per week. By November 1945, men in England and Wales classified as 'Skilled Fellers' earned 93*s* per week, 55 per cent more than the group of women classified as 'Labourer', who earned 60*s* per week. There was no group of female workers classified as 'Skilled Fellers' or even 'Fellers' in this book.

Among sawmill workers, men called 'Skilled Sawyers' were paid 1*s* 11½*d* per hour, 19 per cent more than women called 'Sawmill Worker on Machine' who were paid 1*s* 5½*d* per hour. In May 1944, the pay gap in Scotland between the men earning 90*s* and women earning 64*s*, per forty-eight-hour week was 40 per cent more, although it does say that some women received the full male rate. The same source says among tractors drivers, both men and women received the same pay across the country.

This meant that according to official figures, except for the rare few females who received the same rate of pay as the men, women were paid considerably less. As a result, it was harder for them to compete with the men for better quality lodging or have spare money for going out or to cover any additional expenses they may have had for clothing or travel.

However, again these official figures seem to be considerably higher than the amounts the women actually reported being paid. For instance, Diana Underwood said, 'My "take home" pay was £4.7.2. a fortnight.' She was a measurer and worked in sawmills in the New Forest and earned less than 44s per week, which is 11s short of the recommended 55s for measurers.

Mary Broadhead was a sawmill operator and earned 60s a week, which was 12s short of the official 72s weekly wage for female sawmill operators:

> You had to pay your landlady with thirty bob a week and wages were only about £3 or something like that and so you didn't know how to make ends meet. You got to learn to look after the money but there was only dancing and going to the pictures, but you couldn't really afford it because it used to be two and sixpence to go into dance hall.

12

Freezing Cold Camps and Nowhere to Stay

Dear Madam, 16th November 1939

<u>Women's Land Army</u>

I understand that Lady Denman is communicating with you regarding the difficulties in obtaining accommodation for members of the Women's Forestry Corps whom it is intended to employ on Timber Control Work at Delamere Forest, Cheshire. The local forester has made some attempts at obtaining billets but has been unsuccessful so far – his main difficulty being ignorance as to the exact requirements of the girls and the amounts which they will pay for the accommodation.[1]

Fourteen women from the Women's Land Army were drafted to work at Delamere Forest, Northwich, as early as November 1939. Not only did it prove very difficult to find them lodgings nearby because of the remote location, there were also no petrol rations to billet them elsewhere. Urgent requests were made far and wide for lodgings and the situation became so desperate that Lady Denman had to deal with the matter personally.

In his letter of reply, A.H. Popert said, 'but the great trouble is finding billets for them, since all possible billets in the district have been taken by the military.'

In South Wales, where thirty women where due to start work in the forest in November 1939, Inez Jenkins reported 'a similar difficulty about billets has been overcome by arranging for the Y.W.C.A. to run a hostel for the workers from which they are able to travel daily to the nurseries'.

In a response to that letter, Mrs Crowther explains: 'The trouble, of course, is billeting them for the amount allowed, namely 14/- per week. In the Delamere district, those people who are accustomed to taking visitors are also accustomed to receiving 20/- to 25/- per week …'

Despite this awareness of the shortage of billets in 1939 for the Women's Timber Corps, the situation persisted throughout the war. On 10 July 1941, in the *Yorkshire Post*, Miss Grace Harrison, organising secretary for the Women's Land Army in the West Riding, reports that although forestry was a popular section of training, 'it was handicapped by billeting difficulties, as forestry work was generally in rather remote places'. It is interesting to note she uses the word 'handicapped', which in other newspapers expressed prejudice against the women.

Discrimination

When we first arrived, we all found a short cut through the fields nearby to get to the forest where we were working. However, the local people complained so we had to go around the long way. We were different people from the towns and they didn't like us at all. It was only when they found out we went to church services that things got better.

There were two forests one at either end of the village where we worked to begin with and eventually we cleared all that out. Then we moved to another forest and there was one big house near to the forest, the people in there looked at us as though we were scum of the earth, like we didn't belong. So, when we worked in that forest we were only allowed to get out of the lorry and go straight to the forest.

As Edna Holland remembers, local communities who were asked to provide bed and board for the new female forestry recruits were frequently prejudiced against housing women who were not from the local area.

In August 1941, *The Scotsman* reported, 'Mr. J.J.M. Hannah, Girvan Mains, said that the utilisation of the Women's Land Army was ruled out because of the lack of accommodation. There was at least one parish in Ayrshire where there was not a single cottage.'

The women certainly felt that the locals were hostile towards them. Edna Holland was trained in the Wetherby camp:

There was a man from the village who was elderly and had retired, he had worked in farms and become our odd job man in the huts. He would come and see to the fires and load them up with logs. But, he used to just walk in at nights when we were all changing out of our working clothes. He would just walk straight in, look around at us all and then poke about in the fire. There was nowhere to cover ourselves; if you wanted to be private you would have to go to the toilets. So eventually we complained to the supervisor and the old man called us a snotty lot. He really thought we were below him.

Despite being educated at grammar school before becoming a Lumberjill, Hazel Collins was made to feel like an unwelcome outsider in one of her lodgings:

We had to sit in the parlour. It was all horse hair leather seats that were all slidey, horrible and uncomfortable. We had to have lunch in there. We couldn't mix with the others; we weren't good enough because we were land army. Her children were all training to be doctors you know. I told her she was an old snob when I left. I said, 'I don't know why you do these things.' She said, 'It's just that my children are all very well educated.' I said, 'Well, I was well educated too.' 'Oh, were you?' she replied. I said, 'Yes, does that make a difference?' Then I said a rude word at her when I left with my suitcase.

Olive Edgley also experienced prejudice:

I remember on a day off we went to the Fox and Hound at Westonbirt and we turned up at the door and asked for a bed for the night and we were turned away. They said they had no room. So we went to the nearest telephone box and put on the poshest voice and said three members of Captain Blunt's acquisition staff were in the district. Was there any chance of finding a room? And to this she replied, 'No trouble, no trouble at all.' When we arrived she said, 'There are ... there are ... three land, err land ... ladies here!' Her parting shot was, 'We DO change for dinner here you know,' and Tessa said, 'Well, we DO have a change of shoes you know.'

The girls lived on very little money, were always on the move and had to find billets at each new place of work. So it was very uncommon for the girls to be able to afford to stay in a hotel. However, like Olive Edgley, if they had saved up their money after staying in many basic cottages, bothies or wooden huts it was a well-deserved and rare luxury.

Affleck Grey, who was in charge of timber operations north of Dingwall in Scotland and is the author of *Timber!*, arrived at a hotel with one group of girls in Scotland, where on asking for accommodation for the night he was greeted with the reply, 'How could I seat rough girls like that in my dining room with such as Admiral Dalton who is retired, but comes here every year for fishing?' He was so angered by this that he refused to stay in the hotel, but not before he had made sure the girls were given rooms and treated with respect.[2]

In another instance, two pole selectors wearily made their way to a hotel, after a long day walking miles across Somerset in search of suitable timber for telegraph poles.[3] All the girls could afford was bread and cheese with their tea. When they sat down in the restaurant they realised that the other guests were in eveningwear. The two diners were so disgusted they left their dinner and walked out. The girls were so hungry they could have eaten those abandoned dinners.

Welfare

Some of the luckier girls who were recruited officially through the Women's Timber Corps had the support from 'Divisional Welfare Officers', who would deal with enquiries on, or more likely problems with, 'billeting and employment conditions', read a letter from Inez Jenkins, Assistant Director of the WLA and TC, sent to all county secretaries on 13 August 1942.[4] A selection of letters between the county secretary and a division welfare officer in Oxfordshire in The National Archives reveals how time-consuming the role of welfare officer was. There were just nine divisional welfare officers for the whole of England and Wales, serving thousands of women.

Aside from finding new billets and arranging accommodation, welfare officers did everything from chasing up unpaid doctors' bills and sick leave, to promotions, transfers, recruitment and arranging new or second-hand uniform supplies. To begin with, the welfare officers were also asked to intervene with complaints of bad behaviour, fallouts between girls, finding clubs for evening entertainment and obtaining flat irons for the girls.

However, the majority of the girls had to deal with all of these things themselves and their biggest problem was finding their next suitable lodging. Some were sent to live in bothies in the far reaches of the Scottish Highlands where they had to brave the winters with nothing but a log stove which they had to use for cooking, heating and to warm water for washing and drying sodden work clothes. Only a few lucky ones stayed at home with the luxury of home-cooked food, family and friends and their local community to support them.

Camps and Hostels

Some of the Women's Timber Corps were billeted in main camps or hostels in England, Scotland and Wales, which were built specifically for the forestry girls because there was such an acute shortage of accommodation for the girls. These included Thetford Forest, Essex, Forest of Dean, Shropshire, Wetherby in the Yorkshire Moors and Hereford in England, Shandford Lodge near Brechin and Park House, Drum Oak in Aberdeenshire in Scotland. Many more camps were needed but money and materials were in short supply. Other Lumberjills boarded in Land Army Hostels or Ministry of Supply Hostels.

In dedicated Women's Timber Corps camps such as Culford in Thetford Forest, the girls lived in Nissen huts made of corrugated iron with an arched roof, sleeping ten to a hut with a log burner in the middle.

Catherine Swanston wrote that the facilities the camps provided, over private billets, with a separate washroom and dining hut for mealtimes, offered many benefits to the girls' health and well-being: 'On the whole camps are more popular than billets and they possess certain obvious advantages, such as the provision of adequate means for drying wet clothes and proper sick bay arrangements for looking after girls who are ill.'[5]

After umpteen addresses, Dorothy Swift won a 'hard fight' to transfer to a Women's Timber Corps hostel in Cheswardine, near Market Drayton, Shropshire:

A group of Nissen huts erected within the wood we'd be razing comprised the hostel. The place name, 'Bishop's Wood', was probably derived from its established tree plantation. Our hostel had two dormitories, a dining room, recreation room and ablutions … Each dormitory had 12 beds and a fuelled stove.[6]

In the Hereford hostel, the girls were lucky:

Built on a large plot of land it had numerous one-storey, alphabetically defined concrete buildings called blocks. Each block had 25 rooms accommodating two people in each, sleeping on bunk beds. It was possible for 50 people to live in one block. Doris and I were put into B block reserved for members of the WTC. Block E was reserved for members of the WLA. In total some 100 land girls were housed in two of the many blocks. In others, munitions factory workers, or indeed, anyone of either sex who was away from home during war work might live in them. Although a sickbay with nursing staff awaited needy hostel dwellers it was rarely used by healthy land girls.

There were two communal dining rooms at our hostel. People whose sleeping blocks were near to either eating-place were less likely to miss meals than those whose blocks were not. Collecting leftovers from vacated supper tables to save long walks to the dining room next day was second nature to us. We also pinched scraps of food to take the prisoners at work. We wash our dungarees at a huge laundry adjacent to a purpose-built theatre-cum-dance hall.[7]

Private Billets

However, for the vast majority of Lumberjills they were left to fend for themselves and find their own billets. The Women's Timber Corps had the same itinerant lifestyle as gypsies or other migrant workers, especially in England and Wales where forests were smaller and more numerous.

Diana Underwood, who worked in the New Forest, found it hard to find digs:

We would go and knock on a door and they would either say, 'No, we are sick to the death of it' or 'Yes'. But we had an awful job to get in anywhere, because they didn't want anyone thrust upon them. They knew they had to take us in, but they were not desperately willing. Sometimes they preferred the girls as the lesser of the two evils, as they thought girls would do more around the house. You got on a lot better if you helped out in the billets, preparing vegetables and other jobs. But men paid more, as they had more to spend from their wages.

Life in the corps was transient and nomadic and the girls had to get used to their ever-changing environment. When a patch of forest had been felled, work began on another area of standing timber. One girl is said to have worked in eighty different locations in her first two years of working in the WTC. Each move meant a new billet and, often, a new set of workmates.

After measuring an area, Olive Edgley had to move again and find new digs every few weeks:

We went from Western Super Mare, Cleveland through to Wiltshire, all around the Malmesbury, Stroud, Gloucestershire, to the top of Somerset, Monmouth. We travelled by bicycle and train, then at the other end we had to find digs which was one of the hardest jobs.

Diana Underwood stayed with ten or twelve families in the New Forest, billeted all over the place from Lyndhurst, Ringwood and Brockenhurst and as far away as Colden Common and West Tytherley near Stockbridge: 'If we found good digs it was better to stay and cycle further as our jobs changed.' This meant she had to cycle huge distances as she lived 20 miles from where she worked.

The women learned about people who came from different backgrounds. In a society divided by class, they experienced what it was like, not only living and working with women from a different background, but also living with families from another class for the first time.

Audrey Broad came from a middle-class family: 'When I left home to join the Women's Timber Corps I had to lodge with all sorts of different people. I stayed with a family in Brighton with children and other girls from the Women's Timber Corps. They were a very working-class family.'

Joan Turner stayed with a woman who had one room with a stove in a cupboard:

This lady had not much, but bare boards and camp beds and charged us half our wages. So from there we were sent to Derby put up in a house where the woman had someone sleeping in our beds in the daytime too, so we couldn't unpack. So we went back to Derbyshire Menon Langley, which is a spa now, and lodged in the garden cottage. From there we moved eleven more times in a few years.

However, when Barbara Beddow moved to the Sawmill House on the Swinton Estate: 'Lady Somebody, who was President of the local L.A. branch invited me to afternoon tea, with the silver tea service, cucumber sandwiches, strawberries and cream served on the Sheraton, or was it Minton china?'[8]

Eileen Mark had a completely different experience when she was reassigned to the Watergate Estate in Sussex:

I stayed in lodgings opposite the estate in the manager's lodge, where there were four camp beds in a tiny room just a bit larger than the size of a double bed. We used to wash up, do the clothes washing and help make the food.

Once a week we were allowed to go to have a bath and a chat in the G-Plan estate manor with the lady of the house. Others called her 'Mi'lady' but I never did. The Land Army and Timber Corps would go there and we used to have beans on toast and sit and chat. She had been married three times. We would walk along the passageway to the bath and used to have to stand behind the door waiting our turn.

In the name of doing their bit for the war, girls like Barbara Beddow were invited into people's homes at their own risk: 'In Markington I stayed with a family, mum and three daughters. Mum was having fun with the local army lads and someone wrote to her husband. He came home and chased her with an axe (mine, used for chopping firewood).'

When Mary Broadhead got off the train at Chartham, she was met by a young woman called Mrs Renee Hazelwood:

When I was with Renee Hazelwood and her son Roy, I would take Roy out in his pram for a walk so that Renee could cook dinner. Renee had a horrible cough and I tried to stop her from smoking, but she fell ill. But she got more ill and went into hospital and later died.

Hazel Collins stayed with a nice couple in Quagmire where 'there were fleas in the bed … I said, "I think you have fleas in the bed" and she said, "Oh no, what again!" I had to stay there a couple of nights and she got out a bottle of methylated spirits to wipe the sheets down.'

Alison McLure recalled, 'One Saturday afternoon there was a terrific noise coming from a hut and upon investigating, I found the girls perched on windowsills, beds and lockers screaming their heads off. The cause? A fast-moving mouse.'[9]

In winter, the primitive living conditions were worse. In Scotland it was so cold at night in their basic shelters that ice would form on the inside of the walls in their wooden huts or stone bothies. Bonny Macadam agreed with the other girls, that the best place for your bed was as close to the wood burning stove as possible:

I was posted to a camp at Kirriemuir on Kinnordy Estate, near Glamis. There I lived in a hut for the first time and realised how cold it became on winter nights. It was not unusual for hot-water bottles to freeze! Instead of undressing to go to bed we piled on all our dry clothes, while the wet, working clothes steamed round the wood-burner.[10]

One of the perks for Nan MacLean was sleeping beside the stove in the Nissen hut, which became very cold in winter: 'There was no coal, but we used to go down the road to the RASC [Royal Army Service Corps] camp, when it was unoccupied, and keep the guards talking while others filed up the bogie with their ration of coal.'[11]

Jean Buntin, from the Scottish Timber Corps, lived in wooded huts, heated by wood burning stoves, which were used to dry their wet clothes in winter:

It was quite comfortable while the stove was going but the temperature dropped very quickly when the last log burned away. Early one morning I awakened to a loud bang and a fizzing noise: a bottle of lemonade had exploded with the cold and by breakfast time it had frozen solid.[12]

Joan Turner had to sleep three-in-a-bed in one bitterly cold house: 'Yet it was unpatriotic to protest during the war. We were glad to escape early to bed by candlelight, cuddling in our undies under a shared sheet to keep warm until morning.'

The majority of private billets were very primitive: none had a bathroom, the toilet was outside if they had one but often a bucket was used, lighting was by oil lamps or candles as there was often no electricity and some households still had to draw water from the village pump.

Irene Snow lived in very basic conditions:

You couldn't imagine what it was like then … Some were good and some not so good. In Dulverton we lived in a stone hut with an outside sink under a lean to, where we had to wash outside with cold water all year round. At least at home we had a bath and basin inside. The toilet was outside but that was normal then.

Rose Burton described the cottage where she lived:

There was no electricity, one oil lamp on table in the living room and one in kitchen. In our bedroom we had a candle sometimes two and no wardrobe, just two upright orange boxes with a curtain across for our clothes. We used an old-fashioned jug and basin to get washed and we had to carry the water from downstairs to upstairs and the dirty water downstairs again.

Many a time Molly and I singed our hair bending forward to see in the mirror. We had to put our great coats on in bed to keep warm. The toilet was outside, through a wooden shed. No sink or running water, had to fill two enamel buckets from across the yard outside Lady Hamilton's garage. The dirty water we opened the kitchen window and flung it into a field at the back where it just stayed stagnant.

It was exceedingly rare to have the home comforts we take for granted today in the billets as Rose Burton discovered: 'What bliss! A bathroom and electricity at last and much better food.'

Personal Hygiene

Olive Edgley had some strange digs, some very uncomfortable and some very nice ones: 'I remember the one in Minety, a little village in Wiltshire, because there was no toilet and we emptied our potty out of the window in the morning onto a slop pond.'

Where Mavis Williams stayed in Hereford there was what she called a 'primitive loo' with the 'bucket and chuck it' arrangement.[13] This was not uncommon in rural living conditions. Peggy Conway remembered, 'There were potties under the bed and a "netty" at the bottom of the garden.'

Dorothy Swift stayed at Mr Bellwood's, where the outside toilet was known as 'the little room' and could be reached via a long pathway leading from the back door of the house:

This amenity had a removable bucket in a hole. When this was full Mr. Bellwood would dig a pit in his back garden, lift the bucket from its hole and bury its contents in their prepared grave. The housekeeper once quizzed me about your body waste. 'Does it always find a fresh tomb, Dot? The garden isn't that big is it?'[14]

The Women's Land Army and Timber Corps rules said that there had to be a bath where the girls stayed, but obviously there often wasn't one. One of the biggest problems the girls had to deal with was how they could stay clean and fresh. The work was often very dirty, aside from the hot and sweaty nature of the hard physical work. Some had to rely on the hospitality of others for a weekly wash, often sharing bath water as there was not enough to go around.

Ethel Oliver, a Chopwell Lumberjill, would go home at weekends for a bath when she could, but the 'transport wasn't great'. This could have become a euphemism for excusing the body odour. Katie Dowson said there was a lovely girl she worked with who lived with her granny, and 'in those days you just had a bath on a Friday and sometimes she did not smell too sweet'.

One day someone said to Hazel Collins they had noticed that 'Joyce smells':

> There was one girl Joyce who was very dirty, very unclean. I had to take her to the clinic; she was much older than us, two or three years older … and I looked in her hair and noticed she had nits. I looked at her straight in the face and said, 'You smell.' She said, 'I can't help it.' and I said, 'You can.' So I took her to a clinic and said, 'Can you clean her up?' and she said, 'Why?' 'Because she smells.'
>
> … I had a girlfriend whose feet stank and she was so embarrassed about it. She used to wash her feet in disinfectant. But hours later the smell was back again.

However, it wasn't very easy to have a wash, and in the winter Nan McLean in the Scottish Timber Corps was reluctant to wash at all because she had to use cold water.[15] When Margaret Finch was granted permission to use a tin bath, with warm water, to her dismay she discovered it wasn't in front of the fire:

> Our first posting was to a sawmill in Kings Langley, near London. We were billeted with an old lady by the name of Mrs Homans. We started at daybreak and finished at dark, and when we returned at night Mrs Homans would not let us use her bathroom, as we were so dirty. So we had to take a tin bath, which she kept in the kitchen hanging on the wall, and pans of boiling water out into the back garden where we had our bath. But the main railway line into London passed at the end of the garden, where anyone on the train could see us. So we got a clothes horse from Mrs Homans and hung the towels on it and stood it around the bath to shield us to a point. Of course we had to use the same water for both of us.

The girls in the Scottish Timber Corps were among those to experience the most extreme living conditions. Chris Turner (née MacDonald) stayed in an empty cottage near the head of the Glen near Achnacarry:

No conveniences of course, not even a latrine, but there was a fine stream nearby and for that we were truly thankful! Now we could bathe each night and cleanse ourselves of the days dirt and sweat. Talk about back to nature! We now knew something of the lifestyle of a cavewoman.[16]

But this was by no means unusual; Mavis Williams, in her book *Lumberjill*, included beautiful photos of the girls bathing in a forest stream in Cornwall, 'our only means of washing': 'At least once a week the girls came armed with toilet bags and towels and sometimes a bathing costume, for in one part of the wood there was a natural deep pool.'[17] This was fine in the summer or warmer months, but would not be possible in the winter.

Mavis Williams was also based in Hereford for a while:

The ancient wooden hand pump outside provided the water which had to be carried upstairs in a bucket [to the marble topped washstand with basin and jug]. When the outside pump was frozen, the ice on top of the metal water butt had to be broken. This water was brick red in colour and, as I found when I washed my hair, harboured many tiny creatures, which had to be combed out. White undies became a paler shade of pink. Hot water from the large black kettle was only allowed at the weekend.

The girls were always grateful for a bath and took up offers, which sometimes came from the most surprising places with many welcome benefits. One evening Mavis Williams happened to dance with a reporter, which resulted in an article in the local paper. When Mavis wrote to thank the editor for his interest, he invited the girls to go and stay at his house for the weekend, a day or just for a bath.

Two of us went to be graciously received and welcomed. His home, after some of our digs, was sumptuous. So began a friendship which lasted many years.

Our friend the editor promised my Ganger and I, before we left the area, that he would make arrangements for us to return to his home for occasional weekends. I was 10 to 15 miles away and Wendy almost as far. However, on a Friday evening a taxi would arrive at the door of my digs. At that time, a taxi could travel only so many miles from its home base. I can't remember just how many miles was the rule, but I had to change into another taxi, which would be waiting when the first taxi reached its allotted limit; it was a masterpiece of organisation.

Lying stretched out on the back seat was most relaxing, even though it was dark, as inside lights were not allowed because of blackout regulations. We lingered in hot baths and had as much as we could eat, cooked to perfection by his housekeeper. Sunday evening the procedure was reversed, the second taxi always waiting when the first arrived. Had it not been for those weekends I would, no doubt, have been very lonely.

13

How We Survived All Day on Jam Sandwiches, I'll Never Know

You really must do something about the food problem at the hostel. I'm speaking for myself as well as the girls. If the girls feel sick and empty as I do, I feel really sorry for them. The menu last evening was two potatoes, half an over sized spring onion and a very small piece of uncooked meat, the afters were tasteless and not enough to fill up on and no second helping.

At supper time, there was only a thin slice of cake, one girl went and asked for some dry bread and it was refused her by Miss Simson. The cook started to cut the girl some bread but Miss Simson stopped her and told her we were not supposed to have any food after our dinner. That really takes things too far, don't you think? Dry bread doesn't come on rations and we have our butter to use as we like.

Breakfast this morning was awful, the porridge was spoilt, we didn't get any milk on it, only water, the bacon was sour, I couldn't eat mine, I took it to show Mr. Underwood, also a slice of bread that was put out for breakfast, that was mildewed, he is writing to tell you himself, all I had to eat this morning was half a slice of fried bread and half a slice of bread and butter, and some of the girls had less than that.

You can't expect the girls to stand this much longer, I myself am not going to, I shall be walking out very soon. The poor kids are only sticking now because they think it will get me into trouble, I won't want them to do that any longer. They are all for the hostel really, but it is not run in the right way. If things were altered, we could be very happy here.[1]

How those Lumberjills were sustained with nourishment throughout the war, while they carried out such hard labour, seems to be more dependent on good luck and resourcefulness than rations. The girls rarely depended on three square meals a day. Often food was in short supply, was of poor quality and their diet was severely restricted, as the letter to Mrs Jackson the divisional welfare officer on 25 July 1944 above shows.

Food rationing began in Britain in January 1940. Each person had a ration card, which could only be used at certain shops. Families had to say which butcher, baker and grocer they would buy food from and the rules were very strict. As the Lumberjills were itinerant, this would have made it more difficult. The rationing was severe, including eggs, cheese, butter, margarine, meat, and (later) sugar. So people kept in with the grocer, swapped and bartered with each other for fresh vegetables, sugar and other luxury items. People would often queue outside shops not even knowing what would be left, so the black-market economy was rife.

All too frequently, the girls away from home had to survive on meagre portions and poor-quality food even in camps or in hostels. Many of the private billets didn't have enough rations to cover the Women's Timber Corps, who stayed with them only a short while. There would be little time to register to increase their rations, so they resorted to offering them food that was not rationed. Bread was a staple for many of the women and some were very lucky if they got anything else for lunch.

In a report on 'The Health of Forestry Workers: A survey of the Women's Timber Corps of Great Britain' by Catherine Swanston, which appeared in the *British Journal of Industrial Medicine* in 1946, it was found common for the girls to have gastrointestinal complaints, such as constipation, which was caused by too much starchy food, such as bread, not enough food or long periods without food and a lack of adequate toilet facilities in the forests.[2] This certainly seems to be consistent with reports from the Lumberjills. Joan Turner said, 'How we survived all day on jam sandwiches, I'll never know.'

Dorothy Swift remembered the hunger she often felt during her working day in the forest:

> The long walk to work each day found us eating our packed lunches prematurely. We each had a 'bait tin' and when both were empty we begged more grub from the men we worked with. Working in the open air made us hungry and considering how hard the men worked too it was amazing how their meagre rations sustained them. Come to think of it, what audacity we had – all three of us – to have cadged extra nourishment from our fellow workers' paltry food rations.[3]

Many foods were rationed, so often Katie Dowson just had bread:

The only thing I would like is a nice white bread because it was all grey. Gladys used to bring a big toffee tin filled with beetroot sandwiches, which used to be lovely. It was the prisoners that didn't have anything for lunch. They just ate dried bread. After that I said I never wanted another picnic ever again. Oh I hate picnics.

Frieda Ellerby used to swap her lunch for one of the forester's; ground rice for a bun: 'Frank Kirby was about 80 but used to bike from Longbridge. I said, "What have you got for your bait today?" He replied, "Just sad cake (pie with no filling just pastry)". I felt sorry for him nothing much tasty like. We did look out for each other.'

Rationing meant that food was fairly monotonous and Deirdre MacKenzie remembered always being hungry: 'we really did not mind as long as the diet was reasonable.'[4]

Bread and Cheese

For many women, the daily diet of bread was often improved by adding cheese. But Olive Edgley did not always agree: 'I can remember vividly in Savernake Forest and she [the landlady] could think of nothing other than bread and cheese to give us.'

This was a common story and an experience that Mary Broadhead shared: 'It was nearly every day that we ate cheese sandwiches so when the army was in the woods exercising we would exchange our sandwiches for their hard biscuits and bully beef it was a change for both of us.'

When Joan Turner joined the Timber Corps, at night she was given cocoa and a piece of bread and cheese: 'But we were so hungry one of us used to distract the girls on the front desk while the other sneaked round the back to pinch some more bread.'

In September 1941 extra cheese rations of 8oz, which were already given to agricultural workers and underground miners, were extended to include Land Girls and forestry workers, among others.[5] However, application forms had to be filled in by employers or other responsible people and they would then have to register with local retailers by 13 September. I wonder how many of the Women's Timber Corps, as itinerant workers, were able to benefit from this? Diana Underwood certainly did not:

We were given breakfast, an evening meal and a packed lunch. Although we had 12oz of cheese instead of the standard 4oz ration, the landladies had difficulty finding filling for our sandwiches. We had our share of beetroot and 'pink paste'! Most foods were rationed and we had to make sure of taking our Ration Books when we moved digs. But not all landladies fed us. We often didn't get bread or cheese. They would say, 'Sorry, we haven't got any bread today, so I can't give you anything.' If I had enough money I could buy something to eat. So sometimes we picked mushrooms, with others who knew and always carried a knife.

Beetroot was a popular sandwich filling among the Lumberjills, but not for Margaret Finch:

We took sandwiches out for midday and the landlady Mrs Homans said, 'Do you like beetroot?' So we both said, 'Yes.' But we had beetroot sandwiches the whole six months we spent with her. Don't forget the rations were very hard and beetroot wasn't on coupons or rationed.

But later the local dinner ladies invited Margaret and the other girls to have school dinners, when they heard of their diet of beetroot sandwiches.

Beetroot wasn't the only thing not on rations – rabbit was also fair game, and served up for Joan Turner all too frequently:

We were sent to Grantham, Burton Cobbles. People took us in, but one lady came out of another century. She was all in black and her husband was the village barber. Lots of people had never seen anything like it. With them we had rabbit seven days a week in different ways. I have never looked at a rabbit since.

But free-range rabbit became one of the staple foods in the countryside during rationing for Mary Broadhead as many others:

One day I decided to walk back to Shalmsford Street through the parkland and Chillingham Castle and on the walk I saw a rabbit crouched in the grass. So I threw my coat over it. Food was rationed, so here I had a meal. As I continued my walk home I met an older man on the road who asked if the rabbit was for sale and would I take half a crown for it. I said, 'Yes,' and he paid two shilling and sixpence.

Pat Frayn also used to appreciate the value of rabbits: 'We used to send rabbits down to my family to eat. I used to put two on the train, labelled up, and they would arrive safely at the other end. They used to be delighted to have a couple of rabbits.'

Those who stayed at home were among the lucky ones to be well fed. Although Molly Paterson was less pleased with the plentiful supply of hare in Argyll, where she lived in Scotland:

We were lucky because we didn't have the usual rations of butter, rabbit and salmon because my parents lived next door to the gamekeeper and always had half a deer or haunch of venison. They had to control Salmon numbers too with licences and rabbit and hares were in plentiful supply. So we used to have Jugged Hare stew. But I hated it when my mother made it. We also had milk from the farm and generally ate quite well.

Irene Snow stayed at home and benefited from living on a farm where food was not in short supply. She was a size 18 in those days:

Sometimes we'd have pork and pickled onions or we have bread with cream on. We made the cream ourselves. It was very down to earth food. Some people got the best they could give you on food rations, but there were no cakes or anything like that.

All together there was probably thirty of us working around that area and we would all meet up at Dulverton in an army hut with a log burning stove and eat our cheese sandwiches. If we ever had a bit of pickle that would be lovely. Sometimes the American engineers would offer to take us back for bread and jam on Sundays. I was always a bit hungry, so I really appreciated this.

Rations

The itinerant nature of the girls' work and their need to find billets so frequently meant that they received basic food at a time of rationing. Often the portion sizes were not enough to feed these hard-working girls, as was the case for all workers. However, there was also an underlying assumption that women needed less food than the men, which meant like Dorothy Swift they went hungry:

By then both Muriel and Jean were now lodging with the local game-keeper while I'd been sent to live in the nearby village of Cowsby with a widowed lady called Mrs Bell, who was posh like shiny furniture. Unfortunately, she ate like a bird and made me do the same. My landlady judged a plate of mashed potatoes and one slice of corned beef, with no greens in sight, to be adequate for my dinner. She would bake a tiny fruit pie on a platter, slice it into four segments and serve one to me. It never occurred to Mrs Bell that her lodger was a manual war worker with an insatiable appetite. How I envied Muriel and Jean their piled-up plates of dinner and second helpings of pudding. Within a week I had wangled myself fresh lodgings.[6]

Mavis Williams was ravenously hungry after a day's work:

The table was always immaculately laid with white linen serviettes in silver rings and flowers. Our dear, sweet landlady had been cooking only for herself for so long that she had no idea just what we could consume. What we did have was beautifully served, but it was not enough. We would gladly have forgone the decoration to enable a plate laden with plenty of 'grub' after a hard day's labour.[7]

Sometimes the girls were better fed on camps, where food rations were fairly provided for the girls and prepared by a cook. Edna Holland spoke about her time on the Wetherby Women's Timber Corps camp:

We left at 7.30 a.m. in the back of a lorry, it took us an hour to get to the forest and we'd be collected at 4.30 or 5 p.m., home in time for evening meal at 6.30 p.m. We didn't have a choice of what we ate because we were hungry. Working like that all day made you very hungry. The choice for lunch was a cheese or meat sandwich, in the evening we had a cooked dinner sometimes stew, slices of meat, very rarely fish, mostly meat but with plenty of vegetables. For breakfast we had eggs or sausages or something like that.

Breakfast was always porridge and dried scrambled egg for Nan MacLean:

Some cooks were good with dried egg and some made it seem like a piece of leather. There was always plenty of bread and butter and marmalade and for dinner at night plenty of potatoes with the boiling beef from the soup filled you up. The girls were so hungry they would sit down to eat without even washing their hands.

Fresh Pickings

The heavy carbohydrate diet with little fresh food meant that Rose Burton tried to supplement her diet with fresh fruit and vegetables, cultivated or growing wild in the countryside:

> I had an army friend Fred, who brought me tomatoes. Molly had an air force friend who picked mushrooms from Tangmere airfield; that helped keep us going. In the woods between Fernhurst and Haslemere, where [we] felled mainly pit props, a fresh stream ran through the wood and we picked the watercress to have with our pack up.

Mavis Williams was delighted when the wild berries, blackberries, strawberries and bilberries began to ripen in the summer sunshine:

> There were blackberries galore, bigger than I had ever seen before. We each had our fill, so within a few days we were hacking them down mercilessly, as they'd lost their appeal. 'I'll turn colour if I have any more,' said Cherry, 'especially as there is usually a blackberry pie for our meal in the digs.'[8]

Joan Turner explained, 'People in the country used to feel sorry for us and leave apples out for us in baskets. There was lots of kindnesses.'

Generous Helpings

In among the many stories of lack, there were thankfully stories of generosity extended to the girls, who expressed delight when they remembered what it felt like to be well fed, looked after and cared for while away from home. From a weekly invite to have beans on toast, to home-made crunch biscuits sent by post, the gift of well-cooked home-made food made a huge difference to the women and stayed fondly in their memory for seventy years.

At Lindford, kind ladies provided individual meat pies for Diana Underwood and all the workers on Fridays: 'I fetched these from a house along the main road. Jolly good they were too!'

On the way to her first billet, Peggy Conway made enquiries at the village garage and was told that Toy Top was 3 miles away: 'The proprietors were very kind and volunteered to drive us but asked us in and gave us tea and toasted tea cake with sugar sprinkled on (a pitman's standby).'

On the way to work, Rose Burton and her colleagues would get dropped off by the lorry just outside the Royal Oak pub, just a short walk from the woods: 'Alfie and Carrie Ainger, the landlord and landlady were very kind to us. We used to take our pack up along and have it either in their garden or if wet inside. She often gave us home-made apple pie. It was lovely.'

In Shandwick the local farmer, George McNaughton, used to deliver lovely fresh milk to the camp and invite Enid Lenton to his house in the evenings: 'We would just walk across, it was not very far away, and his wife used to cook a meal for one or two of the girls. We would sit in the house and it was warm and cosy and they always made us very welcome.'

It is often said a good meal is the way to a man's heart and this was no less the case for Lumberjills, like Mavis Williams, when she was well fed at one of her billets: 'Meals here were very good for there were plenty of eggs, milk, fowls, meat and cream. Breakfast consisted of two or three thick slices of homemade bread, covered with homemade jam and heaped with freshly made cream.'

When Margaret Finch was posted to Epping Green Corner and billeted on a farmhouse with a lovely couple who made her the most wonderful breakfasts, she could not have been happier: 'We had home produced bacon fried with buttered potatoes, eggs, sausage, tomatoes, mushrooms and fried bread. Oh, I can taste them now!'

In Middleton, Jean and Dorothy Swift stayed with Charlie and Edna Walton and their two little boys. Charlie was a fireman, and his wife was a former pastry cook at a local manor house: 'Edna was like a second mother to us. Her professional cooking was plentiful, and we were made warm and welcome.'[9]

14

Prejudice: The Female 'Forestry Handicap'

The *Western Morning News* ran the story on 3 January 1940 that women were to be recruited into forestry through the Women's Land Army. The headline read 'Forestry Handicap in South-West'.

On Thursday, 4 January 1940, the *Western Daily Press* and *Bristol Mirror* reported on a committee meeting of the south-western branch of the Home Grown Timber Marketing Association and referred to the introduction of the Women's Land Army, students and schoolboy volunteers as 'an interesting scheme for the recruitment of forestry workers in the South Western counties'.

It was a great disappointment to the timber trade that it had not been given priority in the recruitment of labour during war.[1] It wasn't decided by people who worked in the industry, the labour priorities where fixed by government instead. But the need for workers was so desperate that the government had to find a way to alleviate the shortage.

The crisis was that forestry workers were needed to scale up timber production in every area of the timber trade, from locating the wood, negotiating prices and calculating quantity to felling, processing trees, working the sawmills and distributing the timber across the country. With all the able-bodied young men being called up to fight in the war, this left the very young or older men to work in forestry.

In addition, forestry and timber supply workers were at risk of being recruited into the forces, and so a Control Labour Officer was appointed and fought hard to retain skilled and unskilled workers to meet the demands of the timber trade during the war. The trade took advantage of the protective measures introduced by the Ministry of Labour under the Essential Work Order for forestry workers.

The objection to women being employed in farming or forestry during the war was so strong that every attempt was made to prevent it. However, it appeared that no one remembered the good work 3,000 women had done in forestry in the First World War. The Control Labour Officer drew up a list of sources of other fresh supplies of men, including British Civil Prisoners, the National Dock Labour Corporation, Italian and German prisoners of war, Irish volunteer workers, Civil Defence workers, the National Fire Service, military, borstal institutions, college and schoolboys.

A Mr Marshall declared in the *Western Daily Press* that 'it was a "crying shame" there should be a Women's Land Army while men on the dole were idling on street corners'. Reluctance to adopt women made employment into farming and forestry painfully slow to begin with.

In March 1940, despite protests, the Minister of Labour in the House of Commons, Mr E. Brown, said male conscientious objectors (COs) would be employed on farms and forestry before the submission of applicants from the Women's Land Army. Many of the Lumberjills did indeed work alongside ostracised groups. Some COs refused to fight in the war for religious reasons, for instance if they were Quakers. Others refused because they did not want to kill another person. Whatever their reasons, they were often regarded as cowards or outsiders to society and the Lumberjills were forbidden to talk to them.

Diana Underwood remembered the conscientious objectors getting 'a bit of flack from the other men, but we didn't take any notice of it'. Molly Paterson worked with two conscientious objectors: 'They were ostracised and the others resented them and kept away from them. But there was no violence.'

A Man's Job

Women were regarded as the weaker sex and unable to cope with the dangers, rugged and harsh environment and heavy physical labour required in forestry. However, it became a difficult subject to discuss when women were volunteering by the hundreds to help and there was a desperate shortage of male forestry workers.

To begin with the timber trade agreed to women measurers, but they were reluctant to employ women for general forestry duties that required more physical endurance and strength. On 3 January 1939 a letter was sent to Miss Brew at Balcombe Place, which said:

> just after receiving your letter of January 1st, I received a call from Mr. Popert, the Divisional Officer for the Forestry Commissioners.

He was very surprised to learn that we had been asked for girls for trimming and lopping pit-props, as he understood the Timber Control Authorities really require the girls at Lydney to take a course as measurers … I shall be interested to have your comments, in view of the rather conflicting information I have.[2]

Shortly after, a large draft of well-educated women arrived at Lydney station on 15 January 1940 to start their training as timber measurers, along with twenty other Land Army girls to be employed as general forestry workers. I suspect this was a deliberate move by Lady Gertrude Denman and the staff at Balcombe Place to skirt around the prejudice against the women, who she believed to be perfectly capable of the job of trimming and lopping trees.

In August 1941, *The Scotsman* reported:

the labour situation as the thorniest and most difficult they had to deal with. Many references had been made to the Women's Land Army. That army's doing good work in many instances, but as they all knew, it was not possible to utilise women for all the work on the farm.

Although this was in reference to farming, the same attitude prevailed in forestry, as the same girls were being recruited for this trade. Another suggestion was that the government should make 'a stand still order to keep men on farms' otherwise there would be 'nothing but chaos resulting'.

The timber trade was also disgusted to hear that women would be considered to do their work. They did not believe women could do the highly skilled and heavy labour of a lumberjack and didn't like idea of women taking their jobs. It was rare for women to wear trousers, and unheard of for them to work in hard manual labour.

A sawmill manager informed Muriel Ward that he had 'never wanted women' working for him.[3] This was all too common among timber merchants. Pat Rouse called her foreman a 'devil' and said, 'The attitude was that women can't do anything. You could see it on the men's faces.'[4]

Olive Edgley was irritated by her boss, Captain Blunt:

His job was to annoy us. We worked so hard and never took lunch breaks, but he would always turn up just the moment we sat down. It was weird we'd been working our butts off and in all sorts of weather and he'd say, 'What are you doing girls?' I remember Tessie Lockey one day saying,

'Have you any quarrel with the figures we send in and the amount of work we do?' 'No.' 'Right then, just leave us alone.'

Frieda Ellerby's patience wore thin with one man who relentlessly criticised the women:

Yes we did get nasty comments from the men sometimes. There was a chap there who was always teasing us, and we got so fed up with him. He said, 'You're hopeless, you're hopeless you lot, just hopeless' … He had a real thin face and long nose and he was such a nuisance. Ooh, I remember him. So, one day as we were in the wagon coming back home I said, 'Do you know you've got a good face to go ratting with, as soon as the rats see it they would just collapse.' I just went like that [to hit him] and well I missed him and punched the chap's face next door to him and knocked his false tooth out. Ooh I was sorry because he was in the Salvation Army. Ratty was lucky I didn't hit him really.

The most difficult thing for Olive Edgley in acquisitions was facing the agents on the estates:

They would look at us and say, 'What the heck are you three young girls doing on this job?' Or, 'Who do you three think you are?' Sometimes a man would follow us and we would find him lingering in the trees. When we took no notice of him, he would eventually disappear. It was always a man of course and they could be very sarcastic.

She continued:

Our green berets were distinctive; if the weather was grotty we used to wear our berets. If the weather was good, we didn't. But people thought WTC was the Women's Tank Corps and would ask 'What are you doing in the Women's Tank Corps?'

Other girls were mistaken for artists, German parachutists, spies and women commandos when out in the forests, because people simply could not believe they were doing the job of a lumberjack.[5] One pair were even reported to the army by some young boys because they believed them to be 'behaving suspiciously with a large map'.

Jessie MacLean expressed her frustration at people's unwillingness to believe they were Lumberjills and counter their prejudices against women in the day:

> How often, when travelling about, were we asked by many members of various military units, 'What regiment are you in?' We thought this very funny indeed and went on to try to explain to them about our work: felling, snedding, peeling – oh the pain! – Saw bench, stacking, horses and tractors. They didn't believe any of this. I remember one sailor listening in amazement to our story and his reaction, as one suddenly enlightened: 'Oh you work for Bryant and May then, making matches.' Talk about the hackles rising, for we regarded ourselves as being very special, which, of course, we certainly were.[6]

This poem by women in the Yorkshire division of the Timber Corps shows how very fed up and angry they felt about the prejudice and treatment they received:

PEP TALK TO LUMBERJILLS EVERYWHERE, 1945
Do You Feel Suicidal and In Despair?

Do you feel suicidal and in despair?
Does the mere sight of woodlands make you swear?
Are you losing your poise and savoir faire?
– 'You need protective underwear'

Do you suspect you've seen more than your share?
Of trees and trees and still more to spare,
Are you simply browned off with this ruddy guerre?
– 'You need protective underwear'

Would you like to make the populace stare?
Make horses rear, and infants blare,
Even frighten the wits out of Burke and Hare?
– 'Then get into protective underwear'

If you think that your Foreman's a bore or a bear,
His most pompous pronouncements just so much hot air,
If one day you must swing for him, what do you care?
– 'You've got your protective underwear'

Does a falling tree give you a scare?
Do you fall down cliffs and invariably tear?
Your second-best breeches, woll you know where
– 'You've always your protective underwear'

Do you think that the answer to a maiden's prayer?
Would be to give you your release this year,
Do you feel that your treatment has not been quite fair?
– 'Well you did get protective underwear'

Dear Lumberjills, this is in the square,
No Gratuities, no Medals, but to prove you were there,
Tough you're wheeled off at last in a homegrown bath-chair
– 'You will have your protective underwear'

Yorkshire Division, Women's Timber Corps[7]

Reputation

At the beginning of the war, the volunteers in the Women's Land Army bore the brunt of the many jokes about their unsuitability to farming or forestry work. In March 1941, the *Whitstable Times* wrote 'People amused themselves by writing like this once':

Lipstick in the stackyard
Mirrors in the barn
Puffs among the poultry
Stockings that don't darn
High falutin' breeches
Shirts of patent weave
And kindred affections
Too foolish to believe.

In April 1941, the *Yorkshire Post* ran this story:

An official of the Forestry Commission went in to the village post office recently to send off a telegram, which read: 'Please send more women measurers.' The girl behind the counter looked at the telegram and said:

'Women measurers?' 'Yes, that's right,' said the official. 'My,' said the girl, 'Don't some people have funny jobs in wartime?'

Although it might be regarded in some instances as light-hearted humour, nonetheless there were many stories of the Women's Timber Corps being the brunt of the joke. Pat Frayn said her second husband was rather amused by her war work: 'He thought it was funny and used to joke that I might chop his legs off.'

Betty Hansford described herself as 'small and slightly built'.[8] And the doctor who conducted Betty's medical laughed at her desire to join the organisation but, since she possessed no physical impairment which prevented her from 'having a go', she did just that, and served out her time in the corps as a measurer.

The *Western Morning News* on Thursday, 4 January 1940, read:

Laughter for Land Army – Farmer says, 'Out too late' – Spirit Defended – West call to make use of services

Mention of the Women's Land Army met with mixed reception from those attending Newton Abbott Farmer's Union annual meeting yesterday. Discussing alternative sources of labour for the farming industry, Mr. W. B. Hallett, vice chairman of Devon Farmer's Union observed: 'There is also the Women's Land Army.' Laughter greeted his remark, Mr. F.J. Marshall, Ashburton, interposing 'Don't mention it.'

The article continued in a way to discredit the reputation of the women in the Land Army. It showed the full extent of the prejudice and ridicule they received, inferring that their sexual promiscuity was to blame for their unsuitability to the job. It quotes Mr Hallet as saying: '"We cannot help admiring the splendid spirit of these girls in offering their services." Mr S. Courtier of Islington replied: "The trouble is they are not home early enough in the morning to get on with the job".'

Rumours were spread about the reputation of the young women in the Women's Timber Corps. Margaret Grant, who stayed in the manse at Ardbrecknish, heard about the reputation of the girls before her: 'Apparently, the women who had been working in Ardbrecknish had got a very bad name for having soldiers in their beds and they were being replaced by six "good" girls from Glen Etive.'[9]

So while older local men and women found the Lumberjills a threat to the local communities, the younger men found them a fascination. There was even suspicion amongst some 'locals' that they were wayward women with a reputation for leading men astray. Their reputation about them being 'easy' and sexually predatory was perplexing to Barbara Beddow:

> We were sent to Fearby in North Yorkshire, our overseer was a Canadian lumberjack, very introverted, certainly not used to having women work-ing for him – so he had as little to do with us as possible. Not so the local village boys, we caused quite a commotion, the wives were very suspi-cious and not at all friendly. We were staying on a smallholding with a couple and their two young children, but we were soon asked to move. We were like beings from another planet to them. We both went to stay in the village pub.[10]

The advertising used to promote the Land Army, 'Back to the land', was often perverted to 'Backs to the land' and created a false reputation about the girls. In fact, the girls in the 1940s in their late teens and early 20s were very uneducated about sex and probably knew less than young teenagers today. The women were not very forthcoming about what they knew about sex in the day, perhaps because they didn't know a lot and besides, it wasn't the thing to talk about.

Before Margaret Finch went into the Women's Timber Corp she was just out of convent school. She explained: 'A friend knew I was very innocent so he just warned me not to let men take advantage of my innocence. But we did not talk about things like that when we were young.' She also said that her best friend was terrified of consummating her marriage because she had heard there were balls on the end of it: 'She said, "However will they get up there?"' It was only when she found out the balls were on the other end that her mind was put to rest.

Winifred Maud Taylor, known as 'Pluckie', who was based in Bodmin, thought the girls were all pretty sensible:

> I don't think anybody got into bed with anybody. It was pretty kind of, you know, a bit of a kiss or a snog here, but nothing really. I mean most of them had boyfriends somewhere else that was the thing. They only did if for a bit of company you know. And Julie wrote every week to somebody called Tom Billingford, but she didn't marry him in the end. I had a rather nice officer that I was friendly with but that didn't come to anything either in the end. But war is a funny business you meet up with so many different people all the time.[11]

Nonetheless, rather than seen as naive or vulnerable to predatory men, a common perception was that the Land Girls and Lumberjills lacked morals and were shameless seductresses. By contrast, the men who predated the girls remained socially acceptable.

Doris Danher, who was based at the Culford camp, near Bury St Edmunds, was attacked one evening:

> We met boyfriends and we were asked out for dates and I must say I was very nearly raped by a Polish airman. I went on a blind date and as we were walking down the lane he just grabbed me into the field and threw me on the grass. And I got up as quickly as possible. But I think perhaps he thought it was an accepted thing. I don't know but I was very glad to get out of that episode.[12]

When she was asked whether she reported it, she said, 'No I didn't. I did not report it because I think if you make a date with someone you go with an open mind and you hope these things won't happen, but they could happen. I never thought of reporting it.' When the interviewer asked, 'How much concern was there for your moral welfare?' She replied, 'I think it was every man for himself really.'

Barbara Beddow took a broader, more philosophical view of the attitude towards women:

> I think many of us enjoyed the freedom from parental discipline and wallowed in friendships of all kinds, girls together, boys and girls, girls with older married landladies etc. I think older local people saw us as a threat, bringing a challenge to their own young people, who were still under discipline; the young ones were jealous of our freedom. We were probably seen as being a bit wild and too free.[13]

But the women needed to assimilate into the new working environment in order to succeed: working outside in all weathers, doing heavy grafting with the foresters, and sitting with their legs astride tree trunks. But, in the wrong company, this behaviour was perceived as being crude, with relatives remarking that the women were 'developing unladylike habits'.

Pat Frayn recalled how the Lumberjills had to adapt to the male environment with tougher attitudes if they wanted to get on in forestry:

There were two Timberjills, one in the office and the lorry driver who used to pick us up in the morning. She was real mannish and we used to call her Jimmy. We had to be out there by 7.30 a.m. If you weren't there she would shout 'Come on you buggers, where are you?'

The very nature of the dirty manual labour out in the forest, and the uniform, would give the girls the appearance of being unlike female stereotypes. It was very uncommon for girls to wear trousers, even on horseback women would still be riding side-saddle in a skirt. So the design of jodhpurs which accentuated the feminine curves of their hips, thighs and bottom may have exacerbated their reputation, and even added to the shock of seeing these young, rosy-cheeked, windswept women walking down the streets. Some girls admitted they turned a bit wild and felt comfortable sitting with their legs astride trees out in the forest.

Margaret Grant realised what made her feel at home in the forest was out of place back at home:

Then, one Friday night, Archie said to me: 'You're a bad-tempered bitch and I'm going to sort you out on Monday morning.' I didn't know what he was talking about! He arrived on Monday with a clay pipe and a twist of tobacco and said, 'Try that!' I thought he had gone mad, but I smoked the pipe for two years and never thought anything of it, until the first time I went home on leave and took out the pipe on the train and, watching the faces, wondered why they were all looking at me so strangely! Then, when I got home my grandmother said, 'You're getting coarse girl.' I had probably developed very bad, unladylike habits, through wearing breeches and, perhaps was sitting with my leg over the arm of the chair.[14]

Proof

With a growing urgent demand for forestry workers and women being made available by Balcombe Place headquarters to start work, the authorities had to work harder to make their case to reject the Women's Land Army's help. So, in 1940, the Forestry Commission sought to examine their case to reject more thoroughly.

They conducted a survey of women already working in forestry in order to assess the potential productivity of an all-female operation.[15] The report conceded that female forestry workers could indeed make an effective contribution, albeit a less able one than their male counterparts when it came to the heavier aspects of forestry.

It concluded, for instance, that while the 'nimble fingers' of female plant-ers cost 14 per cent less than if the work had been completed by a man, heavier work like notch planting cost 67 per cent more than the normal cost for men's labour. There was still, however, ample evidence to suggest that women could make a significant contribution to lighter, less strenuous forestry work should they be employed in greater numbers.

Catherine Swanston reported that:

> Forestry work is strenuous and to the stresses of the job itself are added the trials of damp and cold. Much of the work requires a sustained physical effort with good muscles and strong limbs. Production Officers have said that two good, hard-working girls can do no more than equal one man's output. And heard the ratio put as low as four to one when the girls are becoming tired. This discrepancy in output is not surprising when it is remembered that a woman's physical strength is only about half that of a man.

There was no mention of a loss of production when men get tired, I note.

It was the Forestry Commission's consensus that women would be confined to 'lighter forestry duties' like planting. This would, therefore, jus-tify the attitude that it was 'a man's job', requiring skill and strength. In November 1939, some fourteen women from the Women's Land Army where drafted to work at Delamere Forest, Northwich, for lighter forestry duties, working in the tree nursery amongst other trimming and lopping duties. In Scotland, a small cohort of women were trained as telegraph pole selectors.

However, in other parts of the country there is no mention of lighter duties, and small groups of Women's Land Army recruits were taken on to work in all areas of forestry, including the heavy work, as early as December 1939. Others recognised there was an urgent timber crisis and there was no other choice but to employ women to increase production. So, a cohort of thirty girls started training and worked in South Wales, and others began training at the Forestry Camp at Culford, Bury St Edmunds, Suffolk, work-ing in all aspects of forestry from felling and haulage to tractor driving and sawmilling.

But the women objected to leaving all the felling to men. Women did not only want to be their auxiliaries and clean up the brushwood after them. Eileen Mark said, 'I wished I could do heavier felling work,' and other women were physically fit and strong enough to take on all types of forestry work.

Enid Lenton joined the Women's Timber Corps in Scotland and was suited to life in forestry from the start:

> My husband, Reg, didn't want me to join the forces, not the army or the air force but he didn't mind the Timber Corps because I was very strong. We were all very sporty in our family. I used to swim competitively and ice skate. My brother, Tom, was the British holder for the one-mile speed skating title in 1939. I nearly went to the Olympic games to compete in swimming and I used to go on stage at the League of Health and Beauty to demonstrate my fitness. Dad was very sporty and played golf, so my parents, my brother and I were all members of the golf club and we played at Gleneagles and all over Scotland.

Women fellers, in fact, played a crucial part in activities of the organisation, and women eventually replaced men in every branch of production from driving tractors and lorries for timber haulage to operating circular saws in sawmills. Bonny Macadam, who was the daughter of a wealthy malt extract magnate, had learned to handle an axe and drive heavy vehicles on the family estate before the war.[16]

Women were able to take over the felling of pit wood stands and could do the job effectively, cutting the pit props neatly and accurately. The gangs were well organised but they did find it harder to maintain the stamina required for bringing down the larger broadleaf trees. So, once many of the pure pit wood stands had been felled and the felling moved to heavier timber later in war, women began to concentrate more on crosscutting after the men.

Respect

Thankfully, the women had a few, important supporters among the men. One of these was Affleck Grey, who became responsible for all timber operations north of Dingwall in Scotland as soon as war was declared. He was also in charge of the very first girls to be recruited into forestry from the Women's Land Army:

At first they were treated with some derision and ribaldry by the male strength and were regarded as more ornamental than useful. Even the operations foreman held the same views as the men. I, however, with recollections of girl students in the Aberdeen University Mountaineering Club, with their ability to climb as sturdily as the boys and their capacity to portage heavy back-packs to a high-level camp, had other ideas and counselled a 'wait and see policy'. 'Perhaps' I added, 'you may be in for a big surprise.' How soon I was vindicated![17]

On 3 January 1940, the *Western Morning News* reported Mr H. Rolf Gardener from the Home Grown Timber Marketing Association regarded the prejudice against the employment of Women's Land Army in forestry as superficial. He stated that:

Nearly every other European country employed female labour in the forests for all except the heaviest work … There is no doubt they can be of much assistance to a farmer and I sincerely hope you will avail yourselves of their help when you are short of labour. We made use of women in the last war, and there is no reason why we should not do so again.

Russell Meiggs referred to a few 'female Amazons' who rivalled men[17] and, likewise, in 1942, James Tait wrote an article in the *Scottish Forestry Journal* which described a memorable encounter with a group of Women's Timber Corps in Scotland:

I have to admit that a mere man will have to take care if he is to be recognised as a forester in future. The woman in charge could lay a tree with the best of men and it is some considerable time since I saw anyone so knacky [proficient] in the handling of an axe.

Mr Marshall started work with the Forestry Commission in January 1944 at 14 years old. He worked alongside thirty Lumberjills, ranging in age from 14 to 60 years old:

At fourteen I was slung in the deep end with the girls and learnt on the job. The girls did everything from loading telegraph poles onto the lorries, cutting timber, brashing up, pruning and more at Rendlesham Forest, Thetford. The girls teamed up in threes on benches lifting and cutting pit props. All girls were local and learnt on the job. The strength of those girls was amazing.

Indeed, it did not take long for the industry to recognise the value of the women who were sent to assist them. The Timber Corps quickly established themselves as 'grafters' who were not afraid of hard work in all weathers. While some members of the Women's Timber Corps were forced to prove their value to a highly sceptical and exclusively male industry, the press showed tentative support for the girls right from the start and this gathered momentum through the war.

Violet Parker had very fond memories of the men with whom she worked: 'The men were lovely and they accepted me.' Edna Holland looked back at her mentorship with the foresters with great admiration and gratitude:

The Forestry Commission men taught us everything they knew. They were going into the forces and just wanted to pass on their knowledge of how to fell a tree and to make sure we knew how to do it properly, so we could carry on their good work when they were gone. They were not prejudiced at all, always accepted us and treated us well.

A Nomadic Life Through All Seasons

The Other Way

There is a land, or so I'm told,
Where timber girls ne'er feel the cold,
Where trees come down all sned and peeled,
And there's no need an axe to wield.

The transport's never broken down,
And Jills go every night to town.
How different here in snow and sleet,
Shivering with wet and frozen feet.

But wait, the sun's come out at last,
And summer's here and winter's past,
The Lumberjills work all the day –
Who'd have it round that other way?

By Hilton Wood, from *Meet the Members*

Travelling Around

The first time we went into town on the bus in the dark you didn't know where you were. One time we found ourselves in the airfield and the troops said, 'What are you doing here?' We had got on the wrong bus and had no idea where we were going. They said, 'Don't worry we'll get you back somehow.' That coastline was black at night and all the airplanes were droning out from Cranwell. The gliders that went out of there were towed. There was one in the field, so Cath and I climbed over the fence and sat in it. It was just like match wood.

Another time we caught a bus from Grantham to Nottingham and Nottingham to Derby. That time it was in a blackout, we walked across the city and slept in a waiting room all night till the milk train came in. My overalls were all stiff with sap from felling the trees. Then we caught a bus to Stoke and another two buses from there. My parents took it for granted when I used to do that trip across the country in the bombing; they would hope I would be home. Going home on leave and travelling by night was normal because we finished work at a certain time and I'd take the bike to the station. You never got cups, so you would have a jam jar of tea and they could be left anywhere so you could have refreshments.

There were no lights on the trains, we travelled in the dark. There were no fires in waiting room, we'd sit on benches and you did not know who you were sitting next to it was that dark. Then you'd wait until the milk train came in at 7.30 in the morning to get home. Nottingham to Derby took an hour but troops were all travelling at the same time. We had to take gas masks everywhere we went when travelling, not into the forest, but we took it for granted, we were not scared. We had to make the most fun out of everything, that's the way we looked at it.

Like Joan Turner, the necessity for travelling far and wide across the country meant the girls had to make long journeys home from time to time, travelling all through the night by train, bus and finally on foot.

Travelling became a way of life for the Lumberjills; often it was the walk to work that became part of their daily routine. In Argyll, Molly Paterson lived at home and had a familiar walk to work, along a road with amazing views where she could see where Loch Awe met the sky:

Every morning I had to walk a mile and a half into the forest to be at work for 7.30 a.m. and so I would get up at about six and set off at about seven. I walked along the road and remember the mist rising like puffs of cotton wool and floating up from the loch.

It was often idyllic out in the forest landscapes, but the girls were not always stationed as close to their work as Molly, so a day's work started with a longer walk or cycle ride that required fitness and stamina in itself. It was not uncommon for the women to cycle 15 to 20 miles a day to work and back. Bikes were issued to the young women but often it was impossible to cycle through the rough and sandy forest tracks, so they had to walk.

Many girls had never owned a bicycle before the war, so they had to learn how to ride a bike first. Molly Paterson had a beautiful bicycle with high handlebars that her father made for her:

> He was very clever at anything mechanical. He would repair cars and clocks and would make all sorts of things for us. Unfortunately I had never learnt to ride it until I started in the Women's Timber Corps at the age of 19. The girls decided to teach me one day and it was such a laugh. They took it in turns to push me and I don't know how many times I fell off and ended up in the ditch. The girls kept running behind and pushing me until eventually I took off on my own and could ride it properly.

Frieda Ellerby never imagined she'd work in the forests: 'I thought how did we do it, biking 5 miles before work, working all day out in the forests and dancing all night? When we were young we had that energy. A lady asked, "Was it hard work?" I said, "No, it was a picnic".'

If they were lucky, the Lumberjills would get a lift on the back of a departmental lorry to their place of work, with the foreman, or cadge a lift from the local farmer. The emphasis was on austerity rather than comfort for workers.

Irene Snow went to forests around Dulverton in an open lorry with a canvas top and little seats:

> To get in you would have to put your foot on the tyre of the lorry. I wasn't very agile and used to nearly fall into the lorry every time. Especially because I was a size 18 in those days and every time I lifted my leg I ripped my dungarees a bit more. I always ordered my clothes in a size too small, so I had loads of pieces sewn into my dungaree bottoms.

During the war, car drivers would give lifts to complete strangers if they were taking the same route as their vehicles. Such sharing was recommended by Churchill's coalition government to make the most of its mandatory petrol rationing.

When Dorothy Swift was working 4 miles from her new billet in Middleton, hitchhiking was not only commonplace but expected during the war: 'So we thumbed it from Middleton to High Force and back again every day. Never once did we break our promise to get to High Force on time.'

Clad in sou'westers, waterproofs and wellies, looking anything but glamorous, Mavis Williams was all 'thumbs and smiles' at any passing traffic: 'Lorry drivers were the most helpful, but often we would have to clamber on top of the load at the back to be blown to bits in a howling gale and hang on for grim death – not very comfortable but quicker than walking.'

But it wasn't just the physicality of the work which required resilience from the Lumberjills. The women worked in forests all over England, Scotland and Wales and they had to be mobile, not knowing where they would be sent next and often finding themselves at the other end of the country.

Even in a small area, women moved each time a new forest was being worked, and when the area was felled they moved again. By its nature, life in the corps was transient and nomadic. Joan Turner worked in many different forests during her time in the Timber Corps: 'You never knew where you were going in back of trucks all day, it was cold, but you'd look after each other.' The women were vulnerable to their ever-changing work conditions and lack of control over their lives, which they had to accept as part of them doing their bit for the war.

Diana Underwood expressed the same sense of stoicism:

You got sent everywhere and you just had to go wherever you were sent. I went from Colden Common to New Park Farm and it took a long time to cycle home from there [a distance of about 20 miles]. We also stayed at Beaulieu, Minstead, Lyndhurst, Rosewood and Brockenhurst.

Officially the girls 'were supposed to work in pairs, two if not more' but Diana Underwood never did:

I always worked alone … As far as I can judge, we were not exploited, rather the opposite. We had no supervision (only a visit about every 3 months) so I was entirely free to work or not. Looking back, I am amazed at what I was expected to do at 21 years of age with no training in how to manage relationships or people's problems. There was no one to turn to for guidance – no guidelines at all about employees' rights, or where legal responsibility lay.

Hazel Collins explained how the transient work and life meant she had to mature, overcome fears and many new challenges alone:

Working away from home changed my attitude; at home you are a bit kept down. I think I am a strong person now, my daughter says I am very strong. We did not meet up very much, that was the trouble, we were all so spread out all over the place and moving to different forests all the time.

Even while they worked within a single forest, if it was a large one, they could find themselves moving every two or three days to find new lodgings. In mid January 1940, the local press reported that a large number of Women's Land Army volunteers would be sent to Hampshire to be put to work in the New Forest, crosscutting pit props and barking shrubs for charcoal. Within a year these girls in the New Forest were confidently managing all the jobs of the seasoned forester.

Orientation was made even more difficult because, in anticipation of a German invasion, all signposts had been taken down, and getting lost was a daily hazard in the forest where all tracks look the same. The women didn't realise the New Forest was so big till they started to walk through it and got lost, so they came to rely on a compass:

> They walked phenomenal distances and became exceptionally fit. One team spent some time in the New Forest, lodging in eight different billets and walked an estimated 600 miles [but they] grew to love the challenge of a free, nomadic existence, living in the heart of these ancient forests, a wild, secret landscape known to few.[1]

The forest landscape, wildlife and beauty of nature became a great strength to the girls.

Sometimes girls had to move and find new billets as often as three times a week and it required a lot of stamina. 'This created problems with laundry, boot repairs and keeping up with the mail, which often arrived weeks late.'[2] Journeys were made even more arduous because they had to carry their belongings with them. One group in the New Forest decided to travel light, 'but after three weeks of rain, in which it rained everyday, and the difficulty of getting things dried', they changed their minds.

Dorothy Naylor, like most women, also had to carry her tools to and from work: 'We just slung the crosscut over our shoulder and off on our bikes we went. Probably quite dangerous but we didn't think of things like that back then.'

Audrey Broad and her friend Winnie travelled by green painted bikes, which belonged to the Land Army:

We could cycle along some forest rides but mainly we walked. We had to carry gear, which was books for writing in, a long tape, with a leather case, the quarter girth tape, scribe knife, timber sword, a curved sword with a wooden handle, which was used to pull the measuring tape around the girth of the tree. We also used to carry a pot of paint and a brush to paint numbers on the butt of the trees. We didn't have baskets on bicycles and all of our equipment went into satchels.

For the fellers like Margaret Finch, there were additional tools which often made it impossible to ride their bikes:

Jean, the other girl with me, couldn't ride a bike no matter how she tried. So we used to walk to the woods, about 4 miles there, with our bikes so that we could carry all the tools of the trade. A 14-pound axe, a 7-pound axe, bill hooks, chains, loppers, crosscut saws and bow saws and wedges, one crosscut saw was over 6 foot in length, and of course the beetroot sandwiches.

All Seasons

Little could prepare the girls for the brutal working conditions in the forest during the winter months, with pouring rain or snow, icy wind and frozen rutted mud. The conditions of winter were punishing for the girls who worked six days a week from 7.30 a.m. till 5 p.m., some days were longer. They even worked in the dark and the pouring rain (unlike the prisoners of war). When it snowed, they carried on working out in the forests with nowhere to eat their sandwiches, but instead they had to stand knee deep in snow and keep moving to stay warm.

Some of them were provided with a hut to protect them from the worst of the weathers, but not Joan Turner: 'We worked in all conditions all the time, in the cold, wet, damp and fog. The cold really got into you.' Katie Dowson remembered the cold Yorkshire winters in the forest: 'If it rained in the morning we couldn't have our pay unless we stayed until 3 o'clock. We used to brash trees and all the snow would come off the trees. Oh, we suffered!'

Frieda Ellerby was lucky enough to have had a little wooden hut:

Sometimes if it was snowing really badly we would stop for a game of knock out whist in the hut and as soon as it stopped we would carry on.

We went out to work in all weathers, we never got soaked through because we had a little shed and stove, a wooden hut. We made a bee line for the hut.

But many of the women, like Barbara Beddow in the New Forest, 'were not allowed to go home whatever the weather'.

In the winter months, conditions became even more testing for Pat Frayn: 'In the winter, when it snowed we carried on working. It was no harder to cut the trees. Yes it was cold; we had to wrap up and used to wear breeches in the winter.'

One day, Audrey Broad could not go out to the forest to do the wages because the forest was so deep in snow: 'We tried to go out in the snow, but it was impossible to count up what they had done. We couldn't even see the stacks of cordwood, so we had to use guesswork and paid them a good wage.'

Snow made the long journeys required for work even more gruelling, as Peggy Conway found:

We'd had instructions to report to the forester at Hamsterley, only to find that was about 5 miles away and there had been a heavy snow-fall overnight. We managed to get a lift in the cab of a coal lorry to Hamsterley. Again the forester's house was miles away. A trek through the snow, knocked on the door: 'Mr Smith is out'.

During the winter of 1944–45 many of the timber camps, especially in Scotland, were completely snowed up. Lorries could not get on to the roads to take the girls to work, and at one camp food had to be fetched several miles by an improvised horse-sleigh.

Morag Shorthouse remembered the winter of 1944–45:

It was very severe, with heavy snowfall and hard frosts. We had to fill basins with snow and melt them on top of a stove to give us water for washing. No cars or vans could get up the road. In the end they were allowed to go home until the thaw set in.[3]

Jessie MacLean recalled:

Wintertime in the stackyard was quite awful, ankle deep in icy mud. The logs to be cut and stacked were encrusted with this chilling, frosty muck. No amount of hand blowing or 'pine needle' tea could alleviate the pain of frozen fingers and not even the muscle torture of peeling helped – nobody's favourite job. Yet our lives in Wallaceton and the woods of Crawfordton, Dalmacallan, Criagdarroch and Drumtreggan remain a twenty-four-carat gold memory.[4]

When Margaret Grant joined the Scottish Women's Timber Corps there was a foot of snow on the ground:

I was just dumped there and by the Friday I was shovelling gravel in a river bed with a big navvy shovel. You are sore, you are tired, you are hungry, and you are unable to think, you just feel things. I shut off completely. That was in January. Then one April morning in Glen Etive was so beautiful, with snow on the mountain tops and a turquoise blue sky with pink fluffy clouds, that I suddenly realised that I was a big healthy lump, about ten stone of muscle, and that life was wonderful.[5]

Campfires were a great comfort in the winter. Doreen Musson and the other girls would light a fire for cleaning up the brushwood and gather round to keep warm.

There was no shelter in the woods and on frosty winter mornings the cold saw handles and metal machinery parts were particularly unpleasant. The girls were, however, permitted to burn the cut tops from felled trees and this made a welcome bonfire on which to boil a kettle, although it was not always easy to light sodden foliage.

A fire-lighting tip Doreen remembered was shown to her by a passing gypsy, and involved gathering furze from beneath the heart of the gorse bushes: 'No matter how wet the weather there was always some spiked pieces, tinder dry and ready to burn.'

When Mary Broadhead worked in the woods, she would clean up the small trimmings from felled trees and burn them to make toast over the red embers of the fire:

to make a toasting fork we would cut a stick in the shape of a Y and put bread on it. We also made tea or Cocoa with a billycan of boiling water heated over the fire or they put a glass bottle into hot ashes to heat the drink inside, but sometimes it would overheat and burst so they had nothing to drink.

Spring brought a renewed enthusiasm and hope for Moira Gaffney and the girls who had endured the hard winter in the forest:

> Spring with all its promise, always came round and I recall what joy it was to see the naturalised daffodils and the wild primroses in the woods, the delights of the long summer evenings and then the glory of the autumn colours, followed all too soon by the dreary winter again. Even then the snow-capped trees, the purity of the distant hills and the deep stillness of it all was uplifting and remains with me still.[6]

Deirdre MacKenzie delighted in spring and summer in the woods:

> The abundance of wildlife and plants interested me greatly. Some of the older men were very knowledgeable and taught the girls a great deal about birds and wild flowers. Since then I have retained an abiding interest in nature. The sound of the first cuckoo never fails to thrill.[7]

During the summer months, when the scenery and the weather were idyllic, Mavis Williams and the young women profited from being out in the beauty of nature, leading a healthy outdoors life:

> At that time in a morning [6.30 a.m.] it was fairly dark, for the early rays of the sun had not penetrated through the dense forest. It was eerie. Often I was startled by a pheasant, flapping off as I disturbed it. However, I came to enjoy the solitude of the wilds, except when it was raining, for the air was fresh and invigorating … The streams provided means of cooling off during very hot weather, so often during the lunch hour the girls departed to one stretch, the men to another, to have a dip. Soaped down we jumped into it, clear but very cold waters, our only means of a bath. Sure we could bath in front of the fire at our digs, but this was far more fun and exhilarating. It was refreshing and we could dive from the small rocks, and swim in the deepest part. However, word got round that as well Lumberjills in 'them there woods' there were also 'water nymphs.'

After a particularly hard morning, on a few occasions, Agnes Morrison was allowed 'to bask in the sun for a few hours with the loch water lapping our aching feet and relaxing tired limbs'.[8]

But the summertime came with its own risks and perils, as Margaret Grant found:

Bovay, the wood of the cow, was an incredible wood. I saw an astonishing thing there. The wood was in such a mess and the river bed, in the summer when we were working there, seemed very low. We often used the stones to walk up because of the mess of the timber until one day when we were threading our way up the river and Jock MacVain suddenly said, 'Get away from the river, get away.' He was shouting his head off and we didn't know what he was on about. However, when Jock spoke urgently we all reacted quickly, scrambling out of that river bed just before the most thunderous sound and this wall of stones, twigs and water came rushing down. If we had stayed there we would have all been killed. Apparently a storm had created a dam away up at the top and it suddenly broke. It was an awesome sight.[9]

Morag Shorthouse was a great nature lover and enjoyed watching birds and insects in the woods:

We loved watching the ladybirds creeping up our arms and even got used to the ferocious looking wood wasps, once we knew they were harmless. A great many moths and butterflies flitted around us; red and brown, blue and white. Sometimes the flies annoyed us and often we were bitten by mosquitoes, midges and clegs. Around some of the bogs at Kinnordy there was a vivid splash of green and blue in the evenings as truly beautiful dragonflies flitted around like helicopters.[10]

When the Forestry Commission was established at the end of the First World War, forestry policy was about protecting and expanding woodland habitat, so there was some harmony with conservationists. The organisation tried to preserve essential rare species of plant and animals, but during wartime this became more difficult. Nonetheless, a wood where kites were still breeding was rescued at the last moment from the axe.

But when one of the few remaining woodlands of the Red Helleborine flower was identified for felling, although the Chief Acquisition Officer was a keen naturalist, his conscience would not let him spare the wood. It contained magnificent beech urgently needed for aircraft construction. The wood was not completely destroyed but only selected trees were taken.

Eileen Rawlinson remembered the plight of the red squirrels:

I well remember how shocked we were when we bought down an Oak tree containing a squirrel's nest [drey]. It's drey, fortunately then empty,

There were the air raids going on. When I went once they showed me a row of houses and the shell had gone in one end and come out the other and the houses were still standing and there was a great big hole in every house. At Canterbury I was there when they had the air raid and I was told to get out of town, get a bus and go. It was a sensible thing to do because of shrapnel and I went straight to a bus stop and went home.

One day, Hazel Collins and the other women heard a *broomph!*:

I said, 'It's a bomb.' So we went and found it and, oh God, there was two boys there dead. It was in a forest near an RAF camp and it upset all of us because we saw the bodies lying there. We also saw a plane crash, which was so frightening, near where we were working and we ran to see if we could help. I could only see one body in RAF uniform, it was terrible. The doctor gave me sleeping pills because I couldn't sleep. I don't think any of us could sleep as it was so near to us.

Others, like Violet Parker, had a narrow escape:

From where I lived I used to watch all the bombers going over. I was going out for a walk with a soldier and he threw me on the floor and I didn't know what was happening. We were machine-gunned and it hit the church, it had cracks everywhere. It was just an old German plane that thought before I go home I'll try and get rid of everyone I can, which he did. He went up through the town machine-gunning. We were very lucky.

She continued:

There were a few German planes that came down and crashed nearby. We used to go out and see them. You used to lie in bed at night and hear vroom, vroom and think God is that a German or one of ours. You had to get on with it; you couldn't do anything about it. It was a little bit frightening, but you didn't get frightened then really.

Olive Edgley was home on leave in the suburbs in Moorside at Fenham one time:

Our parents wanted us to go down to the shelter and we refused because we were so tired from forestry work and had carried our kit bag on our back all the way back from the station. When they dropped a land mine not far away and we were in bed at the time, the bed shook, the house, everything.

Whilst in London there was an air raid, and as Margaret Finch hadn't been in one before, she didn't know what to do: 'So we took everything with us into a shop doorway and put the bikes in front of us. Then an air force bloke came up and said you cannot stay there, come with me. He managed to get us into a tube station before they closed it.'

The women in Scottish Women's Timber Corps, like Molly Paterson, had all the buzz of war, with military personnel and troops in the area, without the fear of being bombed:

There was always lots of military activity in the Western Highlands. Dalmally was our nearest railway station, which was 7 miles away from Cladich. I always remember it being an extremely busy and noisy place both day and night with the steam trains coming and going all the time. It always seemed full of troops moving in or moving out. We saw soldiers from many different countries, Canadians, French, Australians together with British troops including the commandos. They all went through there to their training camps.

All Army and Navy traffic for the training camps in this area of the Highlands had to go up and down the road through Cladich to Inveraray. At Inveraray in the winter of 1943–44 there was lots of amphibious landing training going on with the soldiers jumping off the craft into the loch in full kit. It was presumably all about the D-Day preparations for the landings in France due to take place in the following June.

As a young girl of 19 I never felt threatened or in any danger walking to and fro from work to home in the dark in spite of all the troops out there on manoeuvres in the woods at night. There were no street lights and all you could see was flickering candle light, but I always felt safe and would walk alone at night in the dark without feeling scared.

One of the worst happenings of all during that period was that every so often we would sadly hear of young boys who had been at the village school with me being killed in action. I remember hearing that David Cowan who I remember as a very tall boy at school being killed in Sicily and also Donald Kennedy died. My school teacher's brother was killed on the Atlantic Convoys. I was to learn in later years that there were several others.

Both of my brothers served in the Army. Walter was a Bevan boy and worked down in the coal mines until he was old enough to join the Army. He then became a motorcycle despatch rider with the Argyle and Southern Highlanders in Egypt and at one stage spent time in Turkey at the British Embassy in Ankara. My other brother Alec was in the Royal Corps of Signals and he took part in the D-Day landings attached to General Patton's Americans and went all the way to Berlin. My father was in the Observer Corps locally watching for enemy aircraft from the top of the hill at Dalmally.

Irene Snow was always worried about her brothers away fighting in the war: 'But I just got on with it. I had one brother who went to Italy, another Iceland and the youngest one stayed in England but got shot in the elbow – he was the only one to get shot but luckily they all came home.'

Molly Paterson, lumberjacks and dog around a fire, Ardbrecknish, Argyll, Scotland.

Lumberjills planting trees.

(Left) Joyce Elizabeth Gaster out on a limb.

(Below) Lumberjills in the Forest of Dean, 1943. (© Crown Copyright, courtesy of Forestry Commission)

Joan Turner.

Hazel Collins by the river bank.

Mavis Williams bathing in a forest stream in Cornwall – 'our only means of washing'. (Mavis Williams)

Joyce Elizabeth Gaster's friends.

Joyce Elizabeth Gaster out in the forest.

Joan Turner and friends.

Loch Awe, Argyll.

(Above) Molly and Edward Paterson.

(Right) Eileen and Wally Mark.

Friend of Joyce Elizabeth Gaster.

Joyce Elizabeth Gaster represented the Women's Timber Corps at the Victory Parade.

(Above) Edna Holland and brother Bill Holland.

(Right) Edith Robothan and Kitty Byett on VE Day outside Gloucester Cathedral. (With kind permission of Ruth Fletcher.)

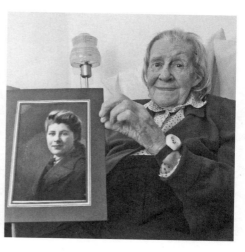

Audrey Broad.

Dorothy Scott. (Richard Darn)

Edna Holland. (Richard Darn)

Ethel Oliver. (Richard Darn)

Frieda Ellerby.

Irene Snow.

Joan Turner.

Katie Dowson and Gladys Fife.

Mary Broadhead.

Pat Frayn.

Violet Parker.

Margaret Finch and Joanna Foat at the *Great British Menu* banquet. (Emma Tunstill, Touch Digital)

Molly Paterson beside the Women's Timber Corps memorial, Aberfoyle, Scotland.

Lifelong Friendship, Love and Romance

Friendships

My allotted niche was next to the warm stove, so an abundance of bodies sat on my bed. It almost collapsed. The girls at Bishops Wood had no qualms about swapping clothes, begging cigarettes, or borrowing cycles from those who had them. Having made new friends I soon settled into my primitive abode. Doris remained my special pal after we had clicked on the train.

For many like Dorothy Swift, it was their close friendships that carried them through the uncertainty of new postings, tough times and hardships of the job. The arduous work in extremes of weather, the loss of friends and brothers at war and missing their families meant that friendships were all the more important and gave them great happiness. The solidarity of the girls was sealed when they faced prejudice and unfair treatment, and their friendships remained strong for life.

Hilton Wood, in *Meet the Members*, said:

I'm perfectly happy for I am being posted with six of my friends. Certainly the camp has an unpronounceable name, and it is situated farther north than I ever thought trees grew, but I guess I said I would be mobile when I joined, so I must make the best of it.

Despite the primitive living conditions, or perhaps because of the living conditions, the girls who were billeted with Dorothy Swift became inseparable:

As roommates thrown together by chance, Joyce and I hit it off straight away. We had the same coloured hair and the same sense of humour.

I nicknamed Joyce 'Hammy'. One would have thought that having to share a tiny room, with a small wardrobe, chest of drawers, wash basin and mirror, would have led to countless quarrels. Not so! Hammy and I never had a cross word.

Edna Holland made very good friends: 'The best thing about the Women's Timber Corps was the friendships we made. Peggy Conway (née Wilkes) came from York, I came from Doncaster and we became great friends.' These women became friends for life.

Meeting all the girls and making friends was the best thing for Peggy Conway:

> The Land Army girls stayed with the farmers and then after they had eaten they had to go to bed and there was no one else there. For us we were all together in the huts, we read books, knitted, talked and it was special. We all sat together and worked together as a team and there was great camaraderie.

A communal and bonding activity for the girls was hair washing. Often with freezing cold water or no facilities, it became a source of despair for both girls and welfare officers, until the girls came up with their own solutions. Dorothy Swift and friends 'boiled rainwater for washing each other's hair'. It became an enjoyable ritual to wash each other's hair, either when the opportunity arose at a new billet or they made special arrangements to wash their hair together.

Getting ready for nights out, Pat Frayn and the other girls brushed or combed each other's hair while having their lunch break: 'We used to light a little fire and put the kettle on and I used to do the other girls' hair in the break, the metal clips in the hair, with the teeth, so it was ready for the evening.'

There was a warm glow of affection between the girls who lived and worked together and their sense of identity as Lumberjills gave Molly Paterson a great purpose, which extended from work to afternoon and evenings out and gave them all *joie de vivre*.

> The girls in the billet were a lively crowd and we used to have great fun together. We all used to go on marches to Glasgow to raise funds for Spitfires and then afterwards go for tea in the council offices or chambers. There was Nancy Spears, a bubbly blonde girl and then there was Dolly

MacKenzie from down the loch. We had a fantastic cook, who came from Ireland, she was young like us and married a forester.

We never had radios in those days but the girls at The Manse had a wind-up gramophone and one record called 'Just One More Chance' and Jean Spence, now Mrs Stewart, tried to teach me the foxtrot. But the other girls said, 'Oh shut that noise down' as she played it over and over again. I have been in touch with Jean all this time.

For many of the girls, they had to make their own entertainment in the evenings and weekends. They enjoyed the camaraderie of living with a bunch of girls and Mary Broadhead enjoyed playing practical jokes:

Some of the girls left the dance early and went into the huts to make apple pie beds. This meant that one of the boards, top, middle or bottom, had been removed from the bed. With your mattress put back on top, so when you got into bed you fell through onto the floor. One night I did not bother to change my position of the mattress and slept with my feet on the floor.

For many girls a good night out was not an option. The main difficulty for welfare officers and the women in forestry was the lack of entertainment for the girls who were in billets far from towns and cities.

Olive Edgley slept in the evening and ate; she didn't want to go out:

We didn't want to go cycling because our bottoms were sore enough from the day. We were an isolated and nomadic lot. We loved it and met lots of people, but by the time we got home at the end of the day, sat down, usually in a little village, had supper and listened to the radio, we were ready for bed.

In the blackout it was black dark. You have to be out on a country road at night when it is really dark to appreciate it. It is intense and doesn't entice you to go out when you are in little countryside digs, in estate houses and cottages. We weren't in posh places. We were very lucky as out on the estates, we got very little of the Bristol bombing other than the odd raid.

Diana Underwood didn't want to go to dances either: 'We didn't have much to do in the evenings, except reading and sleeping.'

The digs were so isolated where Dorothy Swift lodged, they could never get out to socialise:

Two weeks was all any of us could stand in that dreary, inhospitable house. Thanks to our forestry foreman who searched for a better place to send us to, we fled like cheetahs to his chosen accommodation in nearby Middleton, promising faithfully that we would always get to work at High Force on time.

The problem was made worse for many of the Women's Timber Corps because, if they did find themselves in a village or town for a few weeks where the Entertainments National Service Association (ENSA) were putting on a concert, they were among the few to be refused entrance. The treatment was ill received by the girls, when they faced the humiliation of being left outside while others went in.

Complaints about the prejudice they received were raised in a letter to the *Yorkshire Post*. But they received no sympathy there. To add insult to injury, the editor explained that the Women's Timber Corps 'is a civilian Service and not a defence Service. That is why, for example, they are not served in Forces' canteens.' Many of the women complained about being turned away from forces canteens and feeling humiliated as others offered to bring out drinks to them.

As a result, often the girls entertained themselves at home by playing cards, sewing or knitting before going to bed. But some progress was made during the war, because entertainment was regarded as important to keep up morale, so more classes, lectures and dances were arranged for the Women's Timber Corps by 1943 and after.

The girls were, however, subject to other restrictions – only one late-night pass. In the National Archives is a letter sent from the County Organiser for Oxfordshire on 27 July 1944 that states:

> The girls, however, are very anxious to have their late-night pass on Tuesday, 1st August, so I have promised to ask whether it would be possible for you to come to Cokethorpe on the following evening, (Wednesday). If you cannot manage this, they have agreed to take their late pass on Wednesday and have a meeting on Tuesday.

The remote and ever-changing location of billets for the girls in the Women's Timber Corps made evening entertainment less reliable. So one can understand the girls' reluctance to lose their late-night pass, which would ensure they would not miss the long-awaited dance, where they could let their hair down, mingle with the forces and dance the waltz, foxtrot or jitterbug.

For some Lumberjills like Molly Paterson, no distance, mountain, loch or valley would separate them from an evening out:

> To get to the dances from our cottage, I would walk the 2 miles on my own to meet the girls and then we would all walk another 2 miles to the Portsonachan Hotel at the loch side. Sometimes my brothers would come and would ride their bikes to the loch and throw them in the bushes. Here we would all clamber into a rowing boat and row the half a mile across to the other side of Loch Awe at Taycreggan. There would be about eight of us in the boat. After that we walked another mile up the hill to Kilchrenan Village Hall, where we would dance from about 9 p.m. until 2 a.m.
>
> After the dance we had to do it all over again to get home. It took about two hours each way and sometimes I would get home just in time to set out on the one-and-half-mile walk to work again, as we had to work on Saturday mornings. I think I must have been pretty fit in those days.
>
> During the summer the trip across the loch was pleasant enough, but in the winter the loch could get a bit rough and very cold. I don't ever remember being scared and no one mentioned life jackets or the like. We did hear of two drunken men drowning doing the journey one night.

So, for all the lucky Lumberjills who made it to dances in churches or village halls, many did not. They drank lemonade and danced the night away to gramophone records or a band. Some dances served dinner, other people brought in beer from the local pub and while many of the younger British men were away at war, there where plenty of home guards, British army and air bases, foreign Allied troops, American GIs and Canadians to dance with too. What a delight!

Violet Parker used to do waltz, ballroom and foxtrot: 'We learnt at the dances, just picked it up with all the forces. There were Dutch and Spanish, black and white Yanks, and they would all come to the dances. It used to be like party time every weekend.'

Going Out

While the remoteness of their billets made it difficult for many girls to go out, if they did venture out on a bike, this was where the adventures began. Joan Turner had fond memories of being someone who 'went anywhere on the cross bar of a bike and a cushion'.

If Dorothy Swift was going into town, perhaps to dance, she would cycle there: 'I can smell the spring blossom we pedalled past when I think of those carefree evenings. My bike soon fell to pieces because it was not made to carry two people at the same time.'

Doreen Musson remembered bringing her bicycle back from home and sharing it with her friends:

We each had a suitcase so one in the saddle with a case in each hand and the other at the handlebar steering! We could only handle the downhill doing that. We went to the local dances and travelled miles literally – found the one bicycle very handy then but mostly downhill.

Thirsk was the nearest town to where Edna Holland was based, and she used to cycle there on her bike with her three friends: 'There was one on the handlebars, one on the pedals, one on the saddle and the other on the carrier at the back.'

But not everyone got away with riding a bike not made for two. A Scottish paper, the *Sunday Post*, reported:

An RAF corporal and a woman from Women's Timber Corps were each fined £1 in Wigtown Sheriff Court, for riding a pedal cycle for one person, with the woman seated on the handlebar which was described as a most dangerous practice. John Owen, corporal, RAF and Norma Pearson, Lumberjill were charged with riding a pedal bicycle which was not constructed or adapted for the carrying of more than one person.

However, the practice in those days was very common, especially among the Lumberjills. But it wasn't always very comfortable, so the girls found ways to improve the ride.

Dorothy Swift met a young feller who had a motorcycle:

on which he sat all three of us plus himself. When this obliging youth drove us home Muriel sat on the tank, I sat on the pillion and Jean squeezed in behind me. The driver then prised himself onto his more comfy seat. Four nincompoops astride one moving motorbike would be seen only in the circus nowadays. I guess no police constables were plodding about to catch us; although you could get away with all sorts of escapades during World War Two.

The mix and diversity of girls and their upbringing may have divided them on whether they went out to pubs in the evening. Some women were adamant they never went to pubs, as if it was not the place for young women and they certainly did not drink alcohol. But for others, a visit to the pub was a place of fond memories and unexpected meetings.

Doreen Musson became friendly with the local people, and 'learned to drink cider at the local pub (only pastime) also play darts, sing songs around the piano and tell tall tales. The pub was a mile down the road and of course we had to walk.'

While Margaret Grant used to enjoy a beer at Portsonachan: 'The blue sky meets the glassy blue loch, shouting our orders for shandies are the occasions never to be forgotten.'[1] When I visited Loch Awe, I made a visit to the Portsonachan Hotel and enjoyed a beer on the terrace one gloriously sunny and cloudless day. I chatted to the locals, and as I looked down the loch I saw exactly what Margaret Grant had described where the cerulean blue sky dissolved into the blue loch with such intensity. It was otherworldly, absolutely beautiful.

There was a training base for sailors in Wetherby, so the little market town was alive at night, near where Dorothy Swift was based: 'having little or no money to spend. Flushed or skint, we were all high-spirited flirts who popped into the local pub for a get together over a shared shandy.'

Going to the cinema was one way that the government could keep people up-to-date with the news during wartime, as while television broadcasting started in the UK in 1936, television sets were not common in homes until after the war. Cinema also provided some entertainment and light relief from war news to lift morale. The Women's Timber Corps up and down the country from Scotland to Cornwall visited picture houses when their wages would allow. Sometimes it was a safe place to visit for those who did not like to dance, away from the servicemen, for others it was a date, but often it led to adventures out and about in the blackout.

Cinemas in rural areas changed their programmes three times a week, so at 6d a seat Dorothy Swift and the girls had plenty of filmed entertainment:

We relied on the cinemas' *Gaumont British News* to keep us visually updated about the war. If I'd been told then that one day I'd sit in my armchair at home watching events as they happened abroad on a television screen, I wouldn't have believed it. I loved every minute spent at the Walton's. We often popped into a small picture house called The Cosy.

One afternoon, Mary Broadhead and the lorry driver had been out together:

> We heard there was a new film at Canterbury pictures. The film was called
> *Five Graves to Cairo* so we decided to go. But it did not end before it was
> time to pick up the others to go home. We stopped to watch the ending
> and so were late back and the boss was standing in the road shaking his
> fist at us saying where have you been? You're late. They never found out
> where we had been all afternoon.

Olive Edgley used to go to the cinema and then felt emboldened to go on
a night-time adventure:

> The three of us dared each other to go onto a balloon site after and all
> the men came over to talk to us and security was absolutely zero and we
> could have cut the ropes of the barrage balloons all around Bristol. We just
> decided we'd walk on to the site and because we were in uniform nobody
> stopped us and we chatted up the boys and they chatted us up.

For the Lumberjills, dancing was a much-loved way to let off steam. They
enjoyed music and the way their fit and strong bodies moved to music. They
learnt a range of dances from the traditional foxtrot or waltz to Scottish
dancing and the American jitterbug. A melting pot of nationalities led to a
rich and vibrant nightlife for those who were lucky enough to live near to
the dances.

Molly Paterson went to dances every Friday night:

> It was all Scottish dancing. A lot of girls did jitterbugging, but I did
> Scottish dancing. So I spent a lot of time in the girls billet and never
> went home. They tried to teach me the foxtrot, which was equivalent to
> modern dancing and I would teach them all to do Scottish dancing.

The girls who went dancing loved every minute of it and danced the night
away with young servicemen of different nationalities from all over the
world. It was a merry time when the young women wanted to enjoy their
new-found freedom away from the rule of parents and enjoy life. It was
all the more precious and euphoria intense when they knew their dance
partners would soon be sent away to fight in the war.

Social life for Barbara Beddow was very good:

We had five aerodromes, all fairly near. So I wrote to ask the Station Commanders to invite the girls to their social activities, with the result that the girls had plenty of parties, dances, concerts, etc. They were also allowed to use the NAAFI at home in Spalding. I was invited to many of the Officers' Mess parties, where crews brought back exotic foods from visits to Africa and Australia, etc.

Edna Holland went to weekend dances in Thirsk:

Where we did ballroom dancing like the waltz and the quick step, which we learnt at the dances. The Royal Corps of Signals where based in Thirsk and they brought a band to the dances, they were big in the area and they could do anything and everything they wanted doing as they knew everybody.

Eileen Mark and her friends used to go to dances in Compton Village Hall:

Sometimes I was picked up by the Canadians on the back of a lorry or we'd go on bikes. One night I got on the back of a lorry to go home from a dance and a bandoleer of bullets had been put in my bag. I don't know how they arrived there. Sometimes there was a 3- or 4-piece band on stage and sometimes just music, like in America. We drank lemonades and it was very busy, full of 18- to 21-year-olds.

As women were outnumbered by men at camp dances in Deerbolt, Dorothy Swift and her friends were in great demand:

These flings finished late so for two shillings we would bed down for the night at a local YWCA. We had some splendid times, but in retrospect married women at home with children, and husbands away in the forces, must have missed out on all the wartime camaraderie enjoyed by the younger generation.

At the Hereford hostel housing 100 land girls, munitions factory workers of either sex who were away from home during war, there was a purpose-built theatre-cum-dance hall. That theatre was superb. No longer did we need to leave home for entertainment. Not only did we have dances at home, we had professional entertainers provided by ENSA and CEMA who put on a variety shows and plays.

The women got good at dancing and Pat Frayn used to enter competitions:

I remember doing a competition dance with the man that Ivy married. He was a lovely dancer. I used to do the Highland fling, there was two of us that used to do it and they used to have concerts and we were asked to get up on stage. We loved to dance the night away. We never lacked partners at local hops because boys in the nearby paratroops regiment liked to dance. Sadly, some of our dancing partners were later killed in action over Arnhem. There were dances at the village hall even on weekdays. Dancing was a must for Muriel and me. On Saturdays we tripped the light fantastic in Barnard Castle.

There was inevitably some drunkenness and high spirits from time to time. Alfie Weir used to work with the Lumberjills:

There was a girl from Tyneside who was an attraction for the local men when there was a dance on at the hall at the top of castle drive, with a dance floor and tea room. A Scottish band used to come and play from Hawick. Every dance there was people drunk as they would go by train to get bottles of beer from Falstone.

Not all the men were desirable dance partners, and Frieda Ellerby found there were some to avoid at all costs:

There was one chap, 'Ooh!' I said to Sheila, 'Ooh!' and he had great big feet and he didn't get a fat chance to stand on our toes. We said, 'Ooh! look here comes his feet, let's go to the powder room at the back instead.' So off we went, he would have flattened you. I don't think for one minute he knew. But I saw him, he was making a right beeline for us like.

There was a dance held at the town hall in Watford about 4 or 5 miles away which Margaret Finch regularly attended:

So off we go on the bike with Jean standing on the cogs of the back wheel. After a couple of weeks someone asked us if we were in the services, we said 'No Women's Timber Corps.' He said, 'Come in uniform and it's half price.' So off we went the following week, with our best on, and the miniature brass axes on our arm. After that whenever we walked in they played 'The Woodchoppers' Ball', a very popular tune in the wartime.

Romance

Although the camp lay in the remote part of the Highlands, the close proximity of a Canadian Forestry Corps unit enabled us to have an exciting social life, as they offered us transport to dances in Alness and the surrounding villages. The renowned Canadian Corps Orchestra played at the dances. Love was in the air for most of the girls and I was no exception. We girls were greatly outnumbered and much sought after.

Oh, how different it was for the girls like Margaret Fraser in the Scottish Women's Timber Corps who were in camps or billets near to the male camps, like the Canadian or New Zealand Forestry Corps or British Air and Armed Forces. With the beauty and romance of a forest landscape, and no orders to stay away from these groups of men, romance blossomed. Stories about their time in the Women's Timber Corps are reminiscent of the excitement and novelty of a teen holiday romance.[2]

Olive Edgley shared her excitement of a flirtation she had with a forester one day down at Bow Wood in the early days:

> I was sitting on the ground, when a New Zealand feller grabbed my ankle and rubbed his axe up my shin and shaved my leg clean as a whistle. It was so quick and was a good job he didn't tell me because I might have moved. Then he took the hairs off the blade and gave them to me. It must have been so sharp.

Violet Parker was based in Lostwithiel during the war; it was an exciting place to live:

> We had lovely Yanks here, black and white, Spanish and Dutch they were billeted all over the place. The village was transformed totally. We had young Dutch officers here who survived a ship that was sunk. When you're young, you get to know everyone. We had a YMCA and used to see them all out and we used to go over there to have a cup of tea. Then there were dances in the evening in the Drill Hall. We always had dancing on a Saturday evening until 11.45 p.m., not later on a Saturday because you had to go to church in the morning.
>
> We used to do waltz, ballroom and foxtrot. We learnt at the dances, just picked it up. There were lots of local timber and land army girls, we weren't outnumbered, as some of the army had wives and some were

stationed here for just a few months. So, I just flirted around and enjoyed myself. It used to be like party time every weekend, more people in the town than normal. How I missed it all after the war when everyone left.

Often the girls who lived on camps were restricted by rules to keep the late-night liaisons to a minimum. Eileen Mark (née Worsell) received a warning from her landlady: 'Worsell, will you tell the ladies to keep boy-friends away a bit earlier in the evening.'

At Invertrossachs, Nan MacLean was responsible for the moral and physical welfare of the girls:

So I arranged for them to have visitors in the camp rather than going out and feeling romantic, with a full moon shining on the loch. There was no trouble that way. Some girls were quite young but I stood no nonsense. The men's camp was 2 miles away which was far enough for safety.[3]

However, night security was not always guarded so keenly. Dorothy Swift was woken up by the screams of a girl named Doreen one night:

'Get out, get out!' she yelled. No locks on the bedroom doors. It later accrued two airmen had lost their way simply seeking shelter for the night. When the commotion died down we invited them in, made up the fire, and allowed them to stay with us all night sharing stories and jokes.

And sometimes the unexpected events did not lead to such positive out-comes. Near Bristol, Olive Edgley was staying near Black Boy Hill at the Soroptimists Club and then at the YWCA at Temple Meads:

One night there was a dreadful raid on and we were scared in a dense blackout. But the worst thing that happened was the three of us were walking along the street when all of a sudden a man grabbed Tessa by the arm and yanked her into a doorway. Then we thought a very nice gen-tleman had rescued her and offered to see us back to our digs, but why? Because he thought at least one of us would go back with him, out of the frying pan into the fire.

Prisoners of War

Emma Vickers reported that there were many thousands of prisoners of war employed in forestry during the course of the war in *The Forgotten Army of the Woods: The Women's Timber Corps during World War Two*:

> In 1942, 3,000 Italians were integrated into timber production and, by 1945, it was noted that 45,000 Germans were employed in agriculture and forestry. Despite the complaints lodged by local Parish Councils and members of the public over the freedom granted to these men, their employment was, according to the MP Sir Alfred Knox, preferable to 'keeping them in camps, eating their heads off and doing nothing.'

In *Forest Service*, George Ryle wrote about POWs:

> German prisoners of war were described as solid, plodding, careful workers. A few score Southern Italian prisoners of war also worked for several months in Radnorshire and the nearby corner of Herefordshire and were described as good poachers, pleasant and always cheerful but both not the stuff of which woodsmen are made.

Their employment was not always welcomed by the Women's Timber Corps, who were often not allowed to speak to or mix with the Germans. Many girls felt annoyed that the POWs received better treatment than they did. The POWs did not have to work in the rain, or walk or cycle to and from the forest; they had larger rations; they complained and received a more consistent supply of vital equipment, including Wellington boots.

One day a lorry load of Italian prisoners of war was delivered to the mill where Diana Underwood worked, without prior instructions or notice:

> These came from a nearby POW camp and were used to do labouring jobs around the forest. They were not allowed to work with the charcoal burners as charcoal was used in the making of munitions.
>
> We set them to make up the roadway to the woods which was badly churned up by the crawler tractors, (which would get stuck on a tree stump in the mud and have to be pulled off by another tractor). We showed the Italians the slab wood and a heap of sawdust. Fortunately they had built this sort of road elsewhere and made a good job of it. They brought us each a bowl of coffee at lunchtime and told us they were in

North Africa and hid from the Germans but ran towards the British with their arms up to surrender. They did not want to fight.

Dorothy Scott worked with Italian POWs in Stapleford and was irritated by their preferable working conditions: 'They seemed to have better rations than the girls and refused to work in the rain'. Irene Snow didn't work with the German prisoners of war on Exmoor nearby, but she was frightened of them and she was equally miffed they didn't work in the rain as she had to.

Margaret Finch also felt an injustice in the preferential treatment the prisoners of war had received:

> Then off we would go with the bikes loaded to the hilt on a 6-mile walk to the forest and back. The only thorn in our walk was the lorries going past loaded with prisoners of war. They used to jeer at us, 'We are winning the war.' And we were the ones that had to walk to work because we had to remove all our tools from the forest every day, in case there was a break out from the POW camp.

One day, when Katie Dowson was in the office, a group of eight German POWs was dropped up at the private gate, bussed in from Eden camp:

> They had orders from the forestry then, but I was the only girl among the men. It was about the same time I was usually going to work but apart from pinching and riding my bike there was no trouble at all.
>
> You can't imagine it now, knowing what you know now, they never ever did anything apart from riding my bike. But, I was very naive and I never would have known what to do, if anything had happened. Being away from home and away from their women, but they never ever did anything. I have always marvelled about that. There was Hans, he was smashing tall, blond and handsome. His wife was next to me in bed when I had my first child.
>
> We were allowed to talk to them; we were all sat amongst them. They were not segregated. They just got their orders from the office at forestry but there was no guard with them. They were just brought and collected. But if they got wet they didn't have to wait till 3 p.m. like us. On the other hand they just had crusts of bread to eat.

Doreen Musson recalled both German and Italian prisoners of war. The former worked under armed guard, but security was more relaxed for the latter, and they were extremely happy when they heard of the Italian surrender: 'The prisoners worked away from where the girls carried out their duties.'

When Joan Turner came into contact with German prisoners of war, she was just left with them: 'We were only allowed to talk to them while we were walking. They were all right.'

Violet Parker worked with German prisoners of war too, but wasn't allowed to talk to them: 'I remember walking home from the lorry past the railway station and I used to see Italian prisoners of war out there waiting to go home in the railway station.'

In Wallaceton, Jessie MacLean worked for a while alongside German prisoners of war:

> much to our surprise, they were just like ourselves. They were 'Germans', they kept on reiterating, not 'Nazis'. Indeed there were four Nazis working in our woods under armed guard and nowhere near us, but like us the Germans were decent, family men with snaps to prove it; hard working and well behaved. How pitifully appreciative they were to receive a cigarette occasionally from the girls. As a way of thanks, they made such clever and lovely, wooden toys for us: dogs with wagging heads and tails. My favourite was one of two girls crosscutting a tree and this too was an action toy.[4]

In Hereford, both German and Italian prisoners of war worked in the same forests as Dorothy Swift and her gang:

> Fraternising with the enemy was strictly forbidden, and any girl seen talking to the enemy would have to suffer the consequences. But we were only human. It was ridiculous to expect young boys and girls to meet every day yet ignore each other. Some prisoners spoke English and relished the chance to improve it. A few girls took the opportunity to polish up their German and Italian. Being a prisoner of war in England was not too alarming because of how the British treated them. Some prisoners preferred it to fighting.
>
> Only rain prevented land girls from working in the woods. Legislation had it work need not continue during rainfall. We used to pray for rain hoping it would not start before we had been taken to work on lorries. That was because if rain started once we were on site we could stay there until it stopped. There was method in the madness. Watched only

by resting timber-hauling horses, we would shelter in huts or under tarpaulins with prisoners we had invited in to stay dry with us.

We would tell the Germans 'Your bombers bombed London last night, but we shot two of them down. We wonder what Lord Haw Haw will say about that?' The prisoners laughed with us. Lord Haw Haw was actually William Joyce, a British-born traitor who broadcast from Germany to England saying 'Germany calling. Germany calling' and would tell people in England how well the war was going for Germany. Of course, we had to keep our eyes open for the foreman and be ready to scarper if he came.

Barbara Beddow said, 'I had more problems when I was told that I was being sent Italian prisoners of war to work with the girls. The problems with that, I will leave to your imagination.'

Dorothy Swift recalled:

Four land army girls in Hereford used to creep out during night-time blackouts for secret meetings with the German boyfriends. Four prisoners used to escape through a barbed wire fence surrounding their POW camp to indulge in careless oblivion on the outside. When rumours of these romps ran rife the police were called to question the girls, so the culprits dug a hole outside 'B' block, put their evidence in tins and buried it. Those love letters might still be there!

Pat Frayn remembered:

There was a girl called Edith. She was the one that met her husband there, a German prisoner of war from across the road from us. They got friendly and when it all closed down they stayed together and got married. The POW used to work on farms and so were free to go. Edith was working on forestry. He was called Charlie, but his German name was Carl. Her family found it very difficult at first, but they accepted him in the end because he was such a lovely man and did a lot for them.

When Hazel Collins was with Nan and Gwyneth, they swapped lunches with the Italian prisoners of war: 'They were very interesting, but I did not have much to do with them, one was a violin maker. We used to flirt with them but never knew their names.' More than sixty years later, Hazel Collins, in her late 80s, went on holiday to San Marino, Italy, with two or three friends:

We were sitting in a restaurant and I saw little violins all round the wall. The proprietor came through and I said I met an Italian once who made me a violin like that. He said, 'Where?' and I said, 'Holsworthy in Devon' and he said, 'That was me.'

He was an old man and I was an old lady by this time. I couldn't get over it and burst into tears. He had all these little matchstick violins around the wall. He was just a prisoner of war based at the end of the road on the Italian prisoners of war camp. I have always remembered the violin and even when I see a violin now I always think of it. It was small enough to fit in a matchbox.

Marriage

Eileen Mark was working at the Forestry Commission's Walderton Down:

There was an anti-aircraft camp with search lights on the other side of the road in Walderton. I was working in the woods opposite putting pit props in sections along the roadside. Then one night we realised that our pit props were gone and we could see the top of a roaring campfire over on the army base. I was furious and decided to go over to the camp, head-strong and fearless I was determined to get to the bottom of it.

I asked who was in charge and was sent to see the sergeant, where I discovered the pit props had been used for the fire. He apologised, offered me a cup of tea and piece of cake, and introduced himself as Wally. Wally later became my husband to whom I was married for fifty-four years.

Inevitably, many of the women fell in love and got married to men they met during their time in the Women's Timber Corps, as Eileen Mark did. Other Lumberjills, like Bella Nolan and Deirdre MacKenzie, married Canadian Lumberjacks and ended up moving to Canada.

When Bella Nolan left the Women's Timber Corps, she married a Newfoundlander, lived in Carrbridge for two years, then went to Newfoundland for two years, before returning to Scotland.[5]

Social life was good on the camps where Deirdre MacKenzie and her Scottish pals worked with Newfies and the Canadian Forestry Corps in the vicinity providing entertainment:

We went to dances, concerts and whist drives at the weekends and it was at a dance that I met my husband, a Canadian lumberjack. These young men in their checked lumber jerkins, were like a breath of fresh air to us with all our own boys away in the war service. The men who remained were according to the song we sang, 'either too young or too old, They're either too grey or too grassy green …' It was no unusual sight to see the lumberjacks pedalling off to a dance with a girl perched on the handlebars of the bicycle. It all seemed very exciting and remote from war.[6]

Other women met their husbands through the Women's Timber Corps, like Irene Snow:

In South Molton they really looked after you. I lived with a nice couple who had time to give and it was a very clean little cottage. We had a tin bath there. The couple rented the cottage from a man called Jack Snow, who later became my husband. The last year in the Timber Corps was when I met Jack, as his father lived next door. He had been away at war but had since come home. I worked with his sister in forestry and went next door to pick her up on the way to a dance one night and Jack was there. This was the first time we ever met.

Other girls, like Molly Paterson, married local boys:

At the age of 18 in 1940, my friend Winnie Bell introduced me to Eddie Paterson, a young soldier from my part of Scotland, who was stationed at Buddon Camp just outside Dundee at Broughty Ferry. We met one day in Dundee's Balgay Park before going to Winnie's aunt's house for tea.

Eddie asked to see me again and we started courting and after about a year he asked me to marry him. We began to make plans and arranged the day when we would go to buy my engagement ring but unfortunately I fell ill with the mumps. I was told that I had to go home to Cladich until I was clear from infection and because of this Eddie had to buy the ring on his own.

I married Eddie on Wednesday, 26 January 1944 in Dalmally Church on a wet winter's day. Eddie was discharged from the army on 8 July 1944 due to ill health. He had contracted typhoid fever and had spent a long time in hospital and was declared unfit to serve due to the condition of his heart. I left the Timber Corps later that year.

Unfortunately for Margaret Grant, not all marriage proposals ended happily:

> I've some very sad memories of Glen Etive too. The lad I was engaged to, from Sussex, suddenly appeared in this isolated Glen to see me. He walked all the way and then I had to wave to him from the top of the mountain, as he was going down to catch Captain Burns' boat. That was the last I saw of him, for he was killed in 1943.[7]

In April 1939, Barbara Beddow married a boy she had known from school days. But in September 1939 he was killed: 'he was in the Irish Guards, in barracks in Dover where they were shelled from across the channel.'
She continued:

> I remarried during my time in Carlton, near Selby, someone from my hometown that I had known over the years. The family I lived with were very good to me and I have remained friends with the children as they have grown up. My landlady taught me to bake bread and to cook Sunday dinner, including Yorkshire puddings, apple pies, cakes, etc.
>
> We had no shortages, one grandpa had a farm where they killed pigs (illegally) and made butter and cheese. The other family had an orchard with apples, pears and plums, he grew asparagus and I will always remember the slices of thick home cured ham and bundles of asparagus dumpling, with butter and home-grown new potatoes.
>
> We had masses of soft fruit in the garden and had raspberries and strawberries with everything, made dozens of pounds of jam and bottled it in Kilner jars. Blackberries grew down the lane, which we gathered, and the children went gleaning after the peas and beans had been harvested, bringing basket loads home to be eaten or put down in jars, layered with salt. Eggs were put in a big crock with isinglass.
>
> The RAF boys that I knew provided the dried fruit for my wedding cake, my landlady baked and iced it. I bought remnants of ivory, shell pink and pale blue satin and we all sewed my wedding underwear and nighties. The gypsies down the lane sold me clothing coupons for my outfit, and a family in the village, whose husband was a farm labourer and had ten children, sold me butter, margarine and sugar and anything else on ration to take home to my mother.
>
> The wedding over, with a honeymoon in Scarborough, where my husband's Battery was stationed and a great party in the Mess, then back to work … Eventually, my husband came on leave, [and] my old jockey

friend, as a great treat, arrived with a hen in a sack. After trying hard to pluck out the feathers, we had to pack up and take it home to mother! Not before I had given my husband a treat ... After that leave I found myself pregnant and so I resigned.

Marriage would often be the end of their time in the Women's Timber Corps, because of the widespread adoption of the Marriage Bar in the UK after the First World War. This affected working women in teaching, the civil service and in large companies. Representative of attitudes to married women working at that time, it was the norm for women to leave work to look after their husbands, do domestic work and raise children instead.

The Marriage Bar was still in effect in the civil service throughout the war. The reasons for its enforcement, although hard to believe today, were reported in *The Spectator* on 23 August 1946 (p.2) that if women only worked for a few years it provided a necessary turnover, married women were 'less reliable and less "mobile"' than other women and there were other people who needed employment more than married women. The Marriage Bar in the civil service was only called into question in August 1946, when there was a dawning that it restricted individual liberty, was a waste of education and training, and women were in fact rather useful for war work.

Three-Quarters Off Sick
for a Month

Tough! I would not hesitate to agree with Bonny Macadam that the Women's Timber Corps worked in one of the toughest, most gruelling and most physically demanding environments, putting their health and their lives at risk on many occasions: 'It was a very tough life: wearing hard, leather boots, swinging heavy axes and living in stark army huts.'

When Edna Barton was asked whether it was hard work, she replied: 'I should say so ... We thought we were tough. But I never heard anybody moaning or wanting to go home.'

It is hard to imagine that girls didn't moan about one of most common complaints – blisters. They got blisters on their hands and feet and some went septic, so they had to take time off work to let their skin heal. On her first day in the corps, Joan Turner 'got blisters, three planks and cushion to sleep on. Ooh the groaning that went on.'

Dorothy Scott swapped scissors and comb for an axe and saw: 'It was all a challenge for me, but I got on and did it. That's what you did back then. You just had to adapt and I vividly remember getting blisters on my hands when I started which were soft because I was a hairdresser.'

When Frieda Ellerby worked in Wales she got eight blisters:

We soaked our feet in saltwater, but one chap said, 'Whatever is the matter with you?' He told me to go to the chemist to buy a jar of rabbits' fat. Anyway, I didn't see him for a while. But when I did he said, 'Just the person I want to see, did it do any good that rabbit fat?' I discovered after a trip to the chemist that there is no fat on a rabbit.

The Women's Timber Corps also endured a range of other skin conditions, from cuts and grazes to allergic reactions and impetigo. Katie Dowson got cold sores in response to the Norwegian spruce: 'But you had never heard of allergies, you just had to get over it. The needles used to prick you, so your arms were really sore especially with the Christmas trees.'

When I began to amass the information on ailments, illnesses, accidents and deaths that occurred in the Women's Timber Corps, I was shocked. I knew these women were among the toughest and strongest women, with an attitude to go with it, which so inspired me from the start. But to read of the prevalence of illnesses and injuries they endured and risks they took saddened me.

The authorities knew the impact it was having on the girls as the war progressed. By 1945, the concerns about their welfare had grown so acute that the Ministry of Supply commissioned a medical assessment of members of the Women's Timber Corps to identify any 'harmful effects'. In the report, more than 17 per cent of the sickness absence was caused by locomotor diseases, including rheumatism, more than double the proportion of days lost by women in the Royal Ordnance factories. Traumatic strains, sprains or accidents caused some of the other absences.

Catherine Swanston reported:

A certain uneasiness had been evinced by Production and Welfare Officers in different parts of the country on account of the rising sickness rate among members of the Corps. In some places production was being seriously affected and there was a growing impression that many of the girls were beginning to feel the strain of several years in the woods and sawmills.

Some 161 girls were interviewed and physically examined from England, Scotland and Wales. Of these, 30 lived in private billets and 131 in camps and hostels, and every type of forestry work done by women was represented, including operating sawmills. The interviews and physical assessment of the girls took place in the summer, just after a heatwave. So the girls looked extremely fit, suntanned, happy and healthy. The report said, 'The girls looked well, with clear eyes and skin, and many of them were deeply tanned through working during the hot weather in a minimum of clothing. They were alert, high spirited and "full of beans."'

Most of the girls were in great shape, some excellent, with great upper body physique. Those who worked in felling or other heavy jobs had hypertrophied shoulder, upper chest wall and arm muscles. The pectoral muscles, connecting the front of the chest with the upper arm and shoulder, used for bringing arms down to the chest, and the deltoid muscles, forming the rounded contour of the back of the shoulder, in particular were large and strong.

As a result of the muscle build-up, three quarters of the girls were either a normal weight or above average. The report makes it clear that there was certainly no problem with obesity. The remaining quarter of underweight girls had a much higher risk of ill health. Among them were girls that suffered from chronic bronchitis, spinal scoliosis and general debility. One in three of the underweight girls said they had 'had enough' and wanted early release from the corps, compared to one in ten of the normal and overweight group.

However, in general, on meeting the girls they appeared to be 'cheerful and contented' and so 'without going further, it would not have been unreasonable to give them a clean bill of health and assume that there was no cause for uneasiness.' Certainly the girls themselves reported, even years later, how healthy they were. This was borne out by my interviews with the women, such as Molly Paterson: 'I think I must have been pretty fit in those days.'

Dorothy Naylor worked at a sawmill just outside York, chopping, trimming and measuring timber, but only served for sixteen to seventeen months before she had to leave because of ill health, but 'would have loved to have served for longer. I loved every moment, rain, wind and shine!'

Sick Leave

While many of the girls loved their new-found life out in the forest with all its freedoms, they were being tested to the extremes of physical endurance in all weather conditions, and so it is not surprising that while they became fit that their bodies and general health suffered. The survey revealed a picture of ill health among the girls from their sickness absence records over one year. It showed that there was a very high level of sickness absence in the Timber Corps, with three out of four girls taking sick leave between the beginning of July 1944 and the end of June 1945. A combined total of 3,242 working days or 20 days per person was lost, and this did not include lost time owing to works accidents, which increased the lost days to 26 per woman over a year.

The most common causes of sick leave were surgical conditions, such as appendicitis, 27 per cent; locomotor diseases including rheumatism, 17 per cent; gastrointestinal complaints such as constipation, 12 per cent; and nervous conditions, 7 per cent.

Although originally there were concerns raised by welfare staff and supervisors about increasing levels of menstrual sickness among the girls, as a result of the extreme physical demands of the job, the survey found that just under a quarter, 23 per cent, said they had worse menstrual cramps, increased bleeding or more irregular periods, and 6 per cent said it was made worse by heavy felling. Yet 9 per cent said they had less painful periods since they began forestry work.

However, looking at sickness absence records over a year, only half a day per person per year was lost as a result of gynaecological symptoms, including menstrual irregularities. This was no higher than other female workers, and during the survey not one woman applied for release for this reason.

Some girls were given a day off when they got their periods. But this caused problems with other camps where this was not the case. So, to clear up the issue, on 25 July 1944 L.M. Jackson, Divisional Welfare Officer for Oxfordshire, wrote, 'I certainly have met no case of a girl being off work regularly on the occasion of the monthly period. In fact, our view point is that where this is necessary, the girl is considered unfit for our work, and release applied for.'

More than one in four girls took sick leave because they required surgery. Within this group there were five cases of appendicitis, totalling half the total absences for this group. Kathleen Hutchby served for two years before suffering from appendicitis. It is interesting to note that one of the main causes of appendicitis is caused by hard stools leading to infection. We also know that constipation was a problem for the girls in the Timber Corps, who had a poor diet that relied upon bread.

Just over 12 per cent of the sickness absence was due to gastrointestinal complaints. These absences notably included constipation, which was caused by too much starchy food, bread, not enough food or long periods without food and a lack of adequate toilet facilities in the forests.

Mrs Lawrie thought she'd give piecework a go, felling timber, earning 10s a week, which was good money: 'But I was covered in blisters and hurt my back, so I went back to the saw bench.'

Rheumatism was reported as one of the most commonly reported reasons for sickness absence on the records. In the past, it was a term used to describe a wide variety of symptoms causing pain and inflammation in the muscles and joints. Edna Barton remembers plenty of aches and pains and like many former Lumberjills, she said she has suffered from rheumatism all of her life.

Today, the word 'rheumatism' is not considered a technical term that is useful, as it is too generic, covering hundreds of different conditions, including arthritis. Yet there is a strong causal link in the survey made between working in cold or wet weather and wearing damp clothes.

Inadequate tarpaulin sheets and makeshift timber shelters or huts provided some protection from bad weather. But it was more problematic that clothes could not be dried after work, so often the girls had to put their damp clothes from the day before on in the morning and this was thought to contribute towards rheumatism. And yet, some seventy years later, decades of medical research has failed to establish the link between wet, cold weather and muscle and joint pain.

Whatever the cause, whether it was the weather or the strenuous work, one in six of the girls took sickness absence as a result of joint and muscle pain. One might deduce that the unappealing prospect of working out in cold, wet weather may have made it more likely that the girls took sick leave. Additionally, the poor living conditions and isolated billets could have contributed towards making the girls feel more miserable and sensitive to aches and pains and to them needing to take time off work.

The survey also reported that chronic crondritis was experienced by a number of girls in the Timber Corps, that was categorised as an underlying health condition, perhaps unrelated to the work the girls were doing. The primary symptom of crondritis is severe chest wall pain, which becomes worse with trunk movement, deep breathing and or exertion.

Again the causes of this condition may not have been fully understood at the time. Today, the most likely causes are thought to include injury, repetitive minor trauma and unusual excessive physical activity. So this diagnosis could easily have been down to the strenuous and repetitive nature of forestry work involving the upper body.

One woman, Bonny Macadam, was discharged because she had rheumatic fever:

> My last winter in the WTC was bitterly cold. I think this accounted for the rheumatic fever with which I landed in hospital. Mrs Stoddart, Red Cross, asked me to stay and help her in the Bank House when I was discharged. There I spent a very happy recuperation.[1]

As a result of higher standards of living and medical care, rheumatic fever is now very rare in the UK, but it is still very common in poorer parts of the world where there is overcrowding, poor sanitation and limited access to medical treatment. The major symptoms include shortness of breath or chest pain, pain and swelling (arthritis) in joints, involuntary movements or emotional outbursts, skin rash or bumps and lumps that develop underneath the skin.

Signed Off

While it was the fourth most common reason for sick leave in the survey, and it was the most common reason for discharge, 'nervous debility' was not explained in the survey at all. Nervous debility in the 1940s was a generic term which today would cover many conditions including unhappiness, anxiety, depression or other mental health issues.

On 18 October 1943, Margaret Crowler wrote that she left her previous employment in Cheshire to come to her present job in forestry: 'Unfortunately I never made contact with the office regarding a transfer for the simple reason I was so terribly unhappy and I wanted to get away, forgetting that I should have kept to the rules of the Land Army ... I also asked Mrs. Hussey if it will be possible for me to join the Timber Corps.'

The report also acknowledges that it was the practice during the war to recommend girls for timberwork because it was considered that they would benefit from an open-air life. Forests were believed to provide a curative environment for what may be described as 'nervous conditions'.

Margaret Grant recalled:

> Mary had been sent to us, as quite a number of people were from Clydebank. After a raid, she was the only one left alive in an Anderson Shelter. Her family, the animals, the big dogs were killed all around her and the doctors decided, when Mary recovered, that working in a job like ours would be good for her.[2]

Both Edna Barton and Pat Frayn suffered from family bereavements and were recommended to join the corps for therapeutic purposes. While the forest environment may be curative, when you consider the gruelling demands of working in forestry all year round, this therapeutic approach to recruitment may have been questionable.

The reality was that disability and illness were not the only downsides of the job; poor living conditions, not enough food, ill treatment and isolated billets would likely contribute towards making the girls feel down and depressed or triggering other mental health issues. Interestingly, far more time, analysis and attention in the report was given to whether they girls were overweight and were suffering worse menstrual sickness.

There is a reference to a high proportion of girls who had 'had enough' and wanted their release from the corps, which increased with length of service:

The Corps at present represents the survival of the fittest, and in the small group which made up this survey there were a number who complained of increasing fatigue and who viewed with some alarm the prospect of spending another winter in the woods.

The most common cause of medical discharges, after nervous debility at 21 per cent, was pregnancy at 20 per cent. After the peak in deaths during both world wars, there was a following peak in the number of births because of fears of population decline. There was also an increasing value put on health in the UK, and in particular maternal health during the Second World War, when pregnant women first benefitted from the National Milk Scheme, and free or inexpensive orange juice, cod liver oil or vitamin A and D tablets. There was also an increase in the hospitalisation of childbirth, with the majority of births taking place in hospital for the first time. So with this increased focus on maternal health, it follows that the Lumberjills would readily be discharged from the heavy work in the Timber Corps when pregnant.

The other most common reason for medical discharge was locomotor injuries such as strained and sprained muscles, 17 per cent; respiratory problems, 11 per cent; and accidents at work, 8 per cent. The survey found that influenza, colds and respiratory conditions, such as bronchitis, accounted for 13.4 per cent of lost time.

In May 1944, Dorothy Swift was placed in a sawmill in Salford:

I loathed this noisy indoor work. It was not what I joined the WTC for. I hated my lodgings too. What's more I had two spells off work with bronchitis, which I put down to breathing in sawdust. As if that was not enough, my bronchitis was the precursor of an unsightly and contagious skin disease called impetigo. The powers that be decided I should go back to my parents in Sheffield and enjoy some sick leave, so at that point both Muriel and I were listed as sick. It should have read 'sick and fed up to the back teeth'.

The survey ends with a rather disparaging note about the Women's Timber Corps:

An occupation which gives rise to so much general sickness cannot be considered altogether suitable or satisfactory work for women. When their relatively low level of output is also taken into consideration it becomes doubtful, apart from any risk to health, whether the employment of women in forestry work can be economically justified.

Accidents

Accidents were a routine aspect of life in the Women's Timber Corps. Muscular strains and sprains gave rise to the most lost-time accidents and 26 out of 161 girls were released because of the after-effects of accidents at work. This is more than the 16 per cent that retired from the Timber Corps because of accidents.

Eileen Mark used cant hooks, which were poles with a hook on one end: 'Once I was improvising with a pole instead of a cant hook, but the pole twisted and I was knocked out. Another time I was using a bill hook and I nearly cut the top of my finger off.'

They worked in sawmills, which even by the low health and safety standards of the 1940s were considered to be exceptionally dangerous. Amputated fingers were the most common injuries sustained while working in the sawmills.

Bonny Macadam recalled:

A trainee, Mary, was being taught by 'Crolly', Betty Creole, to feed the big saw with huge trees and was told why she should never wear gloves. Unfortunately she forgot this good advice and one day a log caught in her glove and carried her hand into the saw. Mr. Allison's wife, Meg, who was a nurse came immediately and wrapped her poor hand in a towel. Then Bob Allison and I rushed the girl off to Brechin hospital, carefully taking the severed finger with us. We tried to keep up Mary's spirits on the way by telling stories and were amazed when she asked if she could tell us one. This involved a man who had been off work from a sawmill and was asked on his return what had happened. He replied, 'Och! I just did that. Oh no, there's another finger away.' I think our laughter was tinged with hysteria.[3]

Violet Parker saw one or two accidents in the sawmill, catching fingers, and worked with a man who didn't have any fingers on one hand, lost on the sawmills, and that was why he wasn't called up.

While Mary Broadhead was working in the sawmill cutting timber, another girl who was meant to be working with her had stayed at home:

That day I was the only one on the small saw. It was a windy day and the wind was blowing across the yard and over the skids causing the sawdust to be whipped up and into my eyes.

I was cutting the spacers for stacking the timber. The saw blade clinched on the saw causing the wood to jump and my hand slipped down the wood. As this happened I tried to pull my hand away. But too late, it caught my left thumb cutting it off at the first joint and also lacerating my fourth and fifth fingers.

After it had happened I walked across the yard to the office. It was found out that there was no transport for me, [and I] had to wait two hours to be taken to the village doctor. He could do nothing for me, so he sent me on to hospital in Canterbury. This took about another 15 to 20 minutes to arrive at the accident and emergency. A doctor on arrival saw me, the doctor asked my age and because I was under 21 they made an effort to contact my parents in West Yorkshire for permission for a full anaesthetic.

But due to a large air raid the telephone lines were fully occupied with calls. This was taking too long so the doctors decided to go ahead with just a local anaesthetic. They needed help with the operation, so they asked the army to help with doctors and nurses.

As I was waiting in A&E I was put on a high stool outside an office. As I sat there a senior nurse, 'Sister', came along and said to the other nurses, 'What is she doing sat there? Find her a bed at once.' And one was found and I was put into it out in the corridor for lack of room.

Joan Turner wasn't the only one to be caught by a falling tree: 'Sometimes the trees would bounce back instead of falling forwards and one fell on my back once and I had to have a bit of leave.'

But the accidents didn't only happen while the girls were at work, they often happened on the way home too. One night, Hazel Collins left her bike at the station and went into Bude, but missed the last train home and had to walk back from Bude: 'So late at night in the dark and wet, I went down the hill head tucked in and smashed into a bridge. See this scar. They looked after me and stitched me up. I didn't mind as long at the vet didn't stitch me up.'

Eileen Mark met up with a lad to go for a dance and spent all night doing the waltz or quickstep:

It was getting very late and while going home a doodlebug came over-head and turned. It was up a steep hill with the forest to its side. We saw it coming towards us and cycled into a ditch going over the handlebars with the bikes on top of us.

213

But Hazel and Eileen were the luckier ones, as on 18 June 1943 the *Derbyshire Times* reported a 'Fatal Cycling Accident of a Chesterfield Girl' called Miss Clara Greatorex, aged 19, who lived at Tupton.

Lost lives

There were Lumberjills who sadly lost their lives in service during the war. A small number of women were killed when trees fell the wrong way, and others by tragic accidents when hauling and transporting timber. The girls that drove Caterpillar and Fordson tractors frequently tipped over on hillsides while extracting trees.

Eileen Mark used to ride on the back of the tractors: 'Once when I was driving I nearly took the tractor and forester over the edge going down a hill around a corner.'

Dorothy Swift heard of a tragic accident that occurred:

Nan, a 19-year-old forestry lass, was being driven back to her wood on the rear of an empty lorry that had delivered timber to the railway station. After dropping its load the lorry's sideboards had not been replaced. Youthful exuberance had failed to comply with the rules and four girls including Hammy, who were enjoying a singsong on the lorry's open platform, were devastated when the vehicle took a sharp bend forcing their mate Nan to fall off it to her death. By chance a photograph had been taken of Nan and the girls just 10 minutes before they set off for the station. On it Nan was smiling.

Betty Morley passed away some years ago but was in the Women's Timber Corps, and she told her son that at one stage she used to travel in an open lorry from the Ollerton area, Nottinghamshire, to Lincolnshire with the other girls. On one of those occasions there was a tragic accident on the railway crossing in Tuxford between the lorry and a train, and there were some fatalities. For whatever reason, luckily she was not on the lorry that day, but at least one other girl from the Women's Timber Corps died:

Another fatal accident happened in Kingussie in June 1942, after which an inquiry into the cause of death was held in Inverness Sheriff Court.

Olive Clarke had been employed in the Home Grown Timber Department of the Ministry of Supply at Kingussie Railway Station in checking all timber sent from there by the nearby Newfoundland Forestry Unit. Sven Hansen, also engaged in checking wood, said that he and Miss Clarke were standing at No. 2 loading bank watching a lorry reversing towards them. It gave a sudden spurt when it was about twenty feet away and he called to Miss Clarke to look out. It was too late and the lorry struck her, causing her to fall between the railway wagon and the buffers. She died the following day.

The sheriff thought the reason for the accident might well have been that the driver's foot had slipped from the brake to the accelerator and a verdict of accidental death was returned.[4]

In Scotland, Ethel Torbet lost her life in 1942 when a tree with a twisted root fell the wrong way and crushed her. She had only been working for the Women's Timber Corps Scotland for five months when she was tragically killed at Mount Wood, Aberuthven, near Perth, during tree-felling operations on 11 March 1942.

> There was an inquest in Perth Sheriff Court following the accident when Lumberjills gave evidence. The foreman at the lumber camp said there were fifty-five people in the working party in Mount Wood and, of these, twenty-two were Lumberjills. They were considered to be experienced in the woods, their duties being mainly felling, crosscutting and snedding. Evidence showed that on the morning of the accident a tree was being felled by two woodcutters who had shouted the warning 'Timber!' as a signal to the girls to keep clear. However, while they were working the saw had jammed and two girls and a man had gone to push the tree in the direction it was meant to fall. As they were pushing, the tree snapped at the roots and began to fall the wrong way. The girls ran for safety, but Miss Torbet ran in the wrong direction and, to the distress of her companions, was crushed by the tree.[5]

The tree fell in the wrong direction because of the twisted nature of its roots, which was only apparent after the tree had fallen.

Wartime Risks

Apart from the women who worked in bomb alley in Kent and the south-east of England during the flying bomb era, in general the girls lived and worked in safer countryside locations away from the enemy bombing of the towns and cities. But this did not exclude them from all danger.

Rose Burton remembered, 'Part of the wood was the firing range used by the army on Thursday for practice. One day a stray bullet caught a girl in the arm and she had to go to hospital but she survived.'

Mr Marshall worked for the Forestry Commission in January 1944 at the age of 14, and worked alongside thirty Lumberjills ranging in age from 14–60:

> There was a girl called Queenie, she was felling along the defence belt at Rendlesham Forest, which was right next to the airfield. Unfortunately a plane jettisoned its fuel tank on its way in to land and killed the lass at work.

And other women experienced abuse, which was normalised in the context of war. A surprising story which came out of a conversation with Eileen Mark:

> An estate manager who was also a Captain in the Home Guard asked me and Pauline to man the telephones and take messages during an exercise and then we went into the gas chamber too, sometimes wearing a gas mask and sometimes without. It made me sick.

However, violence against women, then as now, was under-reported and reduced in importance. On 22 April 1944, The *Liverpool Daily Post* reported on a murder as a 'double tragedy':

After Dance Tragedy

A Liskeard (Cornwall) Coroner's jury last night, investigating the double tragedy of a farm worker and a land girl found dead at Rilla Mill, returned a verdict that Joyce Recover, aged 21, of the Women's Timber Corps, a native of Kingston (Surrey), was strangled by Raymond Bartlett, aged 22, who afterwards committed suicide by shooting.

Witnesses stated that the two young people went to a Salute the Soldier dance last Tuesday, but the girl did not return to her lodgings. After Bartlett had been questioned he shot himself. The police found the girl lying dead under a pile of straw in a cowshed.

18

Praise and Jubilation at the End of the War

Praise

At the beginning of the war there was praise for the women fulfilling the lighter forestry work, such as planting and measuring. These early reports were frequently written by the one female journalist on the paper or by a lady of note from high society and were often idealistic in tone, perhaps part of the propaganda of war.

In January 1940, the *Bury Free Press* reported: 'Women's Land Army Doing Splendid Work' on the afforestation at Culford with at least 200 women working in collaboration with the Timber Control section of the Ministry of Supply.

In March 1940, the *Gloucestershire Echo* reported: 'The official added that those girls who had taken up forestry were doing excellent work in helping the Forestry Commission to plant new trees to replace the timber which was now being cut for war purposes.'

In November 1940, in the *Cheltenham Chronicle and Gloucestershire Graphic's* 'Gloucestershire Woman's Gossip of the Week' column, the wife of the Postmaster-General and organiser for the Gloucestershire Woman's Land Army was reported as saying she was:

Very pleased with progress of the Land Army in Gloucestershire, which is now the fourth largest employing county.

Many of the girls had had no experience whatever of land work before. They came from city shops and offices, and after a few weeks training got on extraordinarily well. Forestry apparently is a favourite branch of the work, which is quite understandable, for a more delightful occupation would be difficult to imagine. Girls who express a preference for forestry go to the hostel school in the Forest of Dean, and from there are sent out in pairs where they are required.

Towards the end of 1941, praise came from the men in charge, especially in Scotland, with attitudes beginning to change and a new confidence in the girls providing strong evidence that a Women's Timber Corps should be established officially.

In October 1941, the *Aberdeen Press and Journal* ran a report with the headline, 'Women Foresters Praised':

From hairdressing and ballet dancing to lumberjacking in remote camps is a big change for girl workers who have never previously had any experience of real manual labour. Yet such girls have so much impressed members of the Select Committee on National Expenditure that the Committee recommend that the training and employment of these girls should be expanded.

From 1942, the press was full of praise for the girls. The *Daily Record* said: 'Cue – The Women's Timber Corps is doing grand work it is reported, so all together, folks! "They are jolly good fellers!"' The *Courier and Advertiser* ran the headline, 'Shopgirls Shine as Lumberjills':

At a press conference at St. Andrews House, Edinburgh, Councillor J.J. Robertson senior labour officer for Scotland to the Ministry of Supply, said that former shop girls were proving to be excellent 'Lumberjills' from the point of view of stamina, as they were accustomed, in their job, to standing for long hours.

'There is an amazing change in the physique of these girls after a short time in forestry work. They worked through all the rigours of last winter in Perthshire clearing a hillside of growing timber. Their production fig- ures compare favourably with the labour which has been used since war began and are much better than anything we could get from any male labour which we could now recruit from the Labour exchanges.'

He admitted there had been some difficulty in breaking down prejudice against using women's labour, especially among the older timber merchants, but Councillor Robertson's experience in visiting camps had convinced him of the suitability of using girls to fell trees. Many members also commented on the size of the women's muscles after a month of felling trees. He said he had asked a girl working zealously in a snow blizzard, why she was working in such appalling conditions and she replied, 'We want to show you men that we can do this job.'

Suggesting a further turn in the tide of prejudice, in September 1942 the *Falkirk Herald* ran a story which put out a plea from collieries for women in preference to the men for stripping pit props. It read, 'Colliery managers are anxious to have women workers, those who employed them before the war say they work more conscientiously than the men', but they also wanted to free up the men to work underground.

It reported, 'Official sources now make it abundantly clear that the women's market provides the only source of labour left which can speed up production. Necessity is gradually wearing down prejudice, which, strangely enough, exists mainly among men themselves.'

By January 1943, the *Western Daily Press* and *Bristol Mirror* had completely changed its tune from the 'Forestry handicap' headline towards a more positive representation of women working in forestry some three years later. It reported: 'Britain's Lumberjills, members of the Women's Timber Corps, are such jolly good "fellers" and foresters, that they are so increasing the output of home-grown timber their organisation may be kept on after the war.'

The success of the women made their skills worthy of a spectator sport. In late 1943, a women's felling competition was announced in Kirriemuir and twelve pairs of girls took part from camps across Scotland. Morag Shorthouse recalled:

Jean put my name forward along with that of Mary Curran, so we had to get in a little practice as we had never felled together ... We were shown the trees we had to fell, the stop watches were set and we started with all eyes on us. Unfortunately, we did not get the first prize of a silver cup but we came second. Mr Scott ... said he would donate ten shillings to the fastest snedder so off we went again and this time I won amid great hilarity and applause.'[1]

By 1944, the Lumberjills in action became entertainment for a show of their felling skills. Six girls for the north-east of Scotland 'doffed their jumpers' and performed a display, felling trees for the Aberdeen holidaymakers. The *Aberdeen Press and Journal* reported that the first tree was felled in three minutes, the branches lopped off and trunk measured and sawn into lengths in fifteen. The tribute paid to them was, 'But for you, the country and the fighting forces would have been much worse off than they have been.'

By 1944, the Women's Timber Corps had made news in the national press. The *Daily Mirror's* headline on a Lumberjill called Marguerite read '[A] slip of a girl' and said that the daughter of a doctor 'pulls with ease ten ton trees'.

Russell Meiggs wrote that 1944 was the peak year for the Women's Timber Corps when it was at its best. There was greater acceptance of the Women's Timber Corps and training improved, which resulted in more efficiency. Welfare officers had learnt their job and the Ministry of Supply department had learnt from its mistakes:

> Special courses were held to train in leadership and increased use was made of members to supervise small working parties. Over fifty members were also promoted to foreman grade, and took charge of complete operations, sometimes controlling men as well as women.

The director in charge of the Home Timber Production Department at the Ministry of Supply, Gerald Lenanton, summarised the success of the women in the Women's Timber Corps and their contribution towards victory:

> Many people would not believe that women could, or would, take the place of men. Experience during the past three years has triumphantly proved how wrong they were.
>
> All honour to the girls who, as volunteers, faced exile from home, the cold and mud of winter, long hours and heavy work, to do a job of first importance to their country.

George Ryle in *Forest Service* praised one of the most successful projects in Wales, where an exclusively female workforce were required to fell a large wood, a couple of hundred acres, of heavy coppice grown oak:

> The Women's Timber Corps provided a fine force, not only for the rather lighter felling, crosscutting and similar physical works, but also for measuring, stock control, despatching and all the necessary onsite duties. With an all-female workforce, it was so successful, that a sawmill was set up to manufacture colliery tramline sleepers to transport the wood.

The wood lay alongside the old Carmarthen–Swansea line, which provided its only means of transport to the pits. But the line was in service six days a week, so timber had to be stockpiled until it could be transported direct to the colliery every other Sunday. So, twice a month, a train of a dozen wagons was filled and despatched to Swansea as many times as possible before 5 p.m.

George Ryle continued:

Great was the competition between small gangs of these girls to fill the biggest number of trucks and it was good to see the engine driver, the stoker, the guard and the safety men all buckling-to with a will to make sure the train got away well loaded up. That was typical of the spirit of the time.

Celebration

It was a wonderful time for us. I remember D-Day, 6 June 1944. It was a beautiful June day, I remember that. Everything was quiet and at that time the Timber Corps seemed to be ending, winding down.

Violet Parker, like millions of others, was relieved that the end of the war was in sight. The Lumberjills had successfully done their bit for the war. They loved both their life in the forest, with the adventures it brought, but were also tired of the extreme work and weather conditions, especially in winter. The end of their time in the Timber Corps crystallised many happy memories of life during the war, which would be remembered fondly for the rest of their lives.

By Victory in Europe Day on 8 May 1945, and Victory in Japan Day on 15 August 1945, signalling the end of the Second World War, women who were married or had domestic responsibilities were free to leave the Women's Timber Corps. Others were able to transfer into under-resourced occupations, such as teaching and nursing. But they did not move on without making the most of the celebrations.

There was national jubilation when Victory in Europe Day was announced, and Mavis Williams was granted two days' leave to celebrate:

Bells were ringing, hooters hooting, anything that could be banged, banging and people singing, arms around each other, pent-up emotions showing at last. Curtains had been drawn back, lights piercing the darkness after over five years of enforced blackout. My ganger and I decided to find a Dance Hall if we could. It was packed, couples dancing 'on the spot'. The air was alive with happiness and excitement. For a couple of hours we sang and danced and fraternised.

On 13 August 1945, Dorothy Swift signed into a hostel known as the Holiday Fellowship in Hereford the day before her 20th birthday. The next day, victory over Japan was announced: 'To celebrate, we had a day off work ... in the city of Hereford. What a joyful birthday that was.'

Margaret Grant recalled:

> When the war finished, we all went mad, we collected timber to light bonfires on the hills up and down Loch Awe and rang bells in every wee church. The owners of Sonachan estate had kept fireworks from before the war, so we had a wonderful fireworks display. He and I pulled the bells until the wires broke when we found out the war was over.[2]

Joan Turner went around the village banging dustbin lids to wake everyone up when the war finished: 'But we were not discharged until Jan. 1946. By that time I had done four years.' The Women's Timber Corps as an organisation was officially disbanded in August 1946.

Victory Parade

Joyce Elizabeth Gaster was one of the longest-standing members of the Women's Timber Corps, receiving a badge for six years' service on 15 May 1946. She joined the Women's Land Army forestry section in 1940 in the Forest of Dean and trained as a measurer. Thereafter, she worked at Haltwhistle in Cumbria, Northumberland and I was particularly delighted to discover she had worked at Alice Holt Forest in Hampshire, where I had worked for four years. She lived in Dockenfield and worked with a dozen girls. She was one of the special few representing the Women's Timber Corps in the Victory Parade in London on 8 June 1946.

An article in Timber Corps Newsletter (division for 4a) read:

> Five members (two from Scotland and three from England and Wales) were chosen to represent the W.T.C. in the Victory Parade in London on 8 June 1946. Members in division four (a) will be interested to know that Miss Joyce Gaster (measurer at Alice Holt Forest unit) was among those chosen to represent England and Wales. Her account of the day is given below. Miss Eileen Hanna (measuring at H Perry unit) very neighbourly stood by in case any of the representatives dropped out at the last minute.

'I was very thrilled to hear that I had been chosen as one of three W.T.C. to represent England and Wales in the Victory Parade. All the W.L.A. contingent were invited to a tea party on Friday afternoon, July 7 at the Land Army clerk in Chesham Street where we were made very welcome and had a lovely tea. As there were over fifty land girls there, it was some time before I found my W.T.C. companions and was so pleased to find they were both girls I already knew.

After the tea party we were conducted to our billet, which was the Royal Palace Hotel, Kensington. We found we were to share this building with the civil defence and there were over 900 people billeted there altogether. I do not know whether they thought the W.L.A. should be the most energetic but our bedrooms were on the sixth floor and as [these were the] only ones left, we usually had to walk up 188 stairs to reach our rooms! Soon after we arrived there the Scottish girls joined us, bringing two W.T.C. to make us five in total.

After supper we had to go outside the hotel and had a rehearsal. The sergeant of the Coldstream Guards did his best to make us look like practiced marchers. It was a good thing he had a lot of patience! Of course we were very disappointed that there were so few of us to represent the W.T.C. The W.L.A. contingent consisted of six rows – 12 abreast and we were in the back row. Even the land girls said how much better it would have looked if there had been a whole row across the back. After the rehearsal most of us retired to bed to get a good night's rest. We were up at 5.30 as breakfast was from 6 to 8 o'clock and we were very thankful to see it was not raining.

At 9 o'clock we were taken in buses to Hyde Park and then marched to the assembly point near Marble Arch. Here we were able to have refreshments from the N.A.A.F.I. canteen and although we had nearly one and a half hours to wait – the time soon went as all the parade was assembling and there were so many strange nationalities and uniforms to be seen.

Then we were off round Marble Arch and down Oxford Street. We had a band just behind us, so it helped us with our marching. It seemed strange to be marching through all those cheering crowds and they really did give the W.L.A. an extra loud cheer along the route but what's gladdened the hearts of the timber girls most of all was to hear someone shout 'Timber' as we went past.

At Trafalgar Square there was a halt for about 20 minutes while the head of the group was joining up with the rest at Nelson's column. It was here that the rain started, but we were quite glad of it as it was cool and refreshing

But despite the valuable experience and knowledge the women had, the prospects for women wishing to stay within the trade were bleak. A small number of women were either employed on the National Census of Woodlands to assess the amount of standing timber that remained, stayed in local sawmills or went into research.

When Jessie MacLean was demobbed, her friend Mrs Simpson, who was the chief welfare officer in Scotland, suggested she apply for the vacancy in the Forestry Research Assessment Party:

> I did and was accepted. Our boss was J.A.B. MacDonald. There were four of us, all ex-Lumberjills, so it was an enjoyable time for me, travelling all over Scotland to woodlands and nurseries and even to a plot in Edinburgh's Botanic Gardens.[3]

After the Women's Timber Corps, Audrey Broad carried on working in a sawmill doing all the measuring for sawn timber, round timber and standing timber:

> Working outside I got very fit and strong. We had soft wood coming in from Germany and it came in on a loader, which was like a lorry with a pole in the middle. I used to measure the timber before taking it off the lorry and so I used to climb up on the lorry and walk along the trunk balancing to show off. What a foolish woman, walking along them at a great height, I was a bit of a daredevil. My husband was a builder and was building new properties for H. Baker and Son. The sawmill borrowed some of the workmen to help produce more timber and this was how I met him. I worked in the Women's Timber Corps for four and half years and then in the sawmill until I got married to Ted Ansell on 14 February 1948.

Ethel Oliver loved being outside and the whole experience left her with very fond memories: 'After moving around the North East I eventually finished in the woods in 1946. That left me with a bit of dilemma because after such an experience I didn't fancy working in an office or shop.'

Irene Snow went home to Yorkshire for a bit after the war:

> But it was awful going back to the woollen mills. I missed being outdoors. As I liked the fresh air and I still love the trees now. So, when I married Jack in 1952, I moved back to South Molton where I had worked in the WTC and had one son.

Achievements

By the end of the war the number of workers in forestry had risen from 14,000 to 73,000 at its peak. With as many as 15,000 being women, they may have accounted for one in five forestry workers. During the Second World War more wood was produced from British woodlands than ever before in history.

Forestry Commission forests produced more than 51 million cubic feet of wood, which accounted for just 10 per cent of the timber used in the war effort. The most mature forests, the Forest of Dean and the New Forest, bore the brunt of wartime felling. By the end of the war the New Forest alone had twenty-six sawmills and the Forest of Dean had fourteen. They became the two major powerhouses of timber production in England during the Second World War. The New Forest alone produced 12.5 million cubic feet of timber and only trees of special silvicultural interest were conserved.

The remaining 90 per cent of timber came from private estates, supplying pit props for mines producing the coal on which so many of the wartime industries depended. Over 9 million tons of wood was produced for use in coal mines, in pit props and sawn timber for pit wood, and a further 9 million tons of wood was required for other wartime commodities, these included railway sleepers, telegraph poles, packaging boxes for carrying everything from vegetables to military supplies and weapons. It was also used for gun butts, cannon carriage wheels, Mosquito and Spitfire combat aircraft, masts for shipbuilding and charcoal for explosives and gas mask filters, to name but a few.

In total, Great Britain supplied 60 per cent of its timber needs during the war. A total of 46 per cent of trees in forests, woodlands and parks were felled and usable standing timber was exhausted. Many roads were left tree-lined to present the appearance that the landscape had not changed. But that thin screen of trees hid the scarred open landscape behind, depleted of trees.

Germany

On 22 February 1946, the chief officer of the Timber Corps, M.E. Hoskyn, sent the following letter to remaining members of the Women's Timber Corps. The letter was received by Joyce Elizabeth Gaster and was provided by her family from her collection of photos and letters relating to her time in the Women's Timber Corps:

Dear members,

When I last wrote to you on 15th of November 1945, we thought that the closing down of production in this country would mean that the Timber Corps would come to an end very early in the New Year. Since then, however, the pit prop position has become so serious that the closedown policy has had to be reversed until supplies of timber can be obtained from abroad. In consequence, members of the Timber Corps are asked to carry on with the job, at any rate until early summer.

As you probably will know, the purpose of the North German Timber Control which has been formed under our director, Sir Gerald Lenanton, is to get supplies of timber from the German forests to this country as quickly as possible, but until the present trickle of imported timber becomes a steady flow, those of you who are remaining in the Corps will still, as in the past, be carrying out work of the first importance.

The North German Timber Control will be largely composed of officers transferred from this department, including about 100 Timber Corps forewomen and measurers, who have been specially selected from the large number of applicants for clerical duties in Germany. Five welfare officers are coming with me to Germany to look after the welfare of the Timber Control staff.

My only regret at accepting this appointment is that I am not able to remain with the Timber Corps to the end. I am glad to say, however, that I am leaving your welfare in good hands, since Mrs. Simpson, chief officer of the Timber Corps in Scotland, has agreed to take over responsibility for the Corps in England and Wales as well.

Mrs. Simpson will spend part of her time in Edinburgh and part in Bristol, and she will try and fit in visits to the divisions so that she may get to know you personally. She has already met your welfare officers.

As some welfare officers are being transferred to Germany, there will be fewer left in this country and though they may not have as many members of the Timber Corps to look after as they have had in the past, most of them will have to cover much larger areas.

I want to ask you now to help your welfare officer as much as you can during the next few months. If you are in difficulty or need advice, write to her at the divisional office and give the particulars of your case as fully as possible. This gives her a chance to make some enquiries find out the answers before she comes to see you and perhaps saves the second visit. And don't feel neglected if you do not see her as often as you have in the past, it may be physically impossible for her to visit each unit in her area very frequently as well as to get through the office work. It will help her enormously if you will keep in touch with her by letter or, if there is anything urgent, if you will ring her up.

I cannot sufficiently praise the way that welfare officers have looked after your interests all through these difficult years when the things that would have made living and working conditions rather more comfortable were 'in short supply'. If you have not had all you wanted, I can assure you that it is not because your welfare officers did not demand it for you. I have every confidence that you and they together will see that the last effort of the Timber Corps is as good as any of those have gone before.

I wish you all happiness and success in the hope that you will retain cheerful memories of your life in the Timber Corps.

Yours sincerely, M.E. Hoskyn,

Chief officer, W.T.C.

I find this letter so telling of the journey made by those in charge of the Women's Timber Corps. He admits it had been a demanding role for welfare officers, who looked after the Lumberjills, and why? Because 'all through these difficult years when the things that would have made living and working conditions rather more comfortable were "in short supply".'

His heartfelt regard for the women and sadness to leave before their work was finished is tender and expressed with great care. This was a man who had learned how to communicate with the women, to make them feel valued and reassured that their interests would not be neglected again. It is such a poignant letter and so heart-warming to read.

The fact was, Britain needed to stop the slaughter of its forests as soon as possible, but when the war was over the need for wood did not suddenly stop. In fact, the demand for wood continued to rise because of the need to rebuild Britain. There was equal demand from mines for pit props, to keep coal seams open and factories operating.

Importing timber from Canada had always been something Britain had done. But now the Ministry of Supply had its eye on the German forests instead, which were closer to home and offered a satisfying retribution after the war. There was plenty of timber in Germany for essential domestic needs, as well as a huge surplus that could be shipped back to Britain.

On 15 May 1946, the *Arbroath Herald* reported on the appointment of Sheila Butchart as the Supervising Measurer over German Labour and Sir Gerald Lenanton as the Director General of the North German Timber Control: 'Sir Gerald Lenanton said "the sky's the limit" for the amount of timber for the allies. Some of the wood will be for houses in Britain, and 10,000 tons are being released for that purpose this month.'

So a select number of more senior measurers and supervisors, such as Sheila Butchart, from the Women's Timber Corps became an essential part of the North German Timber Control team in the summer of 1945. Their task was to requisition equipment from the sawmills and undertake secretarial work for the Control Commission in the North German Timber Control, which was organising timber supplies to support the reafforestation of Britain.

Miss Sheila Butchart was appointed as Supervising Measurer over German Labour with the North German Timber Control. With considerable experience in the Women's Timber Corps, as Chief Measurer for Scotland, she was well qualified for the post and left for Germany at the end of March 1946.

Jean Smith was one of the women who went out to Germany:

On the last day of the war, I heard that my husband had been killed on active service in Germany. Afterwards, when we were given the opportunity to go to Germany, I decided to try that. The Control Commission required girls, familiar with timberwork, to do secretarial work in North German Timber Control.

There was a big detachment near Brunswick, the nearest town to the Russian home, to which I was posted. I was also in Hanover, Hamburg and a lovely place called Wolfsburg, where the Volkswagen Beetles were made. It was my favourite place.

There was no antagonism in the offices in which I worked. In Brunswick the woman in charge of the office was a German who was extremely efficient and had an excellent grasp of languages. With my experience of consigning loads of timber in Scotland, I was often given the task in Germany. We tried to see as much of the country as possible and the devastation was terrible in cities such as Hamburg.

One thing, which pleased us, was to find a dressmaker who ran up skirts and dresses for social occasions. We had been issued with some clothing by the Control Commission; a blue suit, two pairs of black stockings, a greatcoat, one pair of black shoes, two shirts, four collars, a cap, shoulder titles, a black tie and a cap badge.

When I decided to go to Germany, I signed up for one year only but in the end stayed for three years. It helped me to get over the loss of my husband.

Hazel Collins was another who went out to Germany in May 1946 and stayed for three or four years:

I went with the Control Commission. They had such a good report of me from the Timber Corps and so they asked me to go with them. Anything to get out of the country. I went with one girl called Florence. She had two false front teeth and she was ill on the way there and was sick over the side of the boat and lost her teeth. So as soon as we landed we had to find a dentist.

I always wanted to be a Wren and so when we were given Wrens uniforms in Germany I was very pleased and wore my uniform to a party. I earned forty-two pounds a month and used to take out six pounds and bank the rest. That six pounds used to last me for the month in cigarettes and brandy. I also had a chauffeur, maid and cook and I thought what am I going to do when I go home without any of them? I enjoyed it and did mostly office work and picked up a bit of German. The Control Commission was forestry, fishing, all in the country and a lot of timber was imported back.

She added:

One awful time was when I went to the YMCA in Hanover, with a Welshman, my boss. This particular day the girls said, 'We haven't got any sanitary towels' and so I said, 'I'll get some for you'. I got them and stuck them in a big bag. He came along and he asked, 'What's this?' and I replied, 'What's this?' and he said, 'Yes, stick it on'. So I put it on top of our bags. Then he tripped and fell, and all the sanitary towels went all over the floor, everywhere. And he said, 'For God's sake!' and I replied, 'For my sake, someone give me another bag?' There were hundreds of them all over the floor.

At the end of Mrs M. Tozer's time with the WTC, she joined the Control Commission for Germany (CCG) for one year:

Very few girls stayed on for another year, when the time came. It was an experience you never forget the sight of the bombed areas of Hamburg, Dusseldorf, Munster etc; in the same way, you did not forget the looks of the German people when they were queuing up for bread (it was the time of the food shortage).

It is not pleasant to feel you are hated, by looking well fed, and having won the war. It was strange to hear the prevalent opinion that we had started the war, not them, as we declared war. The CCG had a bad name with the troops also, especially the girls. However, our six WTC in Dusseldorf were always very welcome at the NAAFI, as we were always prepared to help

Mrs Tozer also spent a couple of weekends while working in Germany by the Mohne Dam, famous for the Dambuster raids by the Royal Air Force in May 1943. They used a specially designed 'bouncing bomb' to cause massive destruction in the region and to German war production. Delivered by a specially modified Lancaster bomber, the bomb span backwards as it hit the water and drove the bomb down the wall of the dam before exploding at its base. Mrs Tozer explained that dam had been mended by the time she visited:

A friend and myself swam across one day, which was frowned on. We became friendly with a family who lived on the lakeside one day when we were swimming nearby. They had been there at the time of the dam breaching. The fact that all the fish had disappeared, had made most impression at the time, as fishing was their livelihood. I must say that I was glad to get back to England.

19

We Hate to Think
We're Forgotten

Forgotten

*We read of ATS, WAAFs, WRNS, and WLA, but never of the 'Lumberjills'
of the Women's Timber Corps. How is that? Aren't we doing a useful
job felling, 'snedding', crosscutting trees, and all other work connected
with forestry? We are out in all weathers, rain, hail, or snow, and have no
shelter of any kind. We live in huts at the 'back of beyond,' no NAAFI,
no canteen, no ENSA, no organised entertainment, and no transport to
the nearest town, 10 miles away. We have to pay board and lodgings, and
our 'digs' are in a cold, draughty hut. We don't want medals – but we
hate to think we're forgotten. – One 'Babe in the wood.'*

On 17 January 1943, the *Sunday Post* in Lanarkshire, Scotland, printed this
letter from a member of the Scottish Women's Timber Corps. It illustrates
the women's deeply held frustration at the time that they were poorly supported and apparently undervalued, or, as she says, 'forgotten'.

Lady Gertrude Denman was well aware of the injustice of how the
Women's Timber Corps and Land Army were being treated. She always saw
the women's work in relation to the needs of the nation at war. Yet her powers
of leadership were always being tested to resolve conflicting demands:

Underlying the administrative drive, the penetrating eye in committee,
the often gloriously caustic comment, and the intolerance of dishonesty,
pomposity, and pretension, there was deep affection for those whose cause
she championed [like the Women's Timber Corps and Land Army].
… She waged constant battles for proper recognition of the Land Army,
and succeeded in securing conditions of employment, which were of last-
ing benefit to agricultural workers as a whole. However, the government

ultimately refused to award the Land Army and Timber Corps the grants, gratuities and benefits which it gave to women in the civil defence and armed services, and so Lady Gertrude Denman resigned in protest on 15 February 1945.[1]

Without formal recognition, the women cherished the pair of brass axes and Bakelite badges; they were lucky if they had not lost them in the forests during their work. They hung on to their triangle arm badges received for every six months of service and their precious release certificate, as evidence of their war work.

The letter from Queen Elizabeth, the patron of the Women's Land Army and Timber Corps, on their release from the corps meant so much to Dorothy Swift: 'In December 1946 I was given my release certificate. I still have it. I also cherish my letter from Queen Elizabeth, now the Queen Mother, thanking me for my wartime service in the Women's Land Army.'

Queen Elizabeth had shown support to the girls throughout the war, inviting them to Buckingham Palace for a party in 1943, a rare occasion when they were invited to spend time indoors, as their work involved spending so much time outside normally.

Mary Ralph was requested to turn up in uniform one day out in the forest as the queen, Princess Elizabeth and Princess Margaret Rose were to be there and had asked to meet the women:

A photograph of the queen speaking to me appeared in the local newspaper. She was very smart, wearing a lovely hat with a little veil and a dress and coat to match. The princesses wore their favourite tweed jackets and kilts. The queen talked to each of us in turn, asking me where we worked. When I told her we had been many times in Ballochbuie forest, she said they knew it well. They all seemed so interested in our work. It was a very warm day we were carrying our overcoats on our arms and Her Majesty asked if we had light, suitable clothing for the heavy outdoor work we did? I replied that we wore dungarees. It was an honour for us to have spoken to the queen for so long.

After that we had another visit from Her Majesty and her daughters while we worked in the woods. They just appeared one day with Mr. Farquhar from Invercauld and again asked a lot of questions and seemed very impressed with our arduous life in the forest. It really made us feel that we were doing something worthwhile for the war effort.[2]

The girls also received recognition during wartime when they went on parade up and down the country. The WLA forestry girls went on parade with their axes in Bury St Edmunds for the National War Effort Parade in August 1941, and they also took part in other Spitfire fundraising rallies, some of which were attended by the Land Army and Lady Gertrude Denman.

In April 1943, Bella Nolan had a march past in Inverness to celebrate the first anniversary of the Women's Timber Corps:

> With about one hundred girls taking part, we paraded along Bank Street in front of the crowd of spectators before being led away by the pipers and drummers of the Air Training Corps along Fraser Street, Church Street, Queens Gate, Academy Street and on to the High Street.[3]

Two women received recognition in Scotland for their services to the Women's Timber Corps. On 23 June 1945 the *Fife Free Press and Kirkcaldy Guardian* reported Miss Margaret Graham Kinlock as having been awarded the British Empire Medal for work done in connection with the Women's Timber Corps since January 1940. In addition, Daisy Mill was also awarded a British Empire Medal for services to the Timber Corps. Mary Broadhead was awarded a Frontline Britain badge and National Service medal, but this was not for her time in the Women's Timber Corps, rather her evening work as a driver for the British Red Cross.

Even though there were members of the Women's Timber Corps who sadly lost their lives in service during the war, as they were not part of the fighting forces, for fifty years after the war the Women's Land Army and Timber Corps were not allowed to take part in the Remembrance Day parades.

A few months after she left the Women's Timber Corps, Audrey Broad received a letter from the queen saying thank you:

> But it was only years later that I began to realise that we were not appreciated for what we had done. It was a long time afterwards that I began to think we should have got some recognition. We didn't get any money. We weren't even allowed to keep our uniforms. I thought that was dreadful because a lot of us stayed in the same business and we could have used those uniforms. I did keep one jacket though that I have still got in the cupboard.

The feeling of being forgotten stayed with the women for years afterwards. Joan Turner went to the press to say that she thought they had been forgotten and she 'never lived it down'. Frieda Ellerby said, 'We felt like we didn't get any recognition at the end of the war, but we just accepted it.'

Official Recognition

In October 2007, more than sixty years later, the Women's Timber Corps received their first formal recognition when the Forestry Commission unveiled a memorial in Aberfoyle, Scotland. It is a permanent memorial statue of a life-sized bronze sculpture of a Lumberjill on Forestry Commission land, dedicated to the members of the Women's Timber Corps. The organisation had found more than 100 women from the Scottish Women's Timber Corps to invite to the unveiling and honour their civilian contribution during the war.

Then, in December 2007, the government announced that the Women's Land Army and Timber Corps would receive formal recognition for the first time with the issue of a special badge of honour. Many of the women agreed with Edna Barton's comment, 'better late than never'. This was thanks to the dedication and work of Stuart Olssen.

In 2008, members of the Women's Land Army and Timber Corps such as Winnie Renshaw and her sister Doreen were offered a badge acknowledging their efforts in the war by the then Prime Minister, Gordon Brown: 'In 2008, Doreen and I received a badge and certificate from the government, as a token of thanks for our services during the war.'

A group of women were invited to 10 Downing Street to meet Gordon Brown to mark the occasion. There were also some other events around the country to award the badges. On 22 November 2008, Geoffrey Cox (MP for Torridge and West Devon) hosted a celebration at Merton in honour of the WLA and WTC. Along with over 700 other women who were in the Land Army and still living in Devon, Doreen Musson and both of her sisters were awarded their badge of honour and presented with a certificate of commemoration in appreciation of their war efforts.

This badge, however, caused some upset among the Women's Timber Corps because it used the Land Army emblem, a wheat sheaf, and not the fir tree or pair of crossed axes worn by the Women's Timber Corps – the emblem they had been so proud to wear. Many of the Women's Timber Corps regrettably did not live to receive this special badge of honour and unfortunately it was not awarded posthumously to their families.

To mark the seventy-year anniversary of the Women's Timber Corps in 2012, I feel proud that I was part of the Forestry Commission's nationwide search to find the forgotten army of Women's Timber Corps from England, to gather their stories and to remember their contribution in the war. At the time Pam Warhurst was the first female chair of the Forestry Commission in nearly 100 years, and she championed the project to find the forgotten army of Women's Timber Corps before it was too late.

The Forestry Commission gave the go-ahead to mount a UK-wide search for the surviving Lumberjills and about 100 came forward. You have heard from some of those women in this book. When I met them they were in their late 80s and early 90s. These marvellous women are some of wartime's greatest unsung heroes.

And after more than seventy years, the first commemorative statue to the Women's Timber Corps of the Second World War was unveiled in England. On 28 October in Dalby Forest in Yorkshire, the Forestry Commission made its tribute to the forgotten army of more than 15,000 Lumberjills who did their bit for the war with an axe and saw.

It was wonderful to see the life-size statue up in front of the glorious autumn colours at Haygate on the main drive into Dalby Forest. I really admired the Forestry Commission team and sculptor Ray Lonsdale for their dedication to achieving something really beautiful and capturing so well what life was like for the Lumberjills – *very* hard work but a lot of fun.

Who They Became

For the women in post-war Britain, it was the norm for them to get married and have children, which many of the Lumberjills did. Dorothy Swift returned home to Sheffield where she began work as a tram conductress before marrying her long-term boyfriend Ben Crofts who, during the war, had himself been away on active service.

Audrey Broad stayed in the Women's Timber Corps, for four and half years, until she got married to Ted Ansell on 14 February 1948. She had two children and stayed at home to look after them. But while she was a mum, fulfilling her teenage ambition, she went back school to finish her education and studied English Language and Maths at night school. When her children were old enough to look after themselves, Audrey went back to work with the Forestry Commission as a forest clerk. She was also a member of the History Society, Horticultural Society and a founder member of the local Women's Institute branch.

Diana Underwood was married and expecting her first baby in autumn 1943, and Park Farm in West Tytherley became her home. She moved in with her husband's family and became a farmer's wife.

> So starts another chapter – married life – while staying with the Underwoods and measuring during the working day, I had plenty of 'free time' in the evenings at this somewhat isolated farm so began to help a bit in the garden where Mr Reg Underwood grew vegetables, and tomatoes in his greenhouse. He grew vegetables in the field, sweetcorn, lettuce, spinach, etc. for sale.

For Diana Underwood, becoming a Lumberjill gave her very useful skills for farm working:

> I had learnt to drive a Caterpillar D2 diesel crawler earlier when I was working in the forest. So I learned to drive the standard Fordson tractor to harrow the fields and grassland. The farm was *c.*120 acres of clay ground and they kept 10–12 cows which were milked twice a day by hand.

It really struck me how their experiences had affected their lives when I met Irene Snow, one of the most humble and modest Lumberjills: 'I really enjoyed my time I spent in the Timber Corps, it gave me a great sense of freedom and the feeling that I could do anything after that.'

After hearing so many of their stories I would say that this was the case for many of them, and they did go on to do anything they wanted to, regardless of any expectations of them as women. Barbara Beddow went on to be a great leader and advocate for young people and women:

> Living, working and having to relate to such a variety of people, developed in me an interest in what makes people tick, so when I came home to start a family, I soon became involved in voluntary work: Sunday School, Brownies, Guide Commissioner, Youth Club Leader, Youth Tutor, Marriage Guidance (now Relate) Counsellor.
>
> After retirement at 59, I went on to start and Chair the Calderdale Volunteer Bureau for ten years. At present [June 2005] I am British President of an organisation 'Internationally Yours', and a Women's Friendship Club founded during the last war, aiming to help establish

peace through interaction with women of different cultures. I also run a Probus Widows' & Wives' Coffee Club in Halifax, plus I am involved in a scheme to help young people, which is being sponsored by Prince Charles Prince's Trust and the Wakeham Trust.

Olive Edgley became a youth leader too and other Lumberjills went into teaching. When Margaret Grant left the Women's Timber Corps in 1946, she decided to go to the Glasgow School of Art to study interior design. This is where she stayed for the rest of her career, first as a lecturer in interior design and eventually as head of the department.

Another Lumberjill from Scotland, Anne Shortreed, graduated from art school before the war and then became a Women's Timber Corps trainer at Park House in Aberdeenshire. She then went to the Anna Freud Institute in London, a charity which pioneered mental health care for children and families facing emotional upheaval in wartime Europe. In 1945 she went with the founding members of the British Embassy to Czechoslovakia, assisting with the resettlement of British women married to men of the former free Czechoslovakia. She won a British Council Scholarship to Prague College of Applied Arts in 1946 and graduated with a degree in 1951. She then became a professional artist in Czechoslovakia before returning to Scotland to teach art in West Lothian secondary schools until she retired.

Another common theme among the women was that after all the traveling around in the Women's Timber Corps, it gave them a taste for travel and adventure in later life. Many of the Scottish Lumberjills ended up moving to Canada with their husbands, whom they met in the Canadian Forestry Corps. And others like Hazel Collins and Olive Edgley travelled widely in their lives, living abroad for many years, and visiting many different countries all over the world.

Jessie MacLean agreed: 'The Women's Timber Corps helped me to discover my love of travelling.' In 1945, Jessie joined the ATS and was posted to Europe: 'I was deeply interested in the arts, opera and architecture, although, at the time, places like Stuttgart and Cologne were just fields of rubble, but Venice, Capri and Vienna still shone with all their legendary magic.'

Wartime was a time of great romance and heightened emotion and while women got married, there were also many who got divorced after the war. The Lumberjills, like other women who worked during the war, felt they wanted to be in charge of their own lives, rather than just looking after their husbands' needs. Virginia Nicholson, author of *Millions Like Us: Women's Lives During World War Two*, felt that although marriage and motherhood was expected of 1940s women, 'deep down, women knew they had exploded the inequality myth.'

Hazel Collins reflected: 'Working away from home changed my attitude. At home you are a bit kept down. I think I am a strong person, my daughter says I am very strong like her.' She did not marry until her late 30s and – although she loved motherhood – she did not stay with her husband, divorcing in the late '60s. Courageously for that era, she raised her two children alone.

Another similarity among the women I interviewed was the incredible talent for anything they turned their hand to. Whether it be gardening, baking, sewing, business or building work, they did it all with great accomplishment, skill and confidence. Audrey Broad was a prize-winning gardener, often winning first, second and third prizes in different categories each year.

Edna Barton's son said his mother could make anything. 'Once she made a tent. She was amazingly capable. She was a big gardener, lived on a council estate and won a gardening prize several times. She used to make preserves, baking whatever fruit she had collected from the countryside, such as apple jelly with cloves.' Edna Barton added, 'And I never had lady's hands, never since,' holding her hands out.

Margaret Finch was also incredibly accomplished. She has had a family, run her own fashion business and built herself an extension on her own house. It included digging a 30m trench by hand for a new sewer from the main street which was so deep she disappeared into it. She replastered the ceiling over her hallway and stairs, standing on planks of wood and ladders, but she was still not able to reach above the stairs so she finished the job wearing her highest heels. Well into her late 60s she showed me pictures of her gravelling her drive, moving tons of gravel by wheelbarrow, and in her 70s she put up fencing around her garden.

She is still a vibrant and charismatic woman, full of humour, laughter and stories. She has experienced sexual harassment and inequality over the years but has always made a stand against it. She embraces her sexuality and still enjoys talking of flirtations and past romances. She recently appeared in the *Great British Menu* and the day I spent with her at this event was filled with hilarity and happiness.

When I met Joan Turner she was so full of stories and memories, which poured out of her at a pace, that I had great difficulty in keeping up. Her memory was incredible. She astounded me by saying she wanted to go up in a helicopter for her 90th birthday. These women really were full of courage, adventure and a passion to do anything they wanted to do. I admire them greatly.

Shortly after I met a Lumberjill called Doreen Morrison, from Hexham, in March 2012 sadly she passed away. I held Doreen's arm for quite some time as we waited to do some filming with the BBC at Kielder Forest. She spoke about how she always feels so at home in the forest and that being in the forest and experiencing the sights, sounds and smells brought all of her happy memories of time in the Women's Timber Corps flooding back, when she had such a wonderful time. She was quite disappointed when the BBC said she did not need to walk up into the forest from the road to see the harvester in action: 'Oh I wanted to go up there.' What an adventurer! I will always remember those special moments with Doreen.

The ladies I met are a real inspiration and it makes me even more resolute to ensure those ladies are remembered by future generations for everything they did during the war.

Fond Memories

The women took a wonderful satisfaction, pride and happiness in what they did during the war. So, I will leave you with their words …

I worked on the Banff Estate afterwards with a group of girls, who came from MacEwans, a large department store in Perth. They were very nice girls. My husband visited once while I was there. He always said I've been trying to cut him down to size ever since I worked in the Women's Timber Corps.

Enid Lenton

The Women's Timber Corps helped me to discover my love of travelling, as well as being responsible for a very great happiness in my life, then and now. True friends, we shared joys and sorrows and helped one another through difficult times. I would not have changed anything. Heart breaking to leave.

Jessie MacLean[4]

I enjoyed the camaraderie of the other girls and have only happy memories of my time as a Lumberjill. I liked being free. They were happy days with all the girls.

Edna Barton

I was always up for a laugh and if anyone was going to get in to trouble it would be me. During my time in the Timber Corps I met people and did things I didn't ever think I would do and thoroughly enjoyed myself.

Eileen Mark

I loved every bit of it … we just wanted to win the war and that's all there was to it … It was very exciting, I really loved it … you knew you were helping your brothers who were fighting in the war. It was just a nice feeling. Working outside, handling the wood all day long, you felt like you were really living, I suppose.

Violet Parker

I had a lot of fun and a great experience in the Timber Corps, it is a chapter in my life that I will always cherish.

Doreen Musson

I think because we were cutting a tree down into pit props and we would see it through from start to finish in a way there was a satisfaction in what we did because we knew how important it was for the war. I felt really, really proud of our contribution to the war effort. There was something really good about it, there was a reason why we wanted those trees.

Edna Holland

I loved the work, I've always had a feeling for nature and the outdoors, and I revelled in the countryside. I learnt many of the birds and much country lore which has remained with me, as I have continued to be a bird watcher and walker.

Barbara Beddow

Well that was my war and I must say I loved that way of life in the fresh air – the smell of the felled trees.

Margaret Finch

As I look back, I think those years I spent in the Timber Corps from 1941 to 1944 were probably some of the happiest days of my life. Like so many others at the time, we just got on with things the best we could and all pulled together to help the war effort, without complaining too much! As a group of girls we all got on so very well and all became good friends. I am happy to be able to say that I 'did my bit'.

Molly Paterson

We were very healthy and happy, out in all weathers, working in the snow and frost, of course in glorious sunshine, well away from the horror of war. I still write to some of my friends after over fifty years. We were very close, more like sisters.

Katie Ann Kennedy[5]

War, Which Has Brought to Others Fear

War, which has brought to others fear,
Pain, sorrow, slavery and death,
To me has brought what I held dear,
And longed for, but could not possess.
Has given me wide stretch of sky,
The sailing clouds, the wind's sharp breath,
A roof of leaves, the wild flower's eye,
Bird song, all woodland loveliness,
Health, vigour, deep content and faith
That at its source our stream runs clear.
What have I done? I never meant
To be a wartime profiteer!

Hebe Jerrold, from *Meet the Members*,
chapter XVII, Poems and Verses

20

First World War: Pioneering Women in Forestry

First Lumberjills

Helen Beatrice Poulter, nicknamed Nelly, was among the thousands of pioneering women to work in forestry 100 years ago in 1918.[1] This was the first time in British history that women had ever worked in timber production with an axe and saw. Nelly stayed in school until she was 14 years old then went to work as a machinist in a leather boot, bag and suitcase factory. She worked 8 a.m. till 6 p.m. sewing men's attaché cases, making friends with Lizzie Fox and Florrie.

Nelly's mother died suddenly in 1917 and as her father had passed away a year earlier, the doctor recommended she took a holiday. She said they could not afford holidays and so he recommended a change. She was 20 years of age when she heard everyone talking about the rally for Women's Land Army at Hyde Park. It was reported in the papers that the government were recruiting thousands of young women to work on the land because men were being called up to fight in the First World War.

Nelly had two sisters she would be leaving behind, but after she passed the medical to join the Land Army it was agreed to let her go with Lizzie Fox. Florrie had wanted to join too but had not been allowed by her father. When Nelly and Lizzie went to the recruitment centre they were asked whether they wanted to work on a farm or in the forest. Lizzie and Nelly looked at each other and both said forestry. Nelly did not like the idea of working with cows and thought it was 'doing something better than picking up the eggs'. Nelly was told that they were replacing men in forestry and that wood was needed for the trenches. But she had never been to the countryside before. 'I didn't know what the countryside was. I was a real Londoner.'

Still mourning for her mother she was sent to billets near Singleton in Sussex to join the Women's Forestry Service. For the first two weeks in the forest she wore her mourning clothes, which consisted of heeled shoes and a black dress with a lace collar. When the uniforms arrived they were either too big or too small and so she had to wait for the next assignment. The uniform was the same as the Land Army: boots, breeches, white overalls and slouch hat. But the foresters had armlets and hat with a distinctive badge. Designed by one of the corps, the measurers' badge was a tree embroidered in green silk on a khaki background, surrounded by the letters WFS. and for the cutters, two crossed woodman's axes, and cross saw, and the letters LATS.

Nelly felt self-conscious wearing trousers to begin with: 'The first time we wore trousers, I felt terrible because we knew people were looking at us and laughing at us. It was most uncomfortable at first but when I left them out, I nearly caught my death of cold.' When they went for a day out in Chichester, 'the old gentleman used to laugh at us in our breeches and hobnail boots'.

A group of twenty-five girls, mostly aged 18 to 25, walked 4 miles to and from their billet in Singleton to the forests each day and were taught how to use an axe and saw on the job. 'We had to shout out "timber" and let it just fall.' They used billhooks to strip the branches off trees and worked tirelessly out in the forests for the war effort: 'The only man we saw was the man who used to collect the pit props once a week. When we saw the man we all used to cheer. Anything that reminded us we were still in the land of the living.'

A First World War Women's Forestry Service Arm Band, displaying the LATS badge.

'Didn't I have some muscles after that!' She recalled the time when she had her first baby in Queen Mary's in Hampstead and she noticed the sisters and the nurses where making a fuss about something. Eventually she asked, 'What's the matter, is something wrong?' They said, 'Well you've got muscles like a man.'

> Somebody said, "What work have you done in your time?' I said, 'Well I've worked in the Land Army felling trees.' 'Oh!' [Nelly cried] they was worried out their life and they went for the matron. The matron came. 'Oh, it's alright matron, it's alright, she has been working in the Land Army felling trees.' Ooh I was the hero of the ward after that.

She added, 'We were walking all those miles every day. It was really men's work and it was really needed. I was never criticised or told it wasn't lady-like. My brothers thought it was just the sort of thing I would do. It just happened. It done me the world of good really.'

History of forests

Looking back in history, women have often worked in the forest, gathering cones for seed and working in nurseries. The women were frequently from travelling families, who were paid by the bushel when their bags of cones were brought to the nursery for kilning and winnowing. It was, however, unheard of for women to work with timber, felling trees with an axe and saw.

It was the norm for small groups of men to manage forests across the country for the pleasure of monarchs, country barons and the court for hunting. There were severe penalties for anyone who infringed the forest statutes. But with the signing of the Magna Carta, there was a change in forest statute towards more relaxed rules. However, these 'excessive liberties' resulted in the rapid destruction of forests, so tighter legislation was reintroduced and imposed 'pains and penalties' on anyone who broke the rules.

The history of forests in Britain had been one of steady erosion over hundreds of years, especially when many of the woods that had stood on fertile soils were felled to make room for crops. There was a steady demand for timber for fuel, for charcoal, shipbuilding and house building in the industrialisation of Britain. In the early twentieth century, warnings came from naval experts, government and timber suppliers to the royal dockyards that the country was eating into timber supplies too quickly. These warnings about the rapid destruction of Britain's forests were ignored and apathy had set in by the time iron warships had replaced wooden warships.

At the outbreak of the First World War in 1914, no official organisation existed to look after Britain's forests and manage timber supplies. As a result, no reliable information was available about timber supplies, except that of Ordnance Survey maps, showing approximately 3 million acres of woodlands.

The Timber Trade

To make matters worse, in peacetime Britain imported 80 per cent of hard woods and 95 per cent of soft woods. The stocks of timber came almost exclusively from the British Empire and other overseas suppliers. But as the Great War progressed, the demand for timber increased and the German submarines made imports increasingly difficult.

Timber was the number one raw material, consumed voraciously during wartime, and for the first time in our history Britain had to rely solely on home-grown timber. There was a demand for wood for pit props to keep the coal seams open in order to fuel wartime industries. More timber was used in trenches, to build army bases, aircraft and in shipbuilding. Railway sleepers, telegraph poles, gun butts, cannon wheels and high explosives, all needed wood for their manufacture.

Oddly enough, there was no immediate anxiety about the supply of wood. It was not until 1916 that vigorous and near panic action had to be taken to augment imports, which could no longer be relied upon, by stepping up home-grown timber production. Prime Minister David Lloyd George famously remarked that Britain came closer to losing the war through lack of timber than want of food. So with the difficulties of importing wood, Britain called upon its foreign timber suppliers to provide a workforce instead. Armies of lumberjacks arrived and the Canadian Forestry Corps was formed to increase production of timber in both Britain and France.

By 1917, a Timber Supplies Department was hastily created with key posts filled by university-trained foresters, which ran 182 sawmills, only 32 of which were in Scotland. There were a further 40 sawmills run by the Canadian Forestry Corps, a New England sawmill unit and Newfoundland Forestry Corps. But there were still not enough men to increase home-grown timber production.

The Suffragettes

Large numbers of women were out of work at the beginning of the war. The Suffragette Movement suspended its political action and offered its organising capacity to help meet the new demands of the nation. Women of independent means, driven in part by patriotism, began to volunteer their services to the war effort in large numbers.

As a result, various women's organisations arose to provide wartime support and services both locally and nationally. Aside from the push for women to work in munitions factories, nursing and the auxiliary services, the Women's Land Army played an important role in the production and distribution of food and timber products from the country's farms and woodlands.

The flow of men who signed up for the Armed Forces left an opportunity and necessity for women to produce the home-grown food for the nation. By 1917, thousands of women started working on the land as part of the Women's Land Army. The vast majority of these 'Land Girls' worked on local farms but for the first time in history a small number went into forestry as part of the Women's Forestry Service or Women's Forestry Corps, as it was also known.

An article shows the response to women working in forestry for the first time ever in the UK in 1917:

In addition to foreign labour, the second half of the war also provided opportunities for women to become practically involved in forestry in an unprecedented manner. This wasn't without reaction – the Treasurer's Remembrancer replied curtly to a Board of Agriculture request for an additional £2,000 to employ women in forestry work by stating he thought there was '… no likelihood of the Board spending the £10,000 on putting women into knickerbockers to work on farms.' (National Records of Scotland Ref. E 824/243) But employ them they did.

Whilst the funding for this enterprise came from central government, it was the private estates that hired women to fill the labour shortage and help supply timber. Eleven such 'ladyworkers' arrived at the Blair Atholl Estate in March 1917, and a further eleven 'ladystudents' a month later, where the former tended to felling, clearing and planting duties alongside men and boys, and the latter to the newly founded garden nursery at Inver. Lord Tullibardine, heir to the Duke of Atholl, noted in a letter to his brother that 'when they are not squabbling, (they) work well.'[1]

It was difficult to recruit women into forestry to begin with, because of the demand for female workers in other wartime industries and the male prejudice against employment of women in forestry. Nonetheless, after several months 'a very virile Women's Forestry Corps had become established' (Russell Meiggs).

Women's Forestry Service

An article in *Land and Water Extra,* April 1919, explains how the organisation was established in 1917:

The Women's Forestry Service was started by Miss Rosamund Crowdy, as one of the three sections of the Land Army. While the Land Army is, as a whole, under the Board of Agriculture, the Women's Forestry Service is directly under the Board of Trade. However, the Land Army and the Forestry Corps have always worked in close co-operation. The former has done all the recruiting work for the latter, and selected and passed all candidates for Forestry work, while the county organisers of the Land Army have worked for the Forestry scheme.

The Forestry Service started with two camps for 'cutters,' each numbering about twenty girls, and one camp for timber 'measurers' of twenty-five. Of course, before this definite training scheme was organised, quite a number of women had been employed in the cutting and measuring of timber. These were, however, local women, without uniform or organisation. The first measurers' camp was under canvas at Penn, in Buckinghamshire, but in September 1917, it was moved into wooden huts at Halton, Wendover, in the same county. Huts have been found by far the most satisfactory way of housing the workers, as the tents seldom withstood the rains of an English summer; in Devonshire, last year, a whole camp of foresters was completely flooded out.

'...Our beds are just off the floor on a wooden frame, a straw mattress and pillow and five blankets ... The camp is miles from anywhere, absolutely isolated ... the snow was too thick to work so we carried wood from the piling stations and sawed it for indoor use ... We have breakfast at 6.30 and another at 9.30 ... After lunch we went to the woods and started our new work. It is great axing at great trees. We were given a bill-hook, an axe, a saw and cord measure ... Today has been grand. Very cold but the work is fine. It is great to watch a grand old tree crash to earth and

feel that you did it alone – Life is just what I have always longed for …'
Miss B. Bennet, Women's Forestry Corps, 1916

About 370 women have passed through the measurers' training camp since its inauguration. Of these, only 5 per cent have withdrawn before completing their contracts. Timber measuring, which includes a knowledge of felling, marking, and so on, is a skilled trade, and the girls who took it up were chiefly drawn from the ranks of school teachers, superior bank clerks and so forth. After their training is completed they are frequently sent out as forewomen in charge of timber gangs consisting of twenty to thirty cutters. Measurers have also been put practically in charge of sawmills, work involving the keeping of accounts, and entailing great accuracy, rather than physical strength. The course of training at Wendover is very complete, and requires both a theoretical and practical knowledge of forestry.

The work of 'cutters' is, of course, less skilled, and calls for a physical strength above the average. This fact accounts for the rejection on medical grounds of 18 per cent of the cutters out of a total of 1,800. Those who can endure are picked girls, and it is these who form the bulk of the Forestry Service. The two inaugural training camps for cutters, started at Newstead in Nottinghamshire and Burnham in Norfolk, were closed down in a month, as they were found unnecessary. The girls now go straight to work, and become in two or three days sufficiently practised for the easier jobs in forestry. In a few months they are usually capable of the actual felling of trees. The cutters are hired to private employers, or work in gangs under their divisional officers.

In July 1918, sadly three of these young women from the Women's Forestry Corps drowned in the Tay near Dunkeld, having gone swimming at a notoriously dangerous spot unbeknown to them.

By August 1918, nearly 2,000 women like Nelly (Helen Beatrice Poulter) were employed in forestry across Britain, mainly based in the south of England. These included 350 measurers and forewomen and 1,500 'loggers'. In addition to these 'official' workers, there were at least 1,000 other women who were employed unofficially in local forests and sawmills. This was the first time ever such a huge number of women moved into paid forestry work in Great Britain.

By the time hostilities ceased, those 2,000 women, with the help of forty-three battalions of Canadian Forestry Corps, assessed, stripped and processed over 450,000 acres of woodland. This astonishing effort proved that women could work very effectively in forestry.

But by the end of the Great War, British forests were hugely depleted, with half the best timber felled. So the Acland Committee was formed in 1918 as a sub-committee of the Ministry of Reconstruction, which recommended setting up a state forestry authority which was responsible for afforestation and increasing the production of timber on home soil. On 1 September 1919, the Forestry Act came into force and the Forestry Commission was established, with responsibility for woods in England, Scotland, Wales and Ireland.

The organisation had a focus on afforestation rather than timber production. So after the First World War the imperative was to replant Britain's forests to safeguard what was left of our forests in the event of another war. The first Forestry Commission trees were planted on 8 December 1919 at Eggesford Forest, Devon, nearly 100 years ago.

Timeline

In 1900, forest cover in Great Britain was at an all-time low in history. Over 600 years since the Domesday Book the area of forested land had reduced from 15 per cent to just 5 per cent of Great Britain, with much of the loss occurring during the Industrial Revolution.

1910–18

The Timber Supply Department provides timber during the First World War.

1916

The British Government appeals to Canada to recruit a battalion of expert lumbermen. In the spring the first draft arrives and by October it expands to become the Canadian Forestry Corps (CFC).

1917

The Women's Forestry Service (WFS) is established under the National Service Department and initially employs twenty-five measurers and forty timber cutters.

May – The Board of Agriculture (Scotland) applies to the government to recruit 200 women for forestry work in Scotland.

1918

The Women's Forestry Service officially employs 2,000 women, working alongside 10,000 men in the Canadian Forestry Corps. A further 1,000 women work in forestry, employed locally. British women over the age of 30 gain the vote and women over 21 could be Members of Parliament.

1919

The First World War has consumed half of the best trees for wartime industries. As a result, the Forestry Commission is formed to plant and protect a strategic reserve of home-grown timber in the event of another war. The first Forestry Commission trees are planted on 8 December 1919 at Eggesford Forest, Devon.

1920s

The stocks of timber have been so depleted by the First World War, especially by trench warfare, that the bedrock of UK forestry policy is amended to expand state forests and plant millions of trees to rebuild a strategic timber reserve.

1928

British women over 21 gain the vote on equal basis with men.

1930s

The Forestry Commission estate covers 1 million acres, with a third newly planted for pit props for coal mines.

1937

The Forestry Commission begins working with the Board of Trade to draw up detailed plans for felling in the event of war.

1938

German troops invade Czechoslovakia. British Government plans for war. Gas masks are distributed to the British population. Lady Gertrude Denman approaches the Ministry of Agriculture to re-form the Women's Land Army (WLA) to utilise women in farming to provide home-grown food during wartime.

April – The Women's Voluntary Service (WVS) forms, with just five members. In just four years, by 1942, membership reached more than 1 million.

1939

At the beginning of the Second World War, Great Britain only produces 4 per cent of its timber. It is the largest wood-importing nation in the world.

June to September – Three and a half million British people, mainly children, are evacuated from cities.

1 June – Lady Denman becomes the honorary director of the re-formed Women's Land Army (WLA). County and regional officers are appointed. Under the jurisdiction of the Ministry of Agriculture and Fisheries, recruitment begins for the Women's Land Army members, known as the 'Land Girls'.

August – The Forestry Commission is split in two, the Timber Production Department (TPD) to increase production of home-grown timber and the Forest Management Department (FMD) to look after state-owned forests.

29 August – Lady Denman sets up the Women's Land Army headquarters at her home at Balcombe Place, Sussex.

1 September – Germany invades Poland and on 3 September Britain, its Empire and France declares war on Germany. The Second World War begins. A further 1.5 million British people, mainly children, are evacuated to the country.

December – About 4,500 women are employed by the Women's Land Army, working through one of the most bitter winters on record. Desperately short of forestry workers, the Timber Production Department urgently request women for work. The first women are recruited from the Women's Land Army into forestry. Some 300 skilled fellers from the Newfoundland Forestry Unit (NFU) arrive to help with home-grown timber production.

1940

Food rationing begins in Britain: butter, ham, bacon, tea, meat, eggs, cheese and sugar are the first to be rationed.

January – Stocks of pit wood are predicted to last for just seven months, so home timber production needs to be increased desperately. Some 2,000 lumberjacks from Newfoundland and Canada are recruited.

15 January – A large draft of women arrive at Lydney Station in the Forest of Dean to begin training as measurers with Forestry Commission at Parkend, Gloucestershire. Altogether 400 women are trained at this centre.

March – The supply of timber from the Baltic is blocked by Germany closing sea routes, following the surrender of Finland, Denmark and the invasion of Norway.

April – The WLA begin publishing *The Land Girl*, a monthly magazine with Mrs Margaret Pyke as editor. Its aim is to keep Land Girls in touch with each other. Circulation eventually reaches over 21,000.

May – Germany invades the Low Countries and as a result supplies of timber from the Balkans and later France are stopped.

June – German troops invade Paris and France falls to Germany, preventing further imports of timber from France. About 6,000 Land Girls are now employed on farms in Britain.

August to September – The Battle of Britain takes place.

September – The Blitz begins, Germany bombs British cities night after night to try to weaken the British resolve by terror.

1941

Timber Production Department is transferred to the Ministry of Supply, employing Forestry Commission staff and timber merchants from the private sector.

May – All British women aged between 19 and 40 are required to register at labour exchanges for war service.

June – Clothes rationing begins in Britain. Germany invades Russia. Some 14,000 women are members of the Women's Land Army and employed on the land.

August – The Parkend forestry training school in the Forest of Dean closes.

December – Churchill's government passes the National Service Act no. 2, allowing for the conscription of women. All unmarried women between the ages of 20 and 30 are called up for war work. This is later extended to include women aged up to 43 and married women. Pregnant women and those with children could be exempt.

December – The Japanese bomb Pearl Harbor. The United States enters the war on the Allied side. The Battle of the Atlantic and the menace of the German submarines puts a stop to imported timber, so Britain has to produce its own home-grown supply.

1942

January – First American GIs arrive in Britain.

April – The desperate need to step up home-grown timber production and the shortage of labour leads to the official formation of the Women's Timber Corps (WTC), recruiting 1,200 women directly from the Women's Land Army who were already working for timber merchants and the Home Timber Production Department of the Ministry of Supply. The WTC becomes a separate organisation from the WLA. The girls become affectionately known as the 'Lumberjills', the 'Timbergirls' or the 'Timberjills'.

April – Each month hundreds of women are sent to Women's Timber Corps training camps in Wetherby, Yorkshire, Culford, near Bury St Edmunds,

Suffolk, Hereford and Shandford Lodge, near Brechin in Angus, Scotland. A census of UK woodlands is carried out using members of the Women's Timber Corps and reveals a high quantity of coniferous woods that could be turned into pit props. The Canadian Forestry Corps is formed to assist in production of timber both in Great Britain and France.

June – The numbers reach 40,000 in the WLA and Lady Denman sets up the Land Army Benevolent Fund to provide financial assistance for Land Girls in difficulty.

3 July – Queen Elizabeth hosts a third birthday party for the Women's Land Army and Timber Corps.

27 July – The Australian Women's Land Army is formed and by 1943 it has 2,382 permanent members and 1,039 auxiliary members.

December – The American First Lady, Eleanor Roosevelt, meets Land Army members during her visit to the UK.

1943

In Britain, nine out of ten single women and eight out of ten married women are employed either in the forces, the Women's Land Army, Women's Timber Corps or other war industries. The number of women in the Timber Corps reaches its peak with more than 12,000 recorded members and many hundreds more recruited unofficially working up and down the country in England, Scotland and Wales. Timber production reaches a peak.

December – The American First Lady, Mrs Eleanor Roosevelt, meets Land Army members during her visit to the UK.

1944

May – The Women's Land Army headquarters moves back to London but returns to Sussex after the doodlebug attacks begin.

June – Allied forces land in France (D-Day landings) and the first German V1 doodlebugs hit Britain.

August – Allies liberated Paris.

September – The first German V2 rocket attacks begin.

1945

February – Allied air attack devastate Dresden, Germany.

16 February – Lady Denman resigns as director of the Women's Land Army in protest at the government's decision to exclude members of the WLA and WTC from post-war financial benefits.

14 April – About 150 Land Girls in North Gloucester call a one-day strike in protest against the government's decision not to grant post-war gratuities to Land Girls.

7 May – Germany surrenders and 8 May is VE Day (Victory in Europe Day).

6–9 August – Allies drop atomic bombs on Hiroshima and Nagasaki, Japan.

14 August – Japan surrenders and the Second World War ends.

15 August – VJ Day (Victory over Japan Day) is celebrated.

During the full period of the war, the Ministry of Supply purchased 142 million cubic feet of standing trees and converted them into hundreds of products for war.

7 December – The queen presents golden armbands to long-serving Land Girls.

31 December – The Australian Women's Land Army is disbanded.

Usable standing timber has been exhausted in Great Britain. But some 60 per cent of timber needed in the Second World War was home grown and 46 per cent of trees were felled. Married women and those with domestic responsibilities are free to leave the Women's Timber Corps or to transfer into other occupations such as teaching and nursing.

1946

8 June – The Land Army and Timber Corps march in the Victory Parade, London.

August – The number of women in the Land Army are now down to 54,000. Some 750 Land Girls and Women's Timber Corps march through the City of London to receive armlets from the queen.

31 August – The Women's Timber Corps is officially disbanded, with each girl handing back her uniform and receiving a letter from the queen, who was the patron of the WTC. Many girls continue to work in forestry until 1948. A small number of women are employed on the National Census of Woodlands to assess the amount of standing timber that remains. Others go to Canada or Germany, requisitioning equipment from sawmills, undertaking secretarial work, organising timber supplies and re-afforestation.

1947

March – *The Land Girl* magazine ceases publication. A free newsletter from headquarters, *The Land Army News*, replaces the magazine and continues until 1950.

1948

The Land Army County Committees are dissolved.

1949

October – Tom Williams, Minister of Agriculture, announces that the Women's Land Army is to be disbanded.

1950

Some 8,000 women are still in the Land Army.

21 October – The Women's Land Army is finally disbanded and 500 Land Girls march past Buckingham Palace in the stand-down parade.

1960s

A mechanical revolution takes place. Technical progress allows planting on previously unplantable land. The axe and crosscut saw disappear and are replaced by the lightweight chainsaw.

1995

19 August – Some eighty former Land Girls wearing Land Army armbands march through London as part of the 50th anniversary of VJ Day.

2000

November – The first time that members of the WLA and WTC are invited to take part in the annual Remembrance Day parade at the Cenotaph in London.

2007

10 October – The first memorial to the Women's Timber Corps is unveiled in Scotland, commissioned by Forestry Commission Scotland. Michael Russell MSP, Minister for the Environment, unveils the memorial at The Lodge Forest Visitor Centre, Aberfoyle.

2008

The Department for Environment, Food and Rural Affairs announces that all surviving members of the WTC and WLA are entitled to receive a badge to commemorate their services during the Second World War. The members of the Timber Corps, while pleased to receive a badge, are disappointed that it bore the WLA emblem of a wheat sheaf rather than the Timber Corps emblem of a fir tree.

2012

Pam Warhurst, first female Chair of the Forestry Commission in nearly 100 years, marks the 70th anniversary of the Women's Timber Corps with the commissioning of a Lumberjills sculpture for England.

11 November – On Remembrance Sunday the BBC's *Countryfile* TV programme broadcast a special tribute to the work of the Women's Timber Corps interviewing veteran members Eileen Mark, Olive Edgley and Irene Snow in the Forest of Dean.

2013

28 October – The Forestry Commission unveils the sculpture in honour of the Women's Timber Corps in Dalby Forest, North Yorkshire.

2014

A memorial statue to both the Women's Land Army and the Women's Timber Corps is unveiled at the National Memorial Arboretum in Alrewas, Staffordshire.

Notes

Introduction

1 Elder, Rosalind, 'The Women's Timber Corps' (2009).
2 Forestry Commission Scotland, 'Women's Timber Corps'.
3 MAF900/164 Women's Timber Corps, Oxfordshire.
4 Grinstead, Sarah, 'Winston Versus the Women', *The Huffington Post* (30 September 2015).
5 BBC News, 'Land Girls receive WWII honours' (23 July 2008).
6 Women's Land Army Timber Corps, *Meet the Members: A Record of the Timber Corps of the Women's Land Army* (Bristol: Bennet Brothers Ltd, 1945).

Chapter 1

1 Bates, Laura, *Everyday Sexism* (London: Simon and Schuster, 2014).
2 Always, 'Always #Likeagirl' (online video).
3 Mackie, Lindsay, 'Equal pay packet – with strings', *The Guardian* (29 December 1975).
4 Johnson, Jamie; Lyons, Izzy; and Molloy, Mark, '1918 vs 2018: 13 things women couldn't do 100 years ago', *The Telegraph* (6 February 2018).
5 Meiggs, Russell, *Home Timber Production 1939–1945* (London: Crosby Lockwood & Son Ltd, 1949).
6 Dines, Joyce, 'To be a Timber Girl', *The Best of British Magazine* (February and March 1999).
7 Beddow, Barbara, 'BBC WW2 People's War, An archive of WW2 memories' (June 2005).
8 Grey, Affleck, *Timber! Memories of Life in the Scottish Women's Timber Corps, 1942–46*, ed. Robertson, Uiga and John (East Linton: Tuckwell Press, 1998).

Chapter 2

1 Extract from Diana Underwood's memoirs, *Experiences as a Timber Measurer 1941–1943*. Reproduced with permission from her daughter Mary Hobbins.
2 Beddow, Barbara, 'BBC WW2 People's War'.
3 Dorothy Scott, interview with Richard Darn.
4 Meiggs, Russell, *Home Timber Production 1939–1945*
5 Huxley, Gervas, *Lady Denman GBE 1884–1954* (London: Chatto & Windus, 1961).
6 Meiggs, Russell, *Home Timber Production 1939–1945*, p. 3.

Chapter 3

1 Grey, Affleck, *Timber!*, p. 114.
2 Huxley, Gervas, *Lady Denman GBE 1884–1954*.
3 Art. IWM PST 6078 Imperial War Museum Collections.
4 The National Archives (MAF 900/162).
5 Huxley, Gervas, *Lady Denman GBE 1884–1954*.

6 Stone, Tessa, 'Denman (née Pearson) Gertrude Mary, Lady Denman (1884–1954), public servant' *Oxford Dictionary of National Biography*.
7 Meiggs, Russell, *Home Timber Production 1939–1945*, p. 3.
8 Women's Land Army Timber Corps, *Meet the Members*.

Chapter 4
1 'To be a Timber Girl', *The Best of British Magazine*.
2 Doreen Musson, letter.
3 'To be a Timber Girl', *The Best of British Magazine*.
4 Grey, Affleck, *Timber!*, p. 46.
5 *Ibid.*, p. 58.
6 *Ibid.*, p. 69.
7 'To be a Timber Girl', *The Best of British Magazine*.
8 House, Frank H., *Timber at War: An Account of the Organisation and Activities of the Timber Control 1939–1945* (London: Ernest Benn, 1965).

Chapter 5
1 Grey, Affleck, *Timber!*, p. 19.
2 Huxley, Gervas, *Lady Denman GBE 1884–1954*.
3 *Ibid.*
4 Meiggs, Russell, *Home Timber Production 1939–1945*, *passim*.
5 The National Archives (MAF 900/162).
6 *Ibid.*
7 Meiggs, Russell, *Home Timber Production 1939–1945*, p. 9; Grey, Affleck, *Timber!*, p. 11.
8 The National Archives (MAF 900/162).
9 Grey, Affleck, *Timber!*, p. 167.
10 *Meet the Members*.
11 Telephone call from Joyce Earl, 2012.
12 Grey, Affleck, *Timber!*, p. 25.
13 Meiggs, Russell, *Home Timber Production 1939–1945*, p. 200.
14 Grey, Affleck, *Timber!*, p. 170.
15 Telephone call from Joyce Earl.
16 Grey, Affleck, *Timber!*, p. 169.
17 Women's Land Army Timber Corps, *Meet the Members*.

Chapter 6
1 British Pathé Limited.
2 Grey, Affleck, *Timber!*, p. 65.
3 Women's Land Army Timber Corps, *Meet the Members*, p. 15.
4 Grey, Affleck, *Timber!*, p. 72.
5 *Ibid.*, p. 143.
6 *Ibid.*, p. 148.

Chapter 7
1 Sackville-West, Vita, *The Women's Land Army*.
2 Meiggs, Russell, *Home Timber Production 1939–1945*, p. 199.

Chapter 8
1 Lady Winnie Renshaw, letter.
2 'To be a Timber Girl', *The Best of British Magazine*.

3 Women's Land Army Timber Corps, *Meet the Members*, p. 20.
4 'To be a Timber Girl', *The Best of British Magazine*.
5 Grey, Affleck, *Timber!*, p. 50.
6 *Ibid.*, p. 129.

Chapter 9

1 The National Archives (MAF 900/162).
2 'To be a Timber Girl', *The Best of British Magazine*.
3 Vickers, Emma, 'The Forgotten Army of the Woods: The Women's Timber Corps During World War Two', *Agricultural History Review*, Vol. 59, No. 1 (June 2011), pp. 101–12 (12).
4 Williams, Mavis, *Lumber Jill: Her Story of Four Years in the Women's Timber Corps, 1942–5* (Bradford-on-Avon: Ex Libris Press, 1994), p. 59.
5 Beddow, Barbara, 'BBC WW2 People's War'.
6 Women's Land Army Timber Corps, *Meet the Members*, p. 8.
7 Meiggs, Russell, *Home Timber Production 1939–1945*, pp. 37–40.
8 Women's Land Army Timber Corps, *Meet the Members*, p. 8.
9 Grey, Affleck, *Timber!*, p. 63.
10 Women's Land Army Timber Corps, *Meet the Members*, pp. 34–6.

Chapter 10

1 'To be a Timber Girl', *The Best of British Magazine*.
2 *Ibid.*
3 Women's Land Army Timber Corps, *Meet the Members*, pp. 21–2.
4 Meiggs, Russell, *Home Timber Production 1939–1945*, p. 49.
5 National Coal Mining Museum, www.ncm.org.uk.
6 Beddow, Barbara, 'BBC WW2 People's War'.
7 Women's Land Army Timber Corps, *Meet the Members*, pp. 38–40.
8 Memoirs of Mrs D.G. Gardner (Imperial War Museum Department of Documents, 88/6/1). Catalogue no. Documents 1915.

Chapter 11

1 The National Archives (MAF 900/162).
2 *Ibid.*
3 *Ibid.*
4 Grey, Affleck, *Timber!*, p. 11.
5 *Ibid.*, p. 58.
6 Meiggs, Russell, *Home Timber Production 1939–1945*, p. 242.

Chapter 12

1 Letter from the Divisional Officer to A.H. Popert, at Timber Control. The National Archives (MAF 900/162).
2 Grey, Affleck, *Timber!*, pp. 84–5.
3 Tyrer, Nicola, *They Fought in the Fields: The Women's Land Army* (Stroud: Tempus, 2007), p. 185.
4 The National Archives (MAF 900/162).
5 Swanston, Catherine, 'The Health of Forestry Workers: A Survey of the Women's Timber Corps of Great Britain', Occupational and Environmental Medicine, *British Journal of Industrial Medicine (BMJ)*, 3(1) (1946), pp. 1–10.
6 'To be a Timber Girl', *The Best of British Magazine*.
7 *Ibid.*
8 Beddow, Barbara, 'BBC WW2 People's War'.

9   Grey, Affleck, *Timber!*, p. 78.

10 *Ibid.*, p. 19.

11 *Ibid.*, p. 92.

12 *Ibid.*, p. 34.

13 Williams, Mavis, *Lumber Jill.*

14 'To be a Timber Girl', *The Best of British Magazine.*

15 Grey, Affleck, *Timber!*, p. 92.

16 *Ibid.*, p. 25.

17 Williams, Mavis, *Lumber Jill.*

Chapter 13

1   The National Archives (MAF 900/164).

2   Swanston, Catherine, 'The Health of Forestry Workers: A Survey of the Women's Timber Corps of Great Britain'.

3   'To be a Timber Girl', *The Best of British Magazine.*

4   Grey, Affleck, *Timber!*, p. 72.

5   *Ballymena Observer* (5 September 1941).

6   'To be a Timber Girl', *The Best of British Magazine.*

7   Williams, Mavis, *Lumber Jill*, p. 34.

8   *Ibid.*, p. 54.

9   'To be a Timber Girl', *The Best of British Magazine.*

Chapter 14

1   Meiggs, Russell, *Home Timber Production 1939–1945*, p. 134.

2   The National Archives (MAF 900/162).

3   'The other "Green Berets"', *Nottingham Evening Post*, 20 March 1995.

4   Vickers, Emma, 'The Forgotten Army of the Woods: The Women's Timber Corps During World War Two'.

5   Women's Land Army Timber Corps, *Meet the Members*, p. 38.

6   Grey, Affleck, *Timber!*, p. 143.

7   Provided by Edna Holland.

8   Vickers, Emma, 'The Forgotten Army of the Woods: The Women's Timber Corps During World War Two'.

9   Grey, Affleck, *Timber!*, p. 129.

10 'BBC WW2 People's War' archive.

11 Winifred Maude Taylor (Imperial War Museum Sound Archives Reel 3). Catalogue no. 31050.

12 Doris Danher (Imperial War Museum Sound Archives Reel 2). Catalogue no. 9526.

13 Beddow, Barbara, 'BBC WW2 People's War'.

14 Grey, Affleck, *Timber!*, p. 129.

15 Swanston, Catherine, 'The Health of Forestry Workers: A Survey of the Women's Timber Corps of Great Britain'.

16 Grey, Affleck, *Timber!*, p. 19.

17 *Ibid.*, p. 9.

18 Meiggs, Russell, *Home Timber Production 1939–1945*, labour costs 1941–45.

Chapter 15

1   Tyrer, Nicola, *They Fought in the Fields*, pp. 149-50.

2   *Ibid.*

3   Grey, Affleck, *Timber!*, p. 157.

4 *Ibid.*, p. 148.
5 *Ibid.*, p. 129.
6 *Ibid.*, p. 39.
7 *Ibid.*, p. 72.
8 *Ibid.*, p. 82.
9 *Ibid.*, p. 129.
10 *Ibid.*, p. 157.
11 Private Papers of Miss M. Coleman, memoir by Mrs E. Rawlinson of her WTC training and work in various parts of the country, 1942–1945, Documents 1652. Imperial War Museum.
12 Grey, Affleck, *Timber!*, p. 153.

Chapter 16

1 Grey, Affleck, *Timber!*, p. 129.
2 *Ibid.*, p. 107.
3 *Ibid.*, p. 92.
4 *Ibid.*, p. 148.
5 *Ibid.*
6 *Ibid.*, p. 72.
7 *Ibid.*, p. 129.

Chapter 17

1 Grey, Affleck, *Timber!*, p. 19.
2 *Ibid.*, p. 129.
3 *Ibid.*, p. 19.
4 *Ibid.*, p. 171.
5 *Ibid.*

Chapter 18

1 Grey, Affleck, *Timber!*, p. 157.
2 *Ibid.*, p. 129.
3 *Ibid.*, p. 143.

Chapter 19

1 Stone, Tessa, 'Denman (née Pearson) Gertrude Mary, Lady Denman (1884–1954)'.
2 *Ibid.*, p. 65.
3 *Ibid.*, p. 148.
4 *Ibid.*, p. 143.
5 *Ibid.*, p. 58.

Chapter 20

1 Anderson, Jane (ed.), *Chronicles of the Atholl and Tullibardine Families*, Vol. 6, 1907–57, (Aberdeen, 1991), p. 110; House, Euan, 'The Impact of the First World War on the Woods and Forests of Scotland', *Forestry Memories*, p. 6.

Bibliography

Bates, Laura, *Everyday Sexism* (London: Simon and Schuster, 2014).

Hendrie, James, 'Lumberjills', *Forestry Journal* (December 2009), pp. 40–1.

House, Frank H., *Timber at War: An Account of the Organisation and Activities of the Timber Control 1939–1945* (London: Ernest Benn, 1965).

Huxley, Gervas, *Lady Denman GBE 1884–1954* (London: Chatto & Windus, 1961).

Kramer, Ann, *Land Girls and their Impact* (Barnsley: Pen and Sword Books, 2008 & 2009).

Meiggs, Russell, *Home Timber Production 1939–1945* (London: Crosby Lockwood & Son Ltd, 1949).

Nicholson, Virginia, *Millions Like Us* (London: Penguin Books, 2012).

Grey, Affleck, *Timber! – Memories of life in the Scottish Women's Timber Corps, 1942–46*, ed. Robertson, Uiga and John (East Linton: Tuckwell Press, 1998). Reproduced with permission of European Ethnological Research Centre.

Ryle, George, *Forest Service: The First Forty-Five Years of the Forestry Commission of Great Britain* (Newton Abbot: David and Charles, 1969).

Sackville-West, Vita, *The Women's Land Army* (reprinted London: Unicorn, 2016).

Sherwell-Cooper, W.E., *Land Girl: A Manual for Volunteers in the Women's Land Army 1941* (Stroud: Amberley Publishing, 2011).

Tyrer, Nicola, *They Fought in the Fields: The Women's Land Army* (Stroud: Tempus, 2007).

Williams, Mavis, *Lumber Jill: Her Story of Four Years in the Women's Timber Corps, 1942–5* (Bradford-on-Avon: Ex Libris Press, 1994).

Women's Land Army Timber Corps, *Meet the Members: A Record of the Timber Corps of the Women's Land Army* (Bristol: Bennet Brothers Ltd, 1945).

Articles

Dines, Joyce, 'To Be a Timber Girl', *The Best of British Magazine* (February and March 1999). Reproduced with the kind permission of *Best of British* magazine. www.bestofbritishmag.co.uk.

Grinstead, Sarah, 'Winston Versus the Women', *The Huffington Post* (30 September 2015). www.huffingtonpost.co.uk/sarah-gristwood/winston-versus-the-women_b_8220120.html.

House, Euan, 'The Impact of the First World War on the Woods and Forests of Scotland', *Forestry Memories*. forestry-memories.org.uk.s3.amazonaws.com/document/3760.pdf.

Johnson, Jamie; Lyons, Izzy; and Molloy, Mark, '1918 vs 2018: 13 things women couldn't do 100 years ago', *The Telegraph* (6 February 2018). www.telegraph.co.uk/women/life/1918-vs-2018-13-things-women-couldnt-do-100-years-of/.

Mackie, Lindsay, 'Equal pay packet – with strings', *The Guardian* (29 December 1975). www.theguardian.com/politics/1975/dec/29/past.comment.

Stone, Tessa, 'Denman (née Pearson) Gertrude Mary, Lady Denman (1884–1954), public servant' *Oxford Dictionary of National Biography*. www.oxforddnb.com/view/10.1093/ref:odnb/9780198614128.001.0001/odnb-9780198614128-e-32781.

Swanston, Catherine, 'The Health of Forestry Workers: A Survey of the Women's Timber Corps of Great Britain', Occupational and Environmental Medicine, *British Journal of Industrial Medicine (BMJ)*, 3(1) (1946), pp. 1–10.

Vickers, Emma, 'The Forgotten Army of the Woods: The Women's Timber Corps During World War Two', *Agricultural History Review*, Vol. 59, No. 1 (June 2011), pp. 101–12 (12).

Journals

Journal of the Forestry Commission no. 35: 1966-67 (Plate 8. Lumberjills, Dean Forest, 1943). Images © Crown Copyright, Courtesy of Forestry Commission.

Journal of the Forestry Commission no. 36: 1968-69 (Plate 3. A Lumberjill of the Women's Timber Corps). Images © Crown Copyright, Courtesy of Forestry Commission.

Imperial War Museum

Doris Danher (Imperial War Museum Sound Archives Reel 2). Catalogue no. 9526.

Helen Beatrice Poulter (Imperial War Museum Sound Archives). Catalogue no. 727.

Private Papers of Miss M. Coleman (Imperial War Museum Department of Documents), Documents 1652, a memoir by Mrs E. Rawlinson of her WTC training and work in various parts of the country, 1942–1945.

Memoirs of Mrs D.G. Gardner (Imperial War Museum Department of Documents, 88/6/1). Catalogue no. Documents 1915.

Winifred Maude Taylor (Imperial War Museum Sound Archives Reel 3). Catalogue no. 31050.

Mrs M. Tozer (Imperial War Museum private papers). Catalogue date 1987-09-15; catalogue no. Documents 1405.

The National Archives

MAF 900/162 Timber Corps. Employment of girls on forestry work 1 folder 1939–1945 Public Records, Open Document, Open Description.

MAF 900/164 Women's Timber Corps, Oxfordshire 1 folder 1942–1945 Public Records, Open Document, Open Description.

Websites

Always, 'Always #Likeagirl' (online video). www.youtube.com/watch?v=XjJQBjWYDTs.

BBC News, 'Land Girls receive WWII honours' (23 July 2008). news.bbc.co.uk/1/hi/uk/7517821.stm.

Beddow, Barbara, 'BBC WW2 People's War, An archive of WW2 memories', (June 2005). www.bbc.co.uk/history/ww2peopleswar/stories/37/a4311037.shtml.

Elder, Rosalind, 'The Women's Timber Corps' (2009). womenstimbercorps.com.

Forestry Commission Scotland, 'Women's Timber Corps'. scotland.forestry.gov.uk/activities/heritage/world-war-two/womens-timber-corps.

Land and Water Extra, 'Women in the War' edition, April 1919. www.scarletfinders.co.uk/160.html.

Index